Truly, Madly, Deadly
The Unofficial True Blood Companion

Becca Wilcott

Published by ECW Press
2120 Queen Street East, Suite 200, Toronto, Ontario, Canada M4E 1E2
416-694-3348 / info@ecwpress.com

LIBRARY AND ARCHIVES CANADA CATALOGUING IN PUBLICATION

Wilcott, Becca
Truly, madly, deadly : the unofficial True blood companion / Becca Wilcott.

ISBN 978-1-55022-933-2

1. True blood (Television program). I. Title.

PN1992.77.T78W54 2010   791.45'72   C2010-901253-4

Developing editor: Jen Hale
Typesetting: Gail Nina
Cover design: Keith Berry
Text and color section design: Tania Craan
Colour section, in order: Jen Lowery/StartraksPhoto; Camera Press/Retna Ltd.; Camera Press/Retna Ltd.;
Digital Focus Intl/Keystone Press; Glenn Harris/PR Photos; Michael Germana/Keystone Press;
Sara De Boer/Retna Ltd.; Sara De Boer/Retna Ltd.
Printed by: Victor Graphics 1 2 3 4 5

This book has been printed on 30% PCW paper

The publication of *Truly, Madly, Deadly: The Unofficial True Blood Companion* has been generously supported by the Government of Ontario through the Ontario Book Publishing Tax Credit, by the OMDC Book Fund, an initiative of the Ontario Media Development Corporation, and by the Government of Canada through the Book Publishing Industry Development Program (BPIDP).

 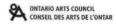

Canada Council   Conseil des Arts   Canadä   ONTARIO ARTS COUNCIL
for the Arts   du Canada   CONSEIL DES ARTS DE L'ONTAR

PRINTED AND BOUND IN THE UNITED STATES

ECW PRESS
ecwpress.com

To Julie Wilson.
Without you, I'm nothing.

Contents

"All play means something."
—Johan Huizinga, *Homo Ludens*

Tell Me, Truebie

"What's your earliest memory of vampires? Was it a literary vampire? A cinematic vampire? A Hallowe'en costume? Was it a dangerous, funny, or sexy vampire? What impact did it have on you?"

After all the people I talked to while researching this book, when it came time to answer my own question, I couldn't recall that initial encounter. In all likelihood, it was the one from *The Hilarious House of Frightenstein*, or Count Chocula, mascot of the General Mills cereal, something I would have had access to as a young person — in other words, a "lower shelf" vampire. It would have been safe, defanged, and frumpy, and, in the case of *Sesame Street*'s The Count, educational. It wouldn't have been hideously monstrous or overly sexual, like Udo Kier in *Blood for Dracula* lusting after the blood of "*wurgens*," or Max Schreck in F. W. Murnau's *Nosferatu* (1922), or Klaus Kinski in Werner Herzog's 1979 adaptation of the same name. Their pointed ears and consistently erect, tubular fangs were not something I was aware of as a child, although they would become my touchstone characterizations later in life any time someone mentioned a *vampyr*, the undead, a nightwalker.

In fact, my earliest notion that vampires were even remotely bothersome was the Bugs Bunny cartoon *Transylvania 6-5000* (1963), in which Bugs engages in a magical duel with Count Blood Count.

("Abacadabra!" "Hocus pocus!") At the time, I had a fear of open waters, so, in my child's mind, I equated vampires with fish nibbling at my feet: relentless, but something to overcome nonetheless. The vampires I envisioned in my childhood weren't killers; they were people with a lot of time on their hands. They were well read, well traveled — cool.

And dude, they had great hair.

They could take whatever they wanted and in the next moment disappear as if nothing had happened. Isn't that a universal fantasy? It's the adrenalin of shoplifting a chocolate bar. (And if I'd been a child vampire, I wouldn't have been caught.)

It never occurred to me that vampires could be violent, remorseless creatures who lived by a savage code. At a young age, while my own sexual awakenings were only just beginning to take form, I had yet to consider the consensual desire to be turned or fed upon, relinquishing your mortality to sustain another's immortality. Nor, even in my advanced appreciation for the subversive, had I yet to make the connection between metaphor and actual flesh-and-bone Real Vampires — sanguine, psychic, psi, or energy — those who feed off the blood or emotional energy of individuals or nature to sustain their health, or the intersection between vampirism and the BDSM (Bondage, Discipline, Sadism, Masochism) lifestyle.

For me, vampirism was a performance enhancer, less a way of life in death than a way to make what life you'd been born into something harder, better, faster, stronger, as Kanye West might say. The contemporary, romantic vampire was a better you, a sexier you, the kind of you even your worst enemy would want to be, at once admired and feared by audiences who were safely off the page, or on the other side of the television or film screen. By the time vampires found me, they'd already evolved into everything from rock stars to sparkling high school students, with Slayers in hot pursuit wielding sharpened stakes and witty comebacks. I spent my efforts considering instead what they mean to others, why they're so pervasive, and, through Alan Ball and *True Blood*, how the metaphor of vampirism could finally be extended to include those of us who are both natural and super — the mortals who love them.

Vampires are the perfect (and endless) fodder for any writer. With all the time in the world, what would a vampire look like in this day and age? Breathtakingly beautiful or a paunchy couch potato?

To state my bias, I don't like all fictional vampires. Namely, those who can survive in sunlight. Don't get me wrong; I enjoy the hot-bodied actors of the *Twilight* series and *The Vampire Diaries*. (See afore-mentioned references to good hair.) But, stake me where I stand, any-thing that normalizes the vampire to the level of a high school student risks de-*everythinging* that which makes vampires the ideal personifica-tion of our more subversive, non-mainstream wants and desires. I say this as a tried-and-true fan of *Buffy* (where we never saw a vampire on campus . . . well, except for that one time that Spike got that ring that allowed him to walk in the sun, and — ahem, never mind about that, you know what I'm saying). You want an ideal coming-of-age metaphor, stick to werewolves and witches. But leave me my deepest, darkest vampires. To be precise, that which is not seen, not surface, and not freakin' sparkling.

Why a book about vampires then? Why *True Blood*? It begins and ends with Alan Ball and everything he brings to Charlaine Harris's novels. In the final moments of *Six Feet Under*, Alan Ball's other little HBO masterpiece, I felt as if an anvil had been dropped on my chest. I distinctly recall sitting on my couch and muttering, "Oh my god, he's going to make us watch." I won't call Alan Ball a god; I'll leave that to the actors who repeatedly praise his approach to writing and directing. But as an audience member, I feel equipped to boast that he is unmatched in his ability to get things so right . . . and so wrong. He's messy. His characters are human to a fault, even the non-humans. You yell at them. You coddle them. You want to jump into the television to show them how it's done. And when Alan Ball jumps the shark, man, you just know that shark has issues. For as much as you might say — as I will in this book — that Jason's season 1 addiction feels forced, that Maryann Forrester's storyline goes on far too long, or that a certain vamp queen casting choice left many viewers agog, you cannot deny the ongoing quality of the production, and the legions of fans who will follow Alan Ball into a shallow grave. I'm amazed how many people have heard of *True Blood* — an international phenomenon — without knowing of Alan Ball's participation, but, once they do, vow to catch up on the series because they loved his previous projects.

Are vampires really a dirty secret? There's certainly enough criticism about the current vampire trend, but is it all that different from the off-shoot of serial killer films that resulted from the immense popularity of Hannibal Lecter? If we killed that beast, we'd be without another of my favorite literary-adapted hero-slash-villains, Showtime's *Dexter*. And what a crime that would be. We love these archetypes because they continue to surprise us, visited in so many new ways, revisited even in the faces of the unexpected. Remember the Tom Cruise *Interview with the Vampire* casting debacle? Because, perhaps the true appeal of vampires is that as surely as I'm sitting here, and you are sitting there, we could both be one. That's the fantasy, isn't it? Whether we want to stay up all night, read everything, see everything, be anything, feed, or, in some cases, fly, we're told that on the other side of a remarkably simple procedure there's not so much an after-life as an endless life, as we are. It's a truly mortal desire.

Which is precisely why you can expect to see a few unfamiliar faces in *Truly, Madly, Deadly*: the faces of the fans. I asked people just like me, just like you, why they love *True Blood*. What I got back was as surprising and multi-faceted as I should have expected. It's not just that vampires are everywhere; it's that everyone has a unique take on their appeal. There's no one vamp for every person. And if the online communities surrounding the series prove anything, it's that the fans make all the difference. During the process of writing this book, I was amazed by how many people said they would wait to watch the show if it meant they could watch it with their friends, some recording each episode then using Skype to connect with other fans around the world, just so they can experience it at the same time. And if you're not a fan of spoilers, stay away from Twitter on broadcast night. It erupts in feedback, outcry, and tweets of joy, with "#TrueBlood" regularly trending in the days leading up to and after each episode.

In a slightly sad turn, when I asked participants of my site's "Interview with a Sympathizer" questionnaire which rituals they had when watching *True Blood*, over 25% of respondents said that they wished they had someone to watch it with, so they could talk about the developments or, as one person said, "just to know that I'm not weird for loving it so much." So those people are in this book: bloggers, podcasters, industry professionals, screenwriters, journalists, academics, authors, artists, critics, roleplayers, vampyres, and vampires — it's the face of the fan like you've never seen it, and what we talk about is as wide-ranging as the interviewees themselves.

How does the book break down? After each episode guide, you'll find some or all of the following extras.

Night Caps: This section could also be entitled Oops, Did You Know, Tidbits, The Deets, or Etcetera. These are additional details that keep the party going after last call has been announced.

Relationship Crypt Falls: These are my shout-outs to the characters as they fumble through their relationships as friends, family, and lovers.

Paging Dr. Creepy: Whether it's a gooey prosthetic device or, in one case, an astoundingly good sound effect, this is my vote for most spine-tingling, cringe-worthy moment of each show.

Location, Location, Location: This feature highlights where some of your favorite scenes were filmed.

Suzuki Sets the Scene: Suzuki Ingerslev is *True Blood*'s production designer, responsible for the lived-in look and feel of all locations used in the series. Each episode takes approximately 10 days to produce; Ingerslev and her team work around the clock to secure locations, build sets, and redress others for the next day's shoot. This segment will showcase some of the considerations taken for many of the sets used in seasons 1 and 2.

Encore: Each show is named after a song. This feature gives you a little background information on the song, its performer(s), and to what effect it was used in the episode.

Within many of the episodes, I'll include "Tribute" sidebars where I wax poetic on some of *True Blood*'s supporting characters, those who carry the storylines to the edges and beyond. These are the true torch bearers of the show's most daring themes. It's unabashed, full geek-on fandom.

What else can you expect? Exclusive interviews with Kristin Bauer (Pam Ravenscroft), Patricia Bethune (Jane Bodehouse), Charlaine Harris, Kevin Jackson (the sharp mind behind *Bite: A Vampire Handbook*), and Karen Walton (who wrote the international cult film *Ginger Snaps*); an overview of HBO's brilliant viral marketing campaign; and in and out of character interviews with the Twitter *True Blood* players. I also have input from Alix Fox of *Bizarre* magazine on being an "Undead Talking Head" celebrity; Stacey May Fowles from *Shameless* magazine on the BDSM nature of Sookie and Bill's relationship; Brian Juergens of CampBlood.org on the intersection between the queer and horror communities; Andy Swist about his incredible *True Blood* paper dolls; some of your favorite fan site admins; and much more!

Finally, a note about terminology. While there is no absolute consensus, many employ "vampire" when referring to both the mythical creatures of films, television, and novels *as well as* those who identify as "real vampires" — sanguinarian, psi, and psychic — and use the term "vampyre" in reference to a subculture of lifestylers (or social vampires) who identify with the vampyric genre. For the purposes of this book, I'll observe these definitions.

So, how shall we proceed? Be sure to watch each episode before reading the guides. They won't spoil anything to follow, but will contain major plot points up to that episode. If you have any feedback — and especially if you'd like to be considered for a future "Interview with a Sympathizer" for my site rebeccawilcott.com — drop me a note at becca@beccawilcott.com. Also stop by for weekly recaps during season 3.

Yours . . . truly,
Becca Wilcott

Immortal Love

The Lingering Appeal of Vampires Throughout the Entertainment Ages

"Throughout the whole vast shadowy world of ghosts and demons there is no figure so terrible, no figure so dreaded and abhorred, yet dight with such fearful fascination, as the vampire, who is himself neither ghost nor demon, but yet who partakes the dark natures and possesses the mysterious and terrible qualities of both."

— Reverend Montague Summer,
from *The Vampire: His Kith and Kin* (1928)

"It's always been blood . . . blood is life . . . Why do you think we eat it? It's what keeps you going. Makes you warm. Makes you hard. Makes you other than dead."

— Spike, *Buffy the Vampire Slayer*

Walking dead. Nosferatu. Upyr. Lampir. Incubus. Pontianak. Drakul. Vampyr. Nosferatu. Vampire. It's believed that the existence of vampires may have been noted as early as 1047 in the production notes of a priest who transcribed the Book of Psalms for a prince, signing his name in Old Russian as "Upir' Likhyi," which loosely translated means "wicked" or "foul vampire." An Austrian account in 1725 refers to the Serbian practice of exhuming dead bodies in order to kill them. Likely derived from the French "vampyre" or the German "vampir," the *Oxford English Dictionary* dates the first appearance of the word "vampire" to 1734 when it appeared in the travelogue "Travels of Three English Gentlemen."

If the term for vampires pre-dates our fictional accounts of them, is it possible they actually exist? Or is it more likely that we've embellished stories over time to create one of the most pervasive myths ever? And, if so, why? Alexander Skarsgård has a theory. "[V]ampires symbolize consistency and something that's permanent in a world where everything is constantly changing," he says. "Humans, animals, nature, and even mountains will change over time. To have something that will stand the test of time is attractive."

While there are many theories that attempt to explain the origin of belief in vampires, there's little room for debate when it comes to the ongoing appeal of vampires. What is it about vampires that popular fiction can't seem to get enough of them? They've even been invited past the tightly guarded gates of educational children's television. Did you know that the Muppet vampire, Count von Count from *Sesame Street*, complete with his obsessive counting, seems to have been based on actual vampire myth? One way to supposedly deter a vampire is to throw seeds (usually mustard) outside a door, or place a fishing net outside a window. Vampires are compelled to count the seeds or the holes in the net, delaying them until the sun comes up! And how can we forget one of the most popular vampires in children's fiction, Bunnicula, the cute little rabbit and vegetarian vampire?

Popular culture reflects a society's prevailing attitudes and perspectives at a given time, its notable distinction from high art that it's changeable, influenced by media, and often urban-based. As such, vampire lore has been reinterpreted to suit the needs of each creator. For instance, that sunlight can kill vampires is a fairly modern invention, possibly started by the U.S. government to scare superstitious guerrillas in the Philippines during the 1950s. This was borrowed by authors such as Anne Rice. Recently, authors like Stephenie Meyer have subverted the genre further. Garlic, holy items, and sunlight don't harm her vampires, traits that will undoubtedly be carried forward into other adaptations of the vampire persona. And Hollywood's vampires are typically pale, beautiful, and aristocratic, whereas in the days before Bram Stoker's *Dracula*, vampires were often peasants, shapeless "bags of blood," not the charismatic, six-pack-ab vampires roaming the courtyards of suburban high schools.

Even Ryan Kwanten, who plays Jason Stackhouse, has his own, slightly fanboyish theory. He thinks the popularity of vampires is due to the fact that they're relatable, "unlike a superhero who, to me, seems out of our reach," he says. Psychologist Andrew Bates adds that vampire stories were created at a time when it wasn't possible to write about sex, which is how he explains the erotic metaphors associated with vampirism, "although," he adds, "they've had to face some pretty grim ironic retelling along the way." Welsh psychoanalyst Ernest Jones drives even deeper, noting in his essay "On the Nightmare" that vampires are symbolic of our edgy emotions — love, guilt, anger — that are employed when a loved one dies. We yearn for their return, he explains, and yearn for them to want the same.

The vampire is also our communal "go-to" creature in times of great loss and vulnerability. For instance, when U.S. President George Bush declared a New World Order after the fall of Communism in Russia and Eastern Europe, his strongest opponents created Operation Vampire Killer 2000 (with Bush painted as the vampire), designed to hinder police and military from becoming involved in what they saw as Bush's attempt to become the one dominant world power. Laurell K. Hamilton is the creator of the Anita Blake series. For her, our connection to vampires isn't just a reaction, it puts us at ease. "[N]othing scares most people like death. Vampires are dead, but they're still people; walking and living . . . I think people find that comforting."

The vampire made its first fictional appearances in 1819 when John Polidori wrote *The Vampyre*. Rumored to be modeled after a domineering Lord Byron (earlier incorrectly believed to be the text's author), Polidori's villain was suave and seductive but evil. Following this, James Malcolm Rymer's horrific and gruesome Varney the Vampire tales were published to great success from 1845 to 1847. In 1871, Sheridan Le Fanu introduced a lesbian vampire to the horror canon with his story *Carmilla*.

Fangtastic Folkloric Facts About Vampires

1. Many scholars argue the word "vampire" is either from the Hungarian *vampir* or from the Turkish *upior, upper,* or *upyr* meaning "witch." Other scholars argue the term derived from the Greek word "to drink" or from the Greek *nosophoros* meaning "plague carrier." It may also derive from the Serbian *Bamiiup* or the Serbo-Crotian *pirati*. There are many terms for "vampire" found across cultures, suggesting that vampires are embedded in human consciousness.

2. Probably the most famous vampire of all time, Count Dracula, quoted Deuteronomy 12:23: "The blood is the life."

3. Prehistoric stone monuments called *dolmens* have been found over the graves of the dead in northwest Europe. Anthropologists speculate they have been placed over graves to keep vampires from rising.

4. A rare disease called porphyria (also called the "vampire" or "Dracula" disease) causes vampire-like symptoms, such as an extreme sensitivity to sunlight and sometimes hairiness. In extreme cases, teeth might be stained reddish brown, and eventually the patient may go mad.

5. Documented medical disorders that people accused of being a vampire may have suffered from include haematodipsia, which is a sexual thirst for blood, and hemeralopia or day blindness. Anemia ("bloodlessness") was often mistaken for a symptom of a vampire attack.

6. One of the most famous "true vampires" was Countess Elizabeth Bathory (1560–1614), who was accused of biting the flesh of girls while torturing them and bathing in their blood to retain her youthful beauty. She was by all accounts a very attractive woman.

7. One of the earliest accounts of vampires is found in an ancient Sumerian and Babylonian myth dating to 4,000 BC, which describes *ekimmu* or *edimmu* (one who is snatched away). The *ekimmu* is a type of *uruku* or *utukku* (a spirit or demon) who was not buried properly and has returned as a vengeful spirit to suck the life out of the living.

8. According to *Egyptian Book of the Dead*, if the *ka* (one of the five parts of the soul) does not receive particular offerings, it ventures out of its tomb as a *kha* to find nourishment, which may include drinking the blood of the living. In addition, the Egyptian goddess Sekhmet was known to drink blood. The ancient fanged goddess Kaliof India also had a powerful desire for blood.

9. Chinese vampires were called a *ch'iang shih* (corpse-hopper) and had red eyes and crooked claws. They were said to have a strong sexual drive that led them to attack women. As they grew stronger, the *ch'iang shih* gained the ability to fly, grew long white hair, and could also change into a wolf.

10. While both vampires and zombies generally belong to the "undead," there are differences between them depending on the mythology from which they emerged. For example, zombies tend to have a lower IQ than vampires, prefer brains and flesh over blood, are immune to garlic, most likely have a reflection in the mirror, are based largely in African myth, move more slowly due to rotting muscles, can enter churches, and are not necessarily afraid of fire or sunlight.

11. A vampire supposedly has control over the animal world and can turn into a bat, rat, owl, moth, fox, or wolf.

12. In 2009, a 16th-century female skull with a rock wedged in its mouth was found near the remains of plague victims. It was not unusual during that century to shove a rock or brick in the mouth of a suspected vampire to prevent it from feeding on the bodies of other plague victims or attacking the living. Female vampires were also often blamed for spreading the Bubonic Plague throughout Europe.

13. According to several legends, if someone was bitten by a suspected vampire, he or she should drink the ashes of a burned vampire. To prevent an attack, a person should make bread with the blood of vampire and eat it.

14. Thresholds have historically held significant symbolic value, and a vampire cannot cross a threshold unless invited. The connection between threshold and vampires seems to be a concept of complicity or allowance. Once a commitment is made to allow evil, evil can re-enter at any time.

15. Before Christianity, methods of repelling vampires included garlic, hawthorn branches, rowan trees (later used to make crosses), scattering of seeds, fire, decapitation with a gravedigger's spade, salt (associated with preservation and purity), iron, bells, a rooster's crow, peppermint, running water, and burying a suspected vampire at a crossroads. It was also not unusual for a corpse to be buried face down so it would dig down the wrong way and become lost in the earth.

16. After the advent of Christianity, methods of repelling vampires began to include holy water, crucifixes, and Eucharist wafers. These methods were usually not fatal to the vampire, and their effectiveness depended on the belief of the user.

17. Garlic, a traditional vampire repellent, has been used as a form of protection for over 2,000 years. The ancient Egyptians believed garlic was a gift from God, Roman soldiers thought it gave them courage, sailors believed it protected them from shipwreck, and German miners believed it protected them from evil spirits when they went underground. In several cultures, brides carried garlic under their clothes for protection, and cloves of garlic were used to protect people from a wide range of illnesses. Modern-day scientists found that the oil in garlic, allicin, is a highly effective antibiotic.

18. The legend that vampires must sleep in coffins probably arose from reports of gravediggers and morticians who described corpses suddenly sitting up in their graves or coffins. This eerie phenomenon could be caused by the decomposing process.

19. According to some legends, a vampire may engage in sex with his former wife, which often led to pregnancy. In fact, this belief may have provided a convenient explanation as to why a widow, who was supposed to be celibate, became pregnant. The resulting child was called a *gloglave* in Bulgarian or *vampirdzii* in Turkish. Rather than being ostracized, the child was considered a hero who had powers to slay a vampire.

20. Folklore vampires can become vampires not only through a bite, but also if they were once a werewolf, practiced sorcery, were excommunicated, committed suicide, were an illegitimate child of

parents who were illegitimate, or were stillborn or died before baptism. In addition, anyone who has eaten the flesh of a sheep killed by a wolf, was a seventh son, was the child of a pregnant woman who was looked upon by a vampire, was a nun who stepped over an unburied body, had teeth when they were born, or had a cat jump on their corpse before being buried could also turn into vampires.

21. In vampire folklore, a vampire initially emerges as a soft blurry shape with no bones. These are "bags of blood" with red, glowing eyes and, instead of a nose, a sharp snout that they suck blood with. If it can survive for 40 days, it will then develop bones and a body and become much more dangerous and difficult to kill.

22. In some vampire folktales, vampires can marry and move to another city where they take up jobs suitable for vampires, such as butchers. That they become butchers may be based on the analogy that butchers are descendants of the "sacrificer."

23. Certain regions in the Balkans believed that fruit, such as pumpkins or watermelons, would become vampires if they were left out longer than 10 days or were not consumed by Christmas. Vampire pumpkins or watermelons generally were not feared because they do not have teeth. A drop of blood on a fruit's skin is a sign that it is about to turn into a vampire.

24. Mermaids can also be vampires – instead of sucking blood, they suck out the breath of their victims.

25. Some historians argue that Prince Charles is a direct descendant of the Vlad the Impaler.

(Reprinted with the permission of RandomHistory.com.)

Without a doubt, though, it's Bram Stoker's novel *Dracula* (1897) upon which most modern vampire portrayals are based. First publishing his book to mediocre response, Stoker died in near poverty 10 years before F. W. Murnau's film adaptation *Nosferatu* (1922) and Hamilton Deane's stage adaptation (1924) brought Stoker's monster to the mainstream, with comparisons between vampirism and contagious diseases such as syphilis, turning Stoker's vampire into an apt contemporary metaphor.

But would the real Dracula stand up? Stoker's protagonist has long been rumored to be based on Vlad Tepes, a bloodthirsty medieval character who impaled his victims and was called Vlad the Impaler. But scholar Dr. Elizabeth Miller has good reason for debate. In her book *Bram Stoker's Notes for Dracula*, she and co-author Robert Eighteen-Bisang dissect Stoker's handwritten notes. They discovered that nowhere in them was there a reference to Vlad. Instead, they discovered a note about a 15th-century ruler named "Dracula," along with an additional notation that Stoker had learned that the Romanian translation for "Dracula" meant "The Devil." Stoker wrote "DRACULA MEANS THE DEVIL," leading the scholars to speculate that Stoker, in fact, did not have Vlad the Impaler in mind when naming his iconic and legendary character.

The vampire often rose again in the 20th century, particularly as more vampire fiction appeared as ongoing series of books, often crossing over into the young adult and romance markets. J. R. Ward's Black Dagger Brotherhood series, L. A. Banks's Vampire Huntress Legend series, Laurell K. Hamilton's Anita Blake: Vampire Hunter series, Kim Harrison's The Hollows series, and Charlaine Harris's Sookie Stackhouse novels all portray vampires in a new light (pardon the pun), many diverging from the original legend of vampires as the ruthless monsters who feed without conscience.

It was Marilyn Ross's Barnabas Collins series (1966–71), based loosely on the television series *Dark Shadows*, that issued in the sympathetic, tragic vampire, less evil than existential, the obvious predecessor to *True Blood*'s Bill Compton. This was followed by Anne Rice's hugely influential and epic Vampire Chronicles (1976–2003), picked up again in Stephenie Meyer's paranormically popular Twilight series (2005–2008).

To put the popularity of vampires into perspective, just think: all four books in Meyer's series made *USA Today*'s Bestselling Books of 2009 list. In the same year, 17% of *all* book sales tracked were vampire and/or paranormal–themed, up from 2% in 2007. Charlaine Harris had nine of the top 100 bestselling books of 2009 from her Sookie Stackhouse series. And the mother/daughter team of P. C. and Kristin

Cast had six of their books from the House of Night series represented. Even Jane Austen found new life with *Pride and Prejudice and Zombies* (by Austen and Seth Grahame-Smith) coming in at #48.

As a film and television character, only Sherlock Holmes has made more fictional appearances than Dracula, with IMDb.com listing over 50 productions that cite Bram Stoker in some writing capacity. *Secrets of House No. 5* (1912) is generally accepted as the first vampire film, with F. W. Murnau's silent black-and-white *Nosferatu* marking the first cinematic depiction of the Count a decade later, in 1922. However, it was Tod Browning's *Dracula* with the erotic, tuxedo-clad aristocrat played by Bela Lugosi that became the hallmark of vampire movies and literature, as well as the first talking film to include a vampire. Based loosely on Bram Stoker's short story "Dracula's Guest," *Dracula's Daughter* came to screens in 1936 as a sequel to *Dracula*.

But it was the Hammer Horror series starring Christopher Lee that breathed new life into the vampire franchise, starting in 1958 with *Dracula*, then followed by seven sequels (of which Lee appeared in five), remarkable even by today's standards. The series re-emerged in 1970 when lesbian antagonists were featured in *The Vampire Lovers*, which was based on *Carmilla*. The genre further diversified in 1972 when the blaxploitation film *Blacula* offered viewers their first African American Dracula, leading to a host of other horror/blaxploitation films such *Blackenstein, Dr. Black and Mr. Hyde, Ganja and Hess*, and *Sugar Hill*.

In 1979, film returned Dracula to his monstrous roots with Klaus Kinski's portrait in Werner Herzog's remake *Nosferatu: Phantom der Nacht*, and again in the television miniseries *Salem's Lot*, made in the same year and based on the novel by Stephen King (the movie was remade in 2004). For a wild ride, set aside a day and drink up this cinematic cocktail: Murnau's *Nosferatu*, followed by Herzog's *Nosferatu: Phantom der Nacht*, followed by *Shadow of the Vampire* — a fictional retelling of Murnau's relationship with Max Schreck during the filming of the original *Nosferatu* — capped off with Herzog's documentary *My Best Fiend*, which details his working relationship with Klaus Kinski who played the second Nosferatu. It's enough to make your head spin, but worth the trip!

Bats, Vampires, & Dracula by Elizabeth Miller

Ever wonder which came first – the bat or the vampire? How did bats become so associated with Count Dracula that the poor maligned creatures are forced to lurk in the recesses of 20th-century popular culture? Is it all the fault of that Irish writer Bram Stoker and his novel *Dracula* (1897)? Hopefully, the following paragraphs will answer these (and other) questions.

As all bat lovers know, there is a species known as the "vampire bat," the most common of which is *Desmodus rotundus.* Found only in Mexico and parts of Central and South America, they feed primarily on the blood of livestock. A vampire bat will bite its prey with razor-sharp teeth while the prey is sleeping. Rather than suck the blood, it laps it up, much as a cat laps milk.

As for vampires (those blood-sucking monsters of fiction and film), these have "existed" since ancient times in the folklore and mythology of most cultures in Europe and elsewhere. It appears that when the blood-lapping bats were first observed by Spanish explorers in Central and South America (their natural habitats), they were given the label "vampire" because of the fact that, unlike all other species of bats, these live off the blood of their prey.

Bats were associated with the mysterious and the supernatural long before Stoker's novel appeared in print. As creatures of the night, bats fit in well with the motifs of Gothic fiction. A bat-like vampire appears, for example, as an illustration in the novel *Varney the Vampire,* which appeared 50 years before *Dracula.*

But it is Bram Stoker's novel that cemented the connection between bats and the vampires of folklore. While he was working on his novel in the 1890s, Stoker came across a clipping in a New York newspaper concerning vampire bats, which directly influenced the following comment by Quincey Morris in *Dracula*: "I have not seen anything pulled down so quick since I was on the Pampas and had a mare . . . One of those big bats that they call 'vampires' had got at her during the night and . . . there wasn't enough blood in her to let her stand up." Stoker obviously did not know (or chose to ignore) the fact that the vampire bat is quite small.

But Stoker's major contribution to the association of vampires with bats was his introduction of the idea that a vampire could shapeshift into the form of a bat (as well as a wolf and mist). For example, in his pursuit and seduction of Lucy, Count Dracula frequently disguises himself in the form of a large bat that flaps at her window. In Stoker's novel such a "vampire bat" is, of course, quite capable of attacking and draining humans.

This motif found its way into the movies. While the first film based on *Dracula*, *Nosferatu* (1922) did not use bats (here the connection was with rats), the 1931 Universal Studios classic *Dracula* starring Bela Lugosi certainly did. This was the movie that provided the 20th century with its most memorable and lasting images of Count Dracula (including the bats), images that survive to this very day.

Even the medical community has latched on to the Dracula-bat connection! A Venezuelan research team has isolated a previously unknown anticoagulant glycoprotein from the common vampire bat. This substance targets activated forms of blood coagulation factors, thus inhibiting them immediately. Named "draculin," this anticoagulant agent promises to be significant in the development of improved drugs to fight heart disease and stroke.

Bram Stoker would certainly be amazed!

Elizabeth Miller is recognized internationally for her expertise on Bram Stoker's 1897 novel Dracula. *She has lectured throughout Canada, as well as in the United States, England, Ireland, Germany, Poland, and Romania. Dr. Miller has been interviewed extensively by major media including the BBC, ABC (20/20), CBC, the* Guardian, *the* New York Times, Entertainment Weekly, *the* Los Angeles Times, *and the* Wall Street Journal. *Her own publications on* Dracula *include dozens of articles and several books including* Reflections on Dracula *(1997),* Dracula: The Shade and the Shadow *(1998),* Dracula: Sense & Nonsense *(2000; rev 2006),* A Dracula Handbook *(2005), and* Bram Stoker's Dracula: A Documentary Journey into Vampire Country and the Dracula Phenomenon *(2009). Visit Dr. Miller at Dracula's Homepage (www.ucs.mun.ca/~emiller) and the Dracula Research Centre (www.blooferland.com/drc).*

Showing no signs of ill health, it's unlikely our insatiable craving for vampires will die soon, as evidenced in the rise of vampire franchises, including the Blade trilogy, based on the vampire-hunter of Marvel Comics; Joss Whedon's cult show *Buffy the Vampire Slayer* (and spin-off *Angel*); *Van Helsing*; the female-fronted Underworld series; Stephenie Meyer's film-adapted Twilight series; *Blood Ties*, featuring the illegitimate (vampire) son of Henry VIII; *Being Human*, which features a vampire, werewolf, and ghost; *The Vampire Diaries*, based on L. J. Smith's series; our beloved *True Blood*; and, in the works, an adaptation of the Anita Blake: Vampire Hunter novels by Laurell K. Hamilton.

Even the short-lived soap opera *Port Charles*, the spin-off of *General Hospital*, featured a vampire, Caleb Morley, who was so popular with fans, he literally would not die, written back into the story arc after he'd already been offed — twice. Vampires are starting to appear more frequently in international productions as well, including Sweden's adolescent vampire drama *Let the Right One In*; Russia's blockbuster *Night Watch*; and Korea's *Thirst*, winner of the Jury Prize at the 2009 Cannes Film Festival.

Vampires have evolved from the stuff of demonic legends to magazine heartthrobs, making stops along the way as existential monsters and pop culture superheroes. They've been played by some of the biggest names in Hollywood — Tom Cruise and Brad Pitt — responsible for elevating foreign imports to the status of North American gods — Alexander Skarsgård and Robert Pattinson — and left a most indelible mark on the career of actors whose contributions to the vampire canon were shaped in part by the eternal hold of an immortal myth — Bela Lugosi and Christopher Lee. Even Martin Landau's career got an unexpected boost when he won an Oscar for portraying Lugosi in Tim Burton's 1994 film *Ed Wood*. (His daughter, Juliet, would go on to play vampire Drusilla on *Buffy the Vampire Slayer*.)

But here's a dire thought. While vampires are destined to live forever, more and more films are asking us just how much longer humanity can keep "sucking" itself dry. If humans have long perished, and with the fictional advent of synthetic blood, courtesy of Charlaine Harris, vampires would truly outlive us all. What would that world look like? And what would it look like without a synthetic replacement? Would it be similar to the scenario in the 2010 film *Daybreakers*, where vampires rule the world and humans are nothing more than living blood banks? What measures would vampires take to sustain themselves?

To those who think now that vampires have (literally) had their day in the sun and perhaps it's time they should retire, I say you may be speaking too soon. I sense a mythical rebirth on the horizon, sunny or otherwise, that echoes a fear far greater than our individual mortality, but something closer to a collective paranoia. Until then, let's enjoy the vampire while it lasts.

The Vampire Touch

Suave Seducer or Sexual Predator?

"In the collective consciousness, over the years, [vampires] have morphed into these really sexy rock stars: dangerous and incredibly hot creatures."

– Alan Ball

This is one of Alan Ball's responses to the oft-asked question regarding the ongoing appeal of vampires. Indeed, with the likes of Eric Northman, Bill Compton, Edward Cullen, Lestat de Lioncourt, Spike, Angel, and Damon Salvatore, one could easily fill a calendar of undead hotties.

I contacted an author, an academic, and a vampire to ask them for their take on Ball's comment. Are vampires inherently sexy, or have we perverted their natures to suit our own desires? Here's what they had to say:

Joe Laycock (academic and author of *Vampires Today: The Truth About Modern Vampirism*)
The vampire has always been sexual, but not necessarily sexy. Stories of nocturnal visits from vampires and demons have been linked to a medical phenomenon called sleep paralysis. It's one thing to wake up in the middle of the night unable to move and feel that you are being violated by a dark, unseen presence. It's quite another to have a crush on Bill

Compton or Edward Cullen. But I don't think the vampire changed so much as we did.

In 1819, when John Polidori wrote *The Vampyre*, his villain, Lord Ruthven, was rich and seductive but still unrepentantly evil. It was not until 1967 that we got our first sympathetic vampire: Barnabas Collins from the soap opera *Dark Shadows*. Anne Rice's reluctant vampires, as well as Nick Knight, Angel, Edward Cullen, and Bill Compton are all descended from Barnabas Collins.

What is interesting is that Barnabas was supposed to get staked after a few episodes. But the vampire saved the show's ratings, forcing the writers to turn him from a villain into a hero. I believe this sympathy for the vampire reflects profound social changes: in ancient times the vampire was often a scapegoat that villagers could blame for any number of problems. Exhuming and burning corpses may have actually brought communities closer together. But in the modern world, we have a much stronger sense of individualism. We now sympathize with the vampire because we too feel alienated. Anne Rice was the first to realize that we now view vampires much as we do rock stars. We know that every rock star from Elvis to Kurt Cobain suffered drug-abuse, heartache, and loneliness, but we want to be them anyway.

Nigel Suckling (author of many books on myths and legends, including *Book of the Vampire*)

Yes, it's curious how sexy vampires have become. General interest in them began in the 18th century when there was a well documented plague of vampirism in Eastern Europe, with the dead apparently rising from their tombs in hordes to attack and infect the living. Vampirism was treated as a very real phenomenon and in fact it still is taken very seriously in rural parts of Greece and the Balkans, but the vampires in question are very different from those in modern fiction. More like zombies in fact, apart from their ability to dematerialize and escape their graves without physically digging their way out. Victorian fiction introduced the notion of the vampire's sexiness, culminating of course in Bram Stoker's *Dracula*, when they became even sexier still. But this wasn't a purely literary invention.

There is a parallel and very ancient and widespread tradition of the sexy vampire, using the term in its broadest sense. In ancient Greece and Rome they had the *lamia*, a beautiful demoness who seduced men in order to drink their blood, and there was a very similar notion about ghouls in the Middle East. In China they have very similar ideas about vampires — some being shambling, zombie-like monsters and others beautiful temptresses looking to drain their victims' blood. In Hebrew tradition the daughters of Lilith, Adam's first wife, took revenge for his rejection of her by seducing his descendants and drinking their blood. So the sexiness of vampires is nothing new and it's tied up with the mystical significance of blood as the carrier of life in more than a purely physical sense. There is a mystery about blood that cannot quite be pinned down or explained away. It's tied up also with power in relationships — domination and subservience — much of which is unconscious and equally beyond easy explanation.

Modern vampire stories tap right into this ongoing dream or nightmare and I think the changing nature of the vampire mythos — their not necessarily being still vulnerable to holy water and crucifixes, for example — reflects one of their most basic talents, which is shapeshifting. They adapt to their circumstances and thus present every generation with fresh, queasily seductive terror, at the same time posing awkward questions about morality.

Michelle Belanger (psychic vampire and author of the *Psychic Vampire Codex*)
The vampire as we know it today has its roots definitively in the folklore of Eastern Europe, and to some extent these vampire beliefs are still in place in rural areas today. The vampires from folklore, on the whole, are not at all what might be expected by people exposed to the pop culture archetype we've all come to know. These vampires are risen corpses. They are unlovely creatures, and many of their distinguishing features stand in direct contrast to the svelte and sexy vampires seen on shows like *True Blood*. One Greek type of vampire, the *vrykolakas*, gets its name from a word meaning "drum-like," and this word is applicable to vampires in general because they were believed to batten in their

graves on the blood sucked from victims in the night, growing large and swollen in their coffins. The vampires of folklore are also frequently described as being red, not pale, because they were thought to grow flushed and ruddy with that self-same blood.

Despite the many differences between the vampires of folklore and the vampires of pop culture today, there are nevertheless some striking similarities. The main similarity is a connection between the vampire and sex. As unattractive as the vampire of folklore might be, a sexual element is still present in many of the tales. Dead lovers were often said to come back to visit their spouses and paramours, exhausting them with sex from nightfall through morning. While these sexual vampires were believed to suck the blood of their victims, they were also literally believed to love their spouses to death, wearing them away with their nightly exertions until they followed the vampire to the grave. Another sexual element appears in several of the official reports penned on exhumed corpses suspected of being vampires. The corpses of male vampires, in addition to having remained whole and undecayed in the grave, were also described as having immense erections. So sex and death are intertwined in the vampire myth even from its very roots.

Once the vampire was transplanted from the folklore of Eastern Europe to the literature of Western Europe, this theme of sex and death became a leitmotif visited by authors again and again. In many ways, the vampire of fiction is used repeatedly as a metaphor for illicit forms of sexuality: from dominance and submission, to sado-masochism, homosexuality, and, in the more horrific instances, penetrative sex forced on an unwilling victim. The vampire as we see him in film is an inescapably Freudian figure: when he gets aroused, his fangs grow long and hard. With these, he penetrates his victim (or his lover); there is a fluid exchange, and sometimes contagion or procreation occurs. A vampire's hunger for blood is further sexualized as a type of lust, a burning need that consumes him whenever he (or she) lays eyes upon the object of desire. Homosexuality, bisexuality, and pansexuality are all topics that can be freely explored within the vampire trope, because the vampire's needs are redirected to something everyone, regardless of gender or orientation, has: blood.

The vampire, as it began in folklore, was in many ways a personification of the primal fear that the living hold for the dead. Once the vampire made its transition from folklore to fiction, the figure morphed and became instead humanity's dark mirror. It represents all of those forbidden hungers and desires that most of us secretly long for: immortal youth, eternal life, inhuman power, and uninhibited sexuality. Once we understand the vampire in these terms, it becomes fairly obvious why this fearsome creature of the night holds such an enduring appeal.

Charlaine Harris

The Woman Behind the Heroine, Sookie Stackhouse

"[These books were] such an escape, and yet there were nuggets of really profound things that [Harris] said about existence and parts of the culture, but it's also wrapped up in a fun amusement-park, gothic, romantic, science-fiction slasher movie . . . Right around [*Dead to the World*] I remember thinking, 'This would make a good TV series. If this show was done right, this would be a show I would watch.'"

— Alan Ball

The power of social media is undeniable. I was over 80,000 words into this book when I finally turned to Twitter for a response (in 140 characters or less) to the one question I was afraid to ask. I needed to know what the Bookies thought, those people who rabidly read Charlaine Harris's novels, back-to-back, before they became converts of the TV series. "Speak now or forever hold your peace," I wrote. "In my book, should I refer to the series as the Southern Vampire Mysteries [the series' original name] or the Sookie Stackhouse novels [the series' informal name]." The answer turned out to be quite simple, but I'm glad I asked.

Everyone thought that Sookie deserved to be front and center, books, series, or otherwise, with the tongue-in-cheek response, "the Sookeh Stackhouse novels," coming a close second. (An inside joke you'll get soon enough, if you don't already.) Sookie is the voice of

Charlaine Harris's blockbuster series about a young, southern, tele-pathic waitress who falls for a vampire in Bon Temps, Louisiana. But even though the books are told entirely from her perspective, the remaining characters — least of which the intense flavor of a humid, southern landscape rife with socioeconomic politics — are far from supporting. The books have had massive commercial success: nine of Harris's novels landed in the top 100 bestselling titles of 2009. If best-sellers don't impress you, how about prolificacy? In her almost 30-year career, Harris has published close to 30 novels, and that's not counting short stories. True, South African writer Mary Faulkner wrote 904 books under six pen names, but it's doubtful she had to meet the demands of today's market or a genre audience that may not have ini-tially taken too kindly to the idea of a mainstreaming vampire.

If we've learned anything about immortality, it's that it allows our imaginations as both readers and writers to adapt, evolve, and just have some fun! But what makes Harris's tales so intriguing? For a start, the novels are gruesome and sexy — "We stumbled into the house, and he turned me to face the couch. I gripped it with my hands and, just as I'd imagined, he pulled down my pants, and then he was in me." They're just as often funny, Sookie's unique, at times, ridiculous voice ringing through the darkness.

The first book, *Dead Until Dark*, was published in 2001, and was met with big success. The novel introduces a number of key characters that feature heavily in the TV series: Bill "Vampire Bill" Compton, Sookie's Civil War–era paramour; Eric Northman, Bill's superior, and Fangtasia bar owner; Jason Stackhouse, Sookie's hapless brother; Tara Thornton, Sookie's friend; Lafayette Reynolds, Merlotte's short order cook; and Sam Merlotte, Sookie's boss. The other titles in the Sookie Stackhouse novels are *Living Dead in Dallas, Club Dead, Dead to the World, Dead as a Doornail, Definitely Dead, All Together Dead, From Dead to Worse, Dead and Gone, A Touch of Dead*, and *Dead in the Family*, with Harris contracted to write another three in the series.

Without spoiling the novels, the remaining characters make up a cast of human and paranormal individuals, all with dramatic conflicts and deep desires. At its heart, the Sookie Stackhouse series is about the

Charlaine Harris rests her signing hand to pose with fan Mitch Obrecht. (Mitch Obrecht)

turmoil of trying to negotiate change, romance, and difference when previously disjointed communities intersect in one small town. The universe in which Sookie lives, her own telepathy included, is a previously uneventful world now brimming with the likes of vampires, weres and shapeshifters, fairies, witches and Wiccans, and, of course, humans, who in many cases are capable of things as miraculous or demonic as non-humans.

Vampires: In the "Sookieverse," vampires attempt to mainstream into society with the advent of a Japanese synthetic blood replacement that acts as a supplement for human blood. With the need to feed on mortals removed, their hope is that they will be treated as equal citizens. Regardless, they remain extremely private about their ways, remaining inflexible on certain mores. The vampires in Harris's world have heightened senses, their fangs appearing when angry, hungry, or aroused. Against traditional vampire lore, they will not die immediately in sunlight, but only after prolonged exposure. Similarly, while garlic and holy water may be an irritant, vampires will not die from them, nor are they unable to enter a house of worship. Silver, however, burns them deeply. Consistent with most lore, a vampire must be invited into a private residence, unable to re-enter should that invitation be rescinded. And if a vampire and human exchange blood, it ties them together so that the vampire may sense the human's most urgent feelings, namely fear. The human can also expect to experience more erotic feelings toward the vampire they've tasted, as well as a sensual connection to the world around them. Humans cannot, however, become impregnated by a vampire.

Weres and Shapeshifters: Weres and shapeshifters assume both human and animal forms. Should a mortal mate with a shifter or were, their were-child will not be able to resist transforming during a full moon. However, if both parents are weres or shifters, their child will be able to change at will like its parents. While shifters are able to transform into any animal, wereanimals are only able to change into one type of animal: werewolves, werepanthers, weretigers, etc. The term "weres" is reserved only for wolves, who consider themselves superior to other shifters. They remain much more secretive about their ways than vampires.

Humans: Among the humans is a collection of groupies — "fang-bangers" — who seek out vampires for sex. Vampire blood is considered an aphrodisiac, extremely addictive and in high demand. Those who capture vampires to retain their blood for black market resale are called "drainers." They bind their prisoners with silver chains, draining the vampire's blood into vials. Depending on the vampire, the blood may have different effects on a human. It's unpredictable. Then there are the evangelists who dislike vampires so greatly that they formed an organization dedicated to the annihilation of the vampire, the Fellowship of the Sun, headed up by the sprightly Steve and Sarah Newlin.

Fairies: Fairies are beautiful, exotic, and extremely strong creatures appealing to humans and vampires alike. Vampires are particularly drawn to fairies, which are near impossible to catch, Sookie describing the attraction as like "watching cats that'd suddenly spotted something skittering along a baseboard." They live in a magical world, but cross over to the human world via portals. While they are age-old, it's undetermined if they are immortal. Those who have fairy blood in them are immune to the adverse effects of iron and lemon — known to kill fairies — but are not full-fledged fairies.

Witches and Wiccans: Witches in Harris's series practice magic rituals, whereas Wiccans follow a pagan religion.

Charlaine Harris was born November 25, 1951, and raised in Tunica, Mississippi. A former weightlifter, she currently lives in Magnolia, Arkansas, with her husband and their three children where she's also a senior warden of St. James Episcopal Church.

In my interview with Harris, she told me that she credited her parents' reverence for books for her lifelong love of reading (she reads about 10 books a month) that also introduced her to the possibility of writing as something more than just a pasttime. "I thought that was the greatest occupation on earth; I still think so," Harris says. "I knew in my heart I was a writer, even when I was working a minimum wage job. It was my secret identity."

In 1973, Harris graduated with a BA in English and communication arts from Rhodes College in Memphis, Tennessee, where she took a creative writing course under a former editor with Houghton Mifflin, which ultimately became Harris's first publisher. She published two mysteries. Then in 1990, she released the first of what would become an eight novel series centered on a librarian-detective named Aurora Teagarden. During this time, Harris also wrote and published five novels in the Lily Bard (Shakespeare) series, set in rural Arkansas.

Harris made a conscious decision to end both series, wanting to try her hand at something new. *Dead Until Dark* was the first of the Southern Vampire Mysteries. It won the 2001 Anthony Award for Best Paperback Mystery. (In 2005, Harris also began another series, the Harper Connelly Mysteries, about a young woman who after being struck by lightning is suddenly able to locate dead bodies, seeing their last moments as they would have seen them.)

Interestingly, for as far as the imagination has taken Harris, she's surprised to learn there are people who actually want to know how to be romantically involved with vampires. "People really want to know that?

Geez Louise." She continues, "I think it would be pretty awful. For one thing, there's that whole daytime ban. That would be inconvenient. Also, there's the whole biting thing. Not a big fan of biting. So, I would have to say, in reality, this would be a pretty bad idea. And, at the risk of sounding like the worst characters in my books, I really wouldn't want my daughter dating a vampire."

How then did this Arkansas mother of three (whose works have been lovingly described as "cozies with teeth") come to write about a love she couldn't endorse? Harris confesses that aside from being bored with writing conventional mysteries she simply wanted to broaden her readership. Citing among her influences H. P. Lovecraft, Edgar Allen Poe, Jane Austen ("the mistress of the small things"), and Shirley Jackson, she made the conscious decision to write cross-genre fiction, blending chick-lit, paranormal romance, and mystery into one story-line. When it came time to construct her protagonist, all she knew was that Sookie dated a vampire. She had yet to determine Sookie's motivations, or those of the vampire for that matter. She devised Sookie's telepathy as a "disability," something that would draw them to one another, united in being outsiders from mainstream society.

Interestingly, Harris doesn't necessarily see Sookie's telepathy as an endearing trait. She told me, "It's the first of many awful things I've done to Sookie. I would not like to know ANY of the things she discovers via her 'disability.'" But it is a great narrative device, certainly in a first-person series. I asked Harris if going to these dark places was liberating for her as an author. "My life has not been an entirely easy one. But I think most writers get rid of their worst doubts and fears by writing about them, even if in an abstract way," she begins. "It's very easy to get to that darker place inside myself, but it's not as dark as it would be if I didn't explore it."

I also suggested to Harris that Sookie's telepathy was a nod to the voyeuristic process of all writers who inherently wonder what makes people tick, what lurks under the surface. Did she agree? "That's the great thing about being a writer, you can live second-hand." She continues, "I don't necessarily think writers have to have first-hand experience of every dark thing they write about — or every happy thing, either."

So, why the Bayou? Harris says she was reacting to famed author Anne Rice, whose Vampire Chronicles series is set in New Orleans, Louisiana, and who made it sound like a mecca for vampires. She thought, "Wouldn't it be funny to take the very prosaic, unromantic *northern* part of Louisiana and put my vampires there?" She's been told that Shreveport has experienced an increase in interest about vampire tours, something Harris finds greatly amusing, her small-town roots showing. "In Shreveport!"

Arriving at Sookie's name was much easier. It's an old southern nickname borrowed from her grandmother's best friend. As for the surname "Stackhouse," Harris pulled it from the phonebook, thinking it a perfect fit with her protagonist's given name.

As for the politics of the books, Harris addresses a lot of larger issues, but similar to Alan Ball's approach, she doesn't see herself as a crusader. "Certainly, there's discrimination and tremendous unfairness in the world . . . [I]f we would like to blame the evil in the world on monsters we need to examine ourselves, because *we* are the monsters. There's a lot of navel-gazing we could do that would make us all better people."

When it came time to settle on a tone, Harris went for something light-hearted against the advice of her agent. She felt her funny take on vampires was as challenging to write as it would have been if she had stuck to the usual ominous fare. For two years, it looked as if her agent might be right. But then the manuscript was sold, proving Harris's instincts correct as one Sookie novel after the other landed on the *New York Times* bestseller list. The television rights were optioned, but the production fell through. Meanwhile, Alan Ball had fallen in love with the books, and threw his hat into the ring along with three other offers. Harris chose Ball. "He understood what the books were about, a mixture of extremes: humor, violence, awakenings."

But it was Ball's polite demeanor that got the deal signed and sealed. Harris had met many players, but had heard nothing but praise from the people who'd worked with Ball over the years. It's perhaps no surprise then that when she first saw the evocative and sexually graphic opening credits she was taken aback. "I thought, 'Oh, my god, I'm going to have to move,'" Harris laughs. "It was so extreme." When HBO sent her the rough edit of the first episode, she settled into the idea that the show could honor her books while taking the stories to new places. "I was riveted. It was so exciting seeing my characters on the screen, and every now and then there was some dialogue straight from the book!" She says she found the sex scenes startling, in particular the viewer's introduction to Jason Stackhouse. "Although I knew Jason's character, I'd never followed him into the bedroom before, since Sookie never did." This sentiment is echoed by Stephen Moyer, who also thrills in seeing the books leap from the page to the screen. "[Charlaine Harris's] books are specifically from Sookie's point of view, and [*True Blood*] isn't just about Sookie . . . When I read *Harry Potter,* I don't want to then go and see *Harry Potter* shot frame to frame . . . If somebody is going to put something in front of me, I want it to be different."

So how *has* Harris — who prefers to go to bed early, get up early, go to the movies with her husband, and watch her daughter's soccer games — adjusted to the life of an international bestselling author? After all, she toiled for almost 25 years before her career trajectory broke through the stratosphere in what must seem to most like an overnight occurrence. But Harris can still remember her first job, working in an offset darkroom for a small newspaper where she "stood on a concrete floor all day and made minimum wage, which then was $1.60 an hour." She agrees that the writing life has rewarded her kindly.

However, the writing life has its dues. More than ever, readers want to connect with their favorite authors. In an industry as competitive as publishing, and loyal independent booksellers closing their doors at a remarkable rate, even authors as successful as Harris need to maintain contact with the loyal fan bases. It's a new world; she could easily pipe in her image over the internet instead of making in-store appearances. But travel is all part of the job. With each new book, Harris is expected to put in her face time, appearing at events, conventions, and on panels, some of which she happily makes her own way to, such as the Romantic Times Booklovers Convention. For a writer who continues to create at an astonishing pace, though, all the coming and going can be discombobulating. "Airplane travel is just not fun anymore," she says on her personal blog. "And when I'm on tour, it's actu-

Sam Trammell and Nelsan Ellis show Charlaine Harris some big love at Comic-Con. (Eileen Rivera, www.BiteClubShow.com)

ally pretty easy to forget where I am. I can't tell you how many times I've woken up in a hotel room and wondered how to find the bathroom . . . Sometimes I feel like a different person when I'm traveling, and it's great to get to a big city and meet lots of wonderful readers. But I always enjoy going home."

In 2005, Barnes & Noble asked Harris to name her favorite book and why. See if you can guess the book (and heroine) that she's talking about: "This book has everything: mystery, unrequited love, class war, illicit sex, madness, and a woman with an unswerving sense of moral rectitude . . . [S]he's devoted to thinking things over carefully before arriving at a rational decision. And yet she's a passionate woman underneath that drab dress that she's decided is suitable for her station . . . extremely conventional, and at the same time unconventional; a prime example of still waters running very deep. She rises above adversity every time, and she has a lot of adversity to rise above. [It's] the basic blueprint for thousands of books that followed." Harris's favorite book is *Jane Eyre* by Charlotte Brontë, which features a protagonist who sounds an awful lot like Sookie.

Ginjer Buchanan is editor-in-chief at Ace Books and Harris's long-time editor. In a promotional video for Penguin USA's *Project Paranormal* series, she recounts how Harris's original manuscript first came to her through an assistant editor who thought there was something special about *Dead Until Dark*. Buchanan gave it a read herself and found the voice and setting fresh and compelling, rendered in a realistic, loving fashion, not as a stereotype. She was also drawn in by Harris's humor and ability to work within the constraints of a plot-driven genre when told only from the perspective of one person. Talking about *Dead in the Family*, the next book in the series, Buchanan shares that the story is, not surprisingly, very much about family and leaves Sookie in a better place than she was in at the end of *Dead and Gone*.

As for the coming installments, Harris has brought on some assistants to create what she calls a "bible" to help her keep track of what's come before in the Sookieverse. She readily admits that the fun of writing comes from creating on-the-go, and that if she herself isn't sure of the answers, she simply works around the questions, even though she already has a pretty good idea how it will all end. With another three novels contracted, she has plenty of time to allow the characters to evolve in ways that are organic and pleasing to Harris. And as for research, she says that it's fairly easy because Sookie's story is set in the fictional town in which Harris imagines she herself actually lives, where she is queen. "Where I rule."

Nothing Is Certain but Death and Sex

Alan Ball's Creative Process

"At one point, HBO asked, 'What is the central theme of this show?' I don't think in those terms. I just think, 'Am I entertained? Am I interested? Am I compelled?' . . . So, I said [*True Blood*] is about the terrors of intimacy. And in retrospect, I think that's kind of true."

– Alan Ball

Alan Ball is no stranger to success, but when he came across Charlaine Harris's Sookie Stackhouse novels, he was a relative stranger to vampires, confessing — oh, the horror! — that he'd never seen an episode of *Buffy the Vampire Slayer* and wasn't particularly a fan of the genre. Why on earth then would he helm a show about vampires? Possibly for the same reason that he created a show about funeral directors? It's a great place to start a story. "A vampire walks into a bar . . ."

Ball was born in Atlanta, Georgia, on May 13, 1957. His father, Frank, was an aircraft inspector and his mother, Mary, a homemaker. He attended the University of Georgia and Florida State University, graduating in 1980 with a degree in theater arts. He joined the General Nonsense Theater Company in Sarasota, Florida, as a playwright. From 1994 to 1998, he worked as a writer on the comedies *Grace Under Fire* and *Cybill*. In 1999, he turned suburbia in on itself, penning the dark satire *American Beauty*. He describes the script as dealing more with the zeitgeist of suburbia than a condemnation of it. He had nothing against suburbia when he wrote the script, realizing regardless that he'd presented "an indictment of the shallowness of American values that [Americans] are basically conditioned from birth to accept as gospel."

American Beauty won an Academy Award for Best Original Screenplay, a Golden Globe Award for Best Screenplay, and a Writers Guild of America Award for Best Original Screenplay. Ball landed a development deal to create the cult HBO series *Six Feet Under*, which, aside from winning a host of awards including a Producers Guild of America Award for Dramatic Series, was responsible for turning morticians into sex symbols. He also wrote and directed the controversial *Nothing Is Private* (a.k.a. *Towelhead*) about a 13-year-old Arab-American girl with a sexual obsession and a strict father.

After *Six Feet Under* ended, Ball signed a two-year development deal with HBO to produce original programming. The resulting project was the pilot for *True Blood*, which Ball wrote, directed, and produced with Anna Paquin, Ryan Kwanten, Sam Trammell, and Stephen Moyer announced as regular cast members in early to mid-2007. They shot the pilot early that summer, with HBO officially ordering the series after Rutina Wesley replaced Brook Kerr as Tara Thornton. Two more episodes into production, the Writers Guild of America strike resulted in the production shutting down until the strike was resolved in 2008. When the show premiered in September 2008 it had one of the lowest viewership of any new HBO series, and yet that audience grew exponentially over the following weeks. After only two episodes had aired, HBO ordered a second season of twelve episodes.

With the Bon Temps vampires, Alan Ball had created a new sex symbol. Well, that's hardly *new*, you might say. But we've never seen vampires like this, especially not like Bill Compton. Complicated. Domestic. Monogamous. And, on the flip side, impulsive, lustful, and hungry. Nor have we seen the metaphor of outsider taken to places rooted so deeply in real life, real lives, and real struggles. By humanizing vampires and demonizing humans, Ball is in fine form: the characters are fresh, fearless, and flawed. "I don't hire people who are traditional hour-long drama TV writers, because I don't want to be hampered by all

Stephen Moyer captivates Anna Paquin and Ryan Kwanten while Alan Ball marvels at his sexy cast. (B. Henderson, www.alexander-skarsgardfans.com)

the preconceptions of what television is," Ball says. "So, I can see how me not knowing the vampire genre in depth could work in that regard. Hopefully, it does."

Ball's conscious decision not to spend a lot of time and effort on CGI vampire effects will leave some fans of *Buffy the Vampire Slayer*'s transforming vampires wanting more, but in keeping with the books, which also focus more on the interpersonal relationships of the characters, less their stereotypical markings. "I always wanted the effects to be minimal . . . it's a little scarier to leave the effects to your imagination," Ball says. "I don't want any of that blue light from the *Underworld* movies, and I'm not going to give the vampires weird contact lenses or have the shape of their heads change when their fangs come out. . . . The effects are just the shorthand to get us from one stage to another . . . [Bill's] been alive for a hundred and seventy years . . . He's in a changing world and he's given up on the idea of having any sort of love in his life until he meets this girl. That to me is way more interesting than what [a vampire's transformation] looks like."

If Ball lost any fans early on for not appearing to be the right fit for the genre — he came off as dismissive of the massive and loyal fan base of the paranormal genre — he quickly proved them wrong with his unabashed love of Charlaine Harris's Sookie Stackhouse novels. "It was an impulse purchase and it was just so much fun . . . I got into Sookie and the world and the characters, and I looked forward to going to bed every night . . . I would tell myself, 'Okay, I'm just going to read two chapters,' and I would read seven." Ball called Harris, who had already given the rights to another producer. But when that producer failed to develop the books, Ball took another stab, with Harris in full agreement. "I trust [Alan's] vision," she's said. "I am sure he will be true to the spirit of the books. I am delighted with the talented cast, Alan's scripts and direction, and the look and feel of the production."

Many fans of the show are also fans of the books, and as the series progresses the question remains as to how the writers will treat each storyline's adaptation. Ball has already diverged from the books in his treatment of Tara and Lafayette, and created larger plots to flesh out the lives of the other characters, whose stories were limited by the novels' Sookie-only perspective. "The main story is the same," he says. "[But] the other characters disappear if they're not in a scene with [Sookie]." But Ball has no plans to stray too far from the original stories. Reading the books, Ball recalls, "I loved the world; I loved how funny it was, how sexy and romantic and dramatic and scary . . . [vampires are] not constrained by conformity and traditional moral codes. You can live vicariously through them."

Psychologist Andrew Bates thinks that Ball's inspiration may hearken back to a repressed Victorian society that once explored sex via the metaphor of the vampire. For his own part, Ball has conceded that America is "weirdly dysfunctional in its relationship with sex," that it's become fetishized, with true intimacy replaced by consumerism, and a denial of sex as an important aspect of our psyches, ideas his characters reflect. "[T]heir sexuality is a way to explore who they are as characters and I feel like that's always [an] underlying part of everything we do." Anna Paquin, Stephen Moyer, Ryan Kwanten, and Alexander Skarsgård have all voiced their beliefs that American culture sees the naked body

A closer peek behind Merlotte's Bar reveals this smiley, happy photo of Charlaine Harris and Alan Ball. (Jodi Ross, courtesy of The Vault www.trueblood-online.com)

and sex as taboo, and that the frequency of nudity and sex on the show doesn't make them uncomfortable. Ball defends all the on-screen nookie, saying, "[I]t's important to show there is this incredible erotic chemistry. [Bill and Sookie] thought that they had no chance to ever have a real love affair and they found each other, and there's something fantastic and mind-blowing about that."

Ball is also the master of death, jockeying effortlessly between images of horrific loss and graceful exits. In the first two seasons of *True Blood* alone, he crafted a series of departures that are fused forever in the imaginations of most viewers as if they witnessed them first-hand. And in the case of Lafayette, he performed a miracle . . . but you'll have to wait and see. If it's true that you write what you know, or, at the very least, write to respond to your surroundings, it's perhaps not surprising to learn that Ball does have a memory to draw from when musing about death, immortality, and what it means to be left behind. He explains, "When I was thirteen years old, I was in a car accident with my sister . . . It was her twenty-second birthday and she died. She died in front of me. She died all over me. [Death] stuck its big old ugly face in my face and my life changed . . . One of my ways of dealing with depressing matters is to make fun of them . . . [I]t has helped me survive a lot."

Perhaps what is most remarkable about Alan Ball is his ability to interweave contemporary politics into these personal narratives in a way that doesn't feel like posturing or grandstanding. He doesn't sugarcoat the issues, allowing bigotry and hypocrisy to fuel the storylines, as they do our lives, creating an allegory that operates successfully under the genre banner. "It seems fun and sexy on the top," says Michelle Forbes who plays Maryann Forrester. "[Yet] it makes us question ideas of compassion and judgment, of ourselves and others . . . how we are terrified of our own thinking, so we'll latch onto group thinking."

Never one for mob mentality, Alan Ball grew up knowing he was gay in a family in which positive body image and sexuality were not discussed openly. That's in part why he responded to Harris's books. "It's certainly not a huge step for LGBT people to identify with any group of characters that are, as a group, outsiders, that mainstream society feels threatened by; that are fabulous and powerful and sexy." He continues, "[And] I know what it's like to be struggling with these feelings and to have these desires for sexual contact, and at the same time to be feeling I shouldn't be having these desires . . ." He best describes the metaphor as "fluid," something that demonstrates the difficulties of co-existing with people who are different and those who can't accept that difference.

It's that respect that keeps Ball's characters from falling into one-dimensional manifestations. And by creating such complex personalities, he asks a lot of his viewers; when you raise the bar that high, it opens up more room for anything to crawl under: the good, the bad, and the ugly. Ultimately, it results in the most interesting, if troubled, characters on television. Jason Stackhouse, for instance, is not a conventional bigot, his self-entitled nature stemming less from a place of hatred than fear that his loved ones' security is at risk. Similarly, while we're never left to forget that Bill is a vampire, Ball has revealed Bill's

Alan Ball models a tasty and refreshing bottle of Tru Blood at Comic-Con. (Eileen Rivera, www.BiteClubShow.com)

self-loathing. He's an immortal who, when human, was proud to fight for the rights of African Americans as he now tries to fight for the rights of his own people even as he struggles with what he's done and is capable of doing again. Tara, cast as a surly, foul-mouthed, self-taught African American woman, is perhaps the furthest from her original depiction in Harris's books, yet Ball manages to rescue her from the stereotype of the proud black woman with a chip on her shoulder. She is all these things, to be certain, but we trust the writing team to show us her story, rather than fall back on the convenience of a cause-and-effect narrative that leads only to her rescue by a knight in shining armor.

Ball's also not one to let his characters rest on their laurels, particularly Stephen Moyer's Bill Compton, who at some point during his 173 years became a fan of Tuvan throat singing quite by accident when Moyer suggested that Bill should be worldly and adventurous in his cultural tastes. The result is a precious scene in which Sookie recoils from Bill's music as a mother might squirm at the sound of thrash metal coming from her son's bedroom. It's these layers of experience that deepen our connection to each character as we find ourselves, perhaps surprisingly, relating to people we'd otherwise never cross paths with.

At the end of the day, though, Ball is here to entertain us. Responding to a statement he once made that *True Blood* is "popcorn for smart people," he defends, "I'm not saying [the show] is shallow; I'm saying it's really entertaining. Part of that entertainment is the emotional connection . . . [W]ithout that, the show couldn't exist." Music, film, food, sex. These are the social traditions that keep us connected to people over time as friends. Even when things get dark, as they often do in *True Blood*, everything about this world — from Merlotte's Bar and Grill, to Gran's kitchen, to Bill's estate, to Lafayette's living room, to Eric's office at Fangtasia — is chockfull of personality, spirit, and lived-in history, the sort of stories and tchotchkes we'd want to poke through if we actually knew these characters. Ball makes us want to spend time with humans and demons alike; we get to know each one from a safe distance while letting them into our homes — onto our couches and into our beds — giving us a rise and a good scare.

ANNA PAQUIN (Sookie Stackhouse)

"I love my job, but this is an extra specially, amazingly personal job to me because I wanted it so bad, and worked so hard to be cast. There's nothing I won't do to make it better or more real."

– Anna Paquin

"It's beautiful to watch [Anna act] because she just channels her inner self out with such ease."

– Sam Trammell

"Hey, you just shut your nasty mouth, mister! You might be a vampire, but when you talk to me, you will talk to me like the lady that I am!"

– Sookie Stackhouse

Anna Helene Paquin was born on July 24, 1982, in Winnipeg, Manitoba, Canada, the youngest of three children. When she was four, her family moved back to her mother's native New Zealand where she attended the Raphael House Rudolf Steiner School, taking up a number of artistic and athletic hobbies, including the viola, cello, piano, gymnastics, ballet, and swimming.

While most actors wait a lifetime for a role that will win them the Oscar, Paquin came to it early, and quite by accident. Paquin had no plans to pursue acting, but, in 1991, director Jane Campion placed an ad in a local newspaper looking to cast a young girl in her next feature film, *The Piano*. Paquin's sister, Katya, decided to audition, and so Paquin tagged along, performing a monologue that so impressed Campion she chose Anna from among the 5,000 other candidates to portray Flora, the daughter of a mute pianist played by Holly Hunter. Campion would later recall, "It is rare to find someone so young with such an instinct for performance." In 1994, at the tender age of 11, a memorably gob-smacked Paquin took to the podium to accept the Academy Award for Best Supporting Actress. Hunter won Best Actress, and Campion won for Best Original Screenplay, making *The Piano* one of the most awarded films of the year. Paquin went on to appear in *Fly Away Home* and Franco Zeffirelli's *Jane Eyre*, amassing an impressive resumé for someone so young.

Following the divorce of her parents in 1995, Paquin, then 16, relocated with her mother to Los Angeles where she continued to act while completing her secondary education at Windward School. During those years, she had roles in such films as *Amistad* (1997), *Hurlyburly* (1998), *A Walk on the Moon* (1999), *All the Rage* (1999), *Almost Famous* (2000), and *Finding Forrester* (2000). But it was a role as a mutant that would catapult Paquin back into the spotlight. Paquin had been cast as Rogue in the highly anticipated film adaptation of the Marvel Comics title *X-Men*, following the exploits of a team of superheroes known for their mutant powers. Rogue has remained one of the most popular of the X-Men characters since the 1980s, landing at #3 on Marvel's list of Top 10 Toughest Females for 2009. Unlike most of the other mutants, Rogue is plagued by her powers, which she sees as a curse. She absorbs

(Byron Purvis/Keystone Press)

the memories, physical strength, and powers of those she comes into contact with. This power can prove fatal to those she touches.

By this time, Paquin had moved to New York where she'd been accepted into Columbia University. She took a break from acting to study liberal arts. "[I]t was the first time I'd ever not worked. So, what did I do? I handed my papers in on time. I went to seminars. I had time to go shopping and socialize with people my own age." It wouldn't be long, however, before Paquin was back on set and on stage, leaving Columbia after one year of study to appear on Broadway in *The Glory of Living*, directed by Oscar-winning actor Philip Seymour Hoffman, and on film in *The Squid and the Whale* (2005). She then reprised her role as Rogue in the 2003 and 2006 *X-Men* sequels.

While Paquin is known as one of the most hardworking and professional young actors in the business, it's doubtful that clairvoyance shows up anywhere among her skill sets, or that she possessed the foreknowledge that her career was about to ascend to new heights, portraying the telepathic waitress Sookie Stackhouse. Paquin also pursued a surprising romantic development with her co-star Stephen Moyer, who portrays her on-screen love interest, Vampire Bill.

Taking the role also meant a move to television, something that Paquin took easily in stride. "It never occurred to me that one form of acting was better than another. I think if you approach your career like that you're limiting yourself to a very boring path. For me, it's about the material."

That Paquin has such clear respect for the character of Sookie, and the challenges that come with playing her, is good news for audiences who would like to see Sookie, and Paquin, on television for many years to come. Paquin understands the appeal: "[Sookie's] so many things in one person. She's tough, and she's courageous, and she's smart, but she's sweet, and she's innocent, and she's naive . . . and she is completely open-minded, which, in her very small town, is a little bit less common, and there's just something about that level of enthusiasm that she has for things that are new, and things that are exciting, as opposed to being frightened . . . I mean, those are the things I love about her."

Does knowing that Sookie will be in Bon Temps for some time to come — we hope! — or the happiness she's found in her engagement to Stephen Moyer, have Paquin thinking about settling down? "I don't want to disappear. I'm done with that. I don't want to be a transient figure in my own life anymore."

STEPHEN MOYER (Bill Compton)

"You've got immortality, you've got blood and you've got sharp, pointed teeth making a hole and sucking from it – that's sexy, man."

— Stephen Moyer

". . . [A]s I have more than 100 years on you, I do not take kindly to you calling me 'son.' So the next time you pull somebody over on suspicion of bein' a vampire, you better pray to God that you're wrong. Because that vampire may not be as kind to you as I'm about to be. I'm not gonna kill you. But I am gonna keep your gun. Does that sound fair?"

— Bill Compton, glamouring a police officer

"Oh, I'm Team Bill all the way. I'm Stephen Moyer *all* the way! I *love* that man!"

— Michelle Forbes

Stephen Moyer was born Stephen John Emery on October 11, 1969, in Brentwood, Essex, UK, where he attended St. Martin's School. A suburban town surrounded by open countryside, Brentwood gained some unfortunate, if slightly humorous, attention in the 1990s when it was dubbed the most boring town in Britain after the former manager of Brentwood Theatre was misquoted as saying that it was hard to pick something interesting about Brentwood. His comment had been completely misunderstood; what he in fact meant was that it would be difficult to choose from among all the interesting events in Brentwood's history. That "Bored Town" is an anagram of Brentwood only added fuel to the fire of a town's name whose actual etymology is "burnt wood."

In 2007, Stephen Moyer, now one of the town's most notable personalities, became Brentwood Theatre's first patron, supporting their

(Dave Longendyke/Keystone Press)

"Reaching Out, Building On" campaign to help fund backstage facilities. And, at long last, the (always perfectly interesting) town can boast something truly memorable — vampires. Well, at least an actor who plays one on TV. Twice, in fact.

Before *True Blood*, Moyer was cast as a vampire in the BBC series *Ultraviolet*. The biggest difference between the two experiences? "I did play a vampire in 1998 . . . and I have these [naturally large] canines that you can see . . . So we decided [in *Ultraviolet*] not to give me fake teeth."

Moyer's roots in the theater community run deep. He founded his own theater company, The Reject Society, and went on to graduate from the London Academy of Music and Dramatic Art, after which he joined the Royal Shakespeare Company, Young Vic, and the Oxford Stage Company, playing Romeo and the lead role in Pete Townshend's rock opera *The Iron Man*.

After making the transition to television, with lead roles in BBC's *The Grand*, *NY-LON* (alongside *Parks and Recreation*'s Rashida Jones), and *Lilies*, Moyer began to land film roles alongside some of the most decorated stars in the business. His first feature was *Prince Valiant* (1997) opposite Katherine Heigl, followed by *Quills* (2000), which co-starred Academy Award–winning actors Geoffrey Rush, Kate Winslet, and Michael Caine. In 2007, Moyer gained familiarity with North American audiences in his starring role in the acclaimed miniseries *The Starter Wife*, with Emmy Award–winning Debra Messing, and a co-starring role in the dramatic thriller *88 Minutes* with Academy Award winner Al Pacino.

By this time, Moyer had traveled all over the world, and was ready to go home. "I wanted to be back in London," Moyer says, "I wanted to be with my kids . . . so I turned down a few scripts." As a teen, Moyer fronted the band The Prophecy. But could he have known what would happen next? Moyer had just settled back in England when a script arrived for a television show about a telepathic waitress living in a small Louisiana town who takes up with a charming, if quite old, vampire. Moyer was unfamiliar with Charlaine Harris and her books, but immediately recognized one name: *American Beauty* writer and *Six Feet Under* creator Alan Ball. He made the tough call to move to Los Angeles, ending his relationship with British journalist Lorien Hayes with whom he has an eight-year-old daughter, Lilac. (Moyer also has a 10-year-old son, Billy, from a previous relationship.)

"I didn't want to come to America straight away . . . [when] I found out it was by Alan, I read it, and put myself on tape the next day. Alan saw it that afternoon, and I flew [to the States] the next morning. As soon as I got the job, I started doing the research, and reading the books . . . I could totally understand what Alan saw in [the books]. Sookie's amazing, Bill's a fantastic character, and the world that Charlaine sets up is just unbelievable."

Perhaps the biggest surprise, however, was his introduction to Anna Paquin, who plays his on-screen love interest and quickly became his off-screen interest, too. On the red carpet at the 2009 Emmy Awards, Moyer talked about what first drew him to the woman he proposed to after two years of quietly dating. "She doesn't take any of my nonsense," he told *E! News*. "She is very funny, and very frank . . . and beautiful."

Life seems good for Moyer. *True Blood* has been a real breakout hit for HBO, he won the 2009 Emmy Award for Breakthrough Performance for his scene in which Sookie meets Bill for the first time, he's working with the best in the business, he's in love, and he's adored by fans worldwide. "There's no other gig I'd rather be doing . . . I'm profoundly happy . . . For the first time in my life, I'm not chasing after anything . . . [and] I'm not running away from anything because I'm not scared of anything."

SAM TRAMMELL (SAM MERLOTTE)

"Seeing yourself run naked is the worst."

— Sam Trammell

"You willing to pass up all your favorite foods and spend the rest of your life drinking Slim-Fast?"

— Sam to Sookie about the impossibility of
a vampire changing its true nature

Sam Trammell was born on May 15, 1971, in New Orleans, Louisiana, and raised in Charleston, West Virginia. He has a brother Paul and a sister Elizabeth. His parents still live in Charleston; his father, Willis, is a surgeon and his mother, Betsy, is an artist. "[Charleston is] such a beautiful, beautiful, beautiful town, which you really realize once you get out and see the rest of the country . . . I loved growing up there," says Trammell.

After graduating from George Washington High School, he attended Brown University, where after a brief flirtation with physics and philosophy, he switched over to semiotics, the study of communication, and took classes on psychoanalysis and linguistic theory. During that time, he spent a year at the University of Paris, returning to the United States looking for a change.

Trammell had never given acting much consideration as a career option; he hadn't even performed in a school play. But when a friend suggested he audition for a play, he came out of the experience changed. "It was a real lightning bolt for me," Trammell says. "It was intense and fulfilling and inspiring."

The acting bug took hold — "I was hooked" — so Trammell took the actor's rite-of-passage bus ride to New York City, hitting the city sidewalks armed with head shots, and taking odd jobs to pay the bills and cover acting classes. Trammell attended auditions, securing a few roles on daytime serials, finally making his primetime debut in the CBS/Hallmark Hall of Fame presentation *Harvest of Fire* (with Jennifer Garner) and *Childhood's End* (both in 1996).

Trammell continued to hone his craft as a stage actor, and in 1998, earned himself a Tony Award nomination for Best Actor in Eugene O'Neill's *Ah, Wilderness!*. The night of the Tony Awards was an evening he recalls as so nerve-wracking that he almost hoped he wouldn't win so he could remain in his seat and avoid having to make a speech. Shortly thereafter, Trammell got his first regular television role on the short-lived ABC series *Maximum Bob*, starring Beau Bridges and based on the Elmore Leonard novel of the same name.

Trammell was getting wider recognition, winning guest roles on such television series as *House, Bones, CSI: NY, Numb3rs,* and *Dexter* — and has since appeared on *Medium* and *Law & Order: Criminal Intent*. Before *True Blood*, he was most familiar to audiences from his co-starring role in *Aliens vs. Predator: Requiem* (2007). "Let me tell you something: that was awesome . . . It's one guy in the [alien] suit, one guy running the electric motor for the mouth, and then one guy doing the tail . . . [G]etting eaten by that thing was one of the coolest things I've ever gotten to do."

Meanwhile, Trammell had heard about a television project that was building buzz around town. When the script for *True Blood* arrived, he immediately took a shine to it. "I realized it took place in Louisiana . . . when I read that, I just thought I'd be perfect for it, because I'm *from* Louisiana." Because the series was attached to Alan Ball and HBO, he acted instantly. "I [said] immediately, 'I'll do it. I don't know even know what it is, but I'll do it.' . . . [And] it's very stressful . . . all of these HBO executives are sitting in these leather chairs, and you go up on the stage . . . But I got a call about two hours later . . . So, it was just, like, a week and a half between getting the script and getting the part . . . I was screaming in my car when I found out. I'll never forget that moment."

(B. Henderson, www.alexander-skarsgardfans.com)

Like many of his other cast members, Trammell was unfamiliar with Charlaine Harris and the Southern Vampire Mysteries, but after reading a few, he quickly came to appreciate the appeal and reach of the bestselling novels, a connection that only deepened upon getting to know Harris.

"[*True Blood*] gave me the opportunity to sort of represent where I really came from and the people I grew up with . . . [And Charlaine

Harris is] very familiar to me because she's from Arkansas, and lives in Arkansas. She's had three kids, and she's like a regular mom, but she writes these crazy books . . ."

Trammell is far from living the dog's life. He's on a hit show, and in a serious relationship with Missy Yager, a former *Mad Men* guest star with connections of her own to Alan Ball, as a guest star on Ball's last character ensemble show, *Six Feet Under*.

Trammell reflects on his good fortune, "I love working with Alan Ball. He's one of the best writers for television, and it's fun. The show is set in an edgy, swampy gothic world. It's scary and bloody, but there's a lot of dark comedy . . . *True Blood* is definitely the biggest thing I've ever done."

RYAN KWANTEN (Jason Stackhouse)

"There are a few models for Jason . . . If people want to read George Bush into him, I think that's fine."

> — Ryan Kwanten on his character Jason Stackhouse

"Sometimes you need to destroy something to save it. That's in the Bible . . . or the Constitution."

> — Jason Stackhouse

"[Ryan Kwanten] was great to work with, because every time he did a take, it was something different, and all brilliant . . ."

> — Michael McMillian (Steve Newlin)

Ryan Christian Kwanten was born on November 28, 1976, in Sydney, Australia. Later in life, he qualified for the World Biathlon in Sweden (2005) and in Italy (2007). So, it should be no surprise that Kwanten was discovered en route to a swimming practice, that his first appearance on camera was as a young surfer, or that many of Kwanten's roles have emphasized some element of physicality, whether it's riding waves, riding horseback, or . . . enjoying the company of a beautiful woman.

Like Anna Paquin, Kwanten came to acting by accident. Kwanten was 15 and waiting in the family car for his brother to come out of an audition so they could continue on to Kwanten's swim training. After some time, he went inside to see how much longer his brother would be. The agent took one look at Kwanten and signed him immediately. His first guest role was on the Australian soap opera *Home and Away*, which has been the training ground for a number of other actors who went on to thriving careers, including Guy Pearce (*L.A. Confidential, Memento*), Oscar-winner Heath Ledger (*The Dark Knight*), Julian McMahon (*Nip/Tuck*), and Melissa George (*Alias*).

(Albert L. Ortega/PR Photos)

From 1992 to 1998, Kwanten had a number of guest appearances on Australian television shows, and appeared in his first film, *Signal One*. In 1998, Kwanten rejoined *Home and Away* as regular Vinnie Patterson, a role that made him an instant heartthrob in Australia, and for which he won an Inside Soap Award for Best Australian Actor. He left *Home and Away* in 2002 to appear in his first lead role in a film, *Liquid Bridge* (2003), after which he moved to Los Angeles to try his hand in Hollywood. "There were [difficult] times . . . I bought a push bike because that's all I could afford, and I was riding for two or three hours from auditions with all the changes of clothes in my backpack."

His hard work paid off, and Kwanten started to secure guest roles on such shows as *The Handler* and *Tru Calling*. In 2004, Kwanten was cast as an Australian surfer in the short-lived series *Summerland*, which also boasts a pre–*High School Musical* Zac Efron among its cast. After *Summerland* ended production, Kwanten appeared with Donnie Wahlberg in *Dead Silence* (2007). But it was a 2006 film about a horse (co-starring Alison Lohman, Maria Bello, and country music artist Tim McGraw) that would draw Alan Ball's attention to this Aussie export. "Alan Ball had seen *Flicka*, and thought the character I played was like a PG version of Jason . . ."

Upon seeing the script for *True Blood*, Kwanten says the devil-may-care character of Jason stood out to him. "[Jason] just tends to fly by the seat of his pants, and I tend to be far too cerebral . . . It's been nice to throw out the textbook and what I thought I knew about acting and life and just go 'OK, this is what I am going to do,' and just do it."

What didn't register immediately with Kwanten was the massive fandom already surrounding the Sookie Stackhouse novels as the team headed into production. "There are otherworldly things that may or may not exist, and I think that level of intrigue is always kind of sexy and mysterious . . . [But] we shot the first season not really knowing what to expect. It's sort of like you're raising a baby, and the baby turns eighteen, and it's time to give it out to the world . . . Fortunately, people seem to like [the series]. We got lucky."

He has, however, understood the crossover appeal of the series from one nation to the next, and from one demographic to another. "Australians are a little more open-minded when it comes to things like sex and body. But Americans, I feel, are probably more used to the violence, and even the supernatural elements. So, the great thing about [*True Blood*] is that it doesn't limit itself to one particular genre. It can go from comedy to supernatural to thriller to drama, all in the space of an episode, catering to not just different demographics but different cultures, too."

So, how does this "cerebral" Aussie feel about the amount of screen time dedicated to his physical attributes, not to mention some of the steamiest sex this side of pay-per-view cable? "When you've got guys like Alan Ball writing the scripts, it's never going to be nudity for nudity's sake. It always comes from a really strong story point. If I get nervous about it, I try to offset that onto the character . . . but Jason's so comfortable with his body, it's just part and parcel with who he is."

Fans of Jason Stackhouse know he's more than skin deep — as beautiful as that skin may be — at times, providing some of the most stunningly simple, straightforward know-how of any of the characters, lessons that Kwanten has picked up on, too. "Without sounding too 'actory,' . . . [I've] opened up parts of myself that I never knew existed. Just in terms of letting things go and not letting every little thing get to me. . . . Life is too short to worry about stuff."

RUTINA WESLEY (Tara Thornton)

"She's just this little flower, this wounded child that needs to be taken care of. And that's where the mouth is coming from, and all that quickfire language."

– Rutina Wesley on Tara Thornton

"School is just for white people looking for other white people to read to 'em; I figured I'd save my money and read to myself."

– Tara Thornton

Rutina Wesley seems bred for show business. With only a handful of acting credits under her belt when she was cast in *True Blood*, Wesley had already spent her life surrounded by the performing arts. Born and raised in Las Vegas, Nevada, Wesley's father is a professional tap dancer, and her mother was a showgirl. Rutina is married to fellow actor Jacob Fishel.

"I was born to be on stage," Wesley confesses. "[As a child,] I loved storytelling. I was always making up stuff. I feel like that was my path."

Growing up, she attended the Las Vegas Academy of International Studies, Performing and Visual Arts and studied dance at Simba Studios before being accepted on a full scholarship into the University of Evansville in Indiana where she received a BFA in theater performance. It was an opportunity she was initially hesitant to take out of a concern that there would be an absence of minorities. Not only was she the only black female in her department, but she spent most of her freshman

(RD/Bishop/Retna Digital)

year dodging questions about what it was like growing up in Las Vegas. "It was like 'Get to Know the Girl From Vegas Week' . . . People would say, 'Is Vegas a real place? Do you live in a hotel?'"

The "huge culture shock" proved beneficial for Wesley, however, with her entire world view evolving alongside the opportunities she was offered, and more she had to fight for. "I've gotten away from feeling I'm too dark. We're all women of color . . . [I]nstead of asking, 'Why didn't I get this?' or 'Why did the light-skinned girl get that?'. . . [I'm] focusing on the positive [and] celebrating all colors and all ethnicities."

Ultimately, going to Indiana was the best choice Wesley could have made for herself. Upon graduating from the program, she landed a highly sought-after place at Juilliard School's Drama Division (along with offers to attend four other of the top programs in the country) where she was put through her paces with roles in such classics as *Macbeth*, *Richard III*, *The Winter's Tale*, *The Marriage of Figaro*, and *In the Blood*. She also spent a summer studying Shakespeare at the Royal Academy of Dramatic Art, where she played Juliet.

Making a name for herself was always the plan for this driven performer. "My family always told me to dream big, so I made sure that I got out of [Las Vegas] and explored new places, because the world is huge." Sage advice, because not long after she graduated from Juilliard in 2005, Sam Mendes (director of Alan Ball's Oscar-winning film *American Beauty*) took notice of Wesley, casting her to star alongside Julianne Moore and Bill Nighy in the 2006 Broadway play *The Vertical Hour* by David Hare. "[A] young actor could not ask for anything more than to work with people of the caliber of Sam Mendes, Julianne Moore, and Bill Nighy . . . I learned so much just by watching them. And they treated me like family . . ."

The following year Wesley stepped into the role of Raya, a young woman trying to raise her tuition by entering a step-dancing competition, in the crowd-favorite *How She Move* by British director Ian Iqbal Rashid. "He met with me over lunch, and I remember I had my natural hair out, so I had this 'fro. I had my braids in, so I wasn't looking very ingenue-ish. We talked about theater, and I told him how I know I seem really hard, with these Angela Bassett arms, but I'm really a flower . . . I won't bite ya. I seem like I will, but I won't." To prepare for the role of a woman of Jamaican descent, Wesley studied with a dialect coach. She also underwent five weeks of intensive dance rehearsal. "The reason I trained so hard in school was so that I could be versatile and play any character. With all these [tricks] in my bag, I'm like a chameleon. I always tell other young actors to go to school, or at least watch movies to learn as much as you can."

Call it hard work, good timing, or plain luck: Alan Ball had already cast the character of Tara Thornton, a fast-talking, surly bartender, in *True Blood* — a character, worth noting, that the novel series writer Charlaine Harris had originally imagined as Caucasian — with *Passions* actor Brook Kerr, but things took a turn in Wesley's favor when Kerr was dropped and Wesley was brought in. "I just took it as sort of a blessing . . . no one wants to lose a job, but everybody wants to work . . . I related to Tara on a level that hit very close to home for me." In the series, Tara battles a number of personal demons, including an alcoholic and evangelical mother who frequently beats and humiliates her.

Alan Ball noted that Wesley was one of the only actors who attempted to show Tara's softer side. "Rutina just nailed the part from the beginning. She traded the toughness for vulnerability. She was really strong, present, and funny in her audition. I didn't see the actress, I saw

Tara." He continues, "I like to work with actors who have been taught. They can come in and know instantly how to play a scene. Rutina trusts the material."

Wesley echoes Ball's sentiment, saying, "I immediately saw past [Tara's] anger . . . You can scream all day long. That would be the easy way to play her. I see Tara more as a flower, a broken woman. People want her to do well, and she doesn't know how. I try to make her softer. She is tortured, incredibly hard to play."

Lest we rest on Wesley's laurels, let's not forget that show business is also about The It Factor. Glenn Edwards, who taught Wesley at both the Las Vegas Academy and the University of Evansville in Indiana, recalls, "Everyone that worked with [Wesley] knew there was something special there — it wasn't just talent." He continues to say that Wesley has always possessed "determination, bravery, self-confidence . . . She had a dream and she was willing to work for it."

Wesley also possesses a sense of clarity in a highly-competitive industry that replaces one actor for another. "[A]n actor shouldn't work from a place of fear, because it'll show in your work. You should work from a place of contentment, relaxation, and coming from your heart, and from the truth of yourself." This conviction positions Wesley as a beacon of hope for other actors of color who are negotiating the same twists and turns that she once did. "It feels good to be a young woman of color leading the way," she says. "I really do think it's possible, and it's what we need to see with this young generation."

NELSAN ELLIS (Lafayette Reynolds)

"[When Ellis steps on the set,] we all just stand back and point the camera in his direction . . . [He] channels from his own planet."

— Alan Ball

"I know every man, whether straight, gay, or George mother-fucking Bush, is terrified of the pussy."

— Lafayette Reynolds

Nelsan Ellis was born in 1978, in Harvey, Illinois. After the divorce of his parents, Ellis, then six, and his mother relocated to Bessemer, Alabama, a poor and violent suburb of Birmingham. Ellis later attended Jess Lanier High School for a year before transferring to McAdory High School. His time spent at Jess Lanier was one of the lowest points of his life. "It was awful," Ellis admits. "It's hard to get an education when teachers spend seventy percent of their time trying to discipline students."

Considering Ellis's backstory for his *True Blood* character, Lafayette Reynolds, a flamboyantly gay short order cook who supplements his income dealing drugs and prostituting himself,

(Matt Sayles/AP Photo)

one wonders how much of Ellis's upbringing plays into his performance. "[T]here are some unfortunate things that happened in [Lafayette's] past that have forced him to live a certain way. I think he's like a starving person stealing food . . . [H]e's basically a good dude who's doing what he has to do to live the lifestyle he wants to live." In creating this backstory, Ellis was able to identify with the character. "I grew up knowing I wanted to escape that life, and the only escape was education."

At 14, Ellis was sent to live with his aunt in Dolton, Illinois, close to his father who works for a grocery distributor, and where he graduated from Thornridge High School in 1997. Thornridge was Ellis's first glimpse at the possibility of a different life, and where he got his first exposure to the acting bug, thanks in large part to teachers Tim

Sweeney and Bill Kirksey whom Ellis credits with reaching out to him; otherwise, "I'd probably have five kids and a rap sheet."

Sweeney says, "Nelsan had such an unusual voice, an unusual manner, and a kind of a cragginess about him that made him a little different from every other kid." He cast Ellis in a lead role in the play *The Colored Museum*, "and I could see the wheels turning and clicking," Sweeney continues. "Once [Nelsan] got hooked, he just decided that was the world he wanted to be in."

Thornridge didn't just introduce Ellis to acting; it placed him in a community of other young black men who were serious about their studies, taught by teachers who were serious about giving their students the tools to succeed. When Ellis graduated, deciding he would continue to pursue acting, he went for the brass ring (not unlike his co-star Rutina Wesley) and auditioned for the Juilliard School in New York City. "It was the best opportunity for acting," says Ellis. But not one that came without its struggles. "The studies were so intense and the institution is so white, and I'm a black man from the South with a very specific vernacular and palate," Ellis recalls. "I felt like an alien . . . But it transformed who I am as an actor and a person."

It was also during this time that Ellis's sister, Alice, was shot and killed, an experience Ellis used to fuel his creativity, reworking his grief in a play about domestic abuse. "[My sister] was in an abusive relationship for about five years," recounts Ellis. "She was pregnant, and my brother-in-law shot her point-blank with a sawed-off shotgun in front of my six-year-old nephew." Ellis's play, *Ugly*, which premiered off-Broadway, was inspired by the events that happened between his sister and brother-in-law, and won the Lincoln Center's Martin E. Segal Award. Of the abuse, he concludes, "You can't ostracize the victims for staying . . . I call it the ugly side of love — you love a person so much you stay with them no matter what." Ellis's brother-in-law was murdered while in jail serving time for his crime.

Undeterred from his quest, Ellis stayed the course, auditioning for and landing guest roles on *The Inside*, *Veronica Mars*, *Without a Trace*, and a role in the football film *The Express*. He poured all of the money from these gigs into remounting productions of *Ugly* and a second play

Darkly, I Die, leaving him homeless for a time and living out of his car.

It's hard to imagine the kind of perseverance it would take for a person to remain optimistic in these circumstances. When he talks about his past, Ellis, who does not consider himself an emotional guy, gets straight to the point. "I don't think I would be in prison, but I definitely think I would be a little shady, only because it's the path that's often taken." And while *True Blood* is graphically violent, the line between fiction and reality is not blurred for Ellis. "Violence, in reality, is strikingly different than what you do on the set."

So, too, is the difference between the questionable moral character of his role as Lafayette and Ellis's personal spirituality. Raised a strict Baptist, his family acknowledges his recent success on *True Blood* but refuses to watch the show. "I come from a very religious family, and I didn't tell my mother about this [role] at all. My mother lives in the woods and doesn't have cable." And Ellis's father is a deacon in the conservative Church of God in Christ. "Truth of the matter is, he don't want his son prancing around in lipstick and makeup, playing some gay dude," Ellis says. "He believes the character is supporting an ideal that Christians don't normally support." Ellis continues, "But I tell him I feel blessed to be playing this character because I love it. I think Alan Ball is a genius," a word Ball has also used to describe Ellis.

Ellis has also worried about the reaction from the African American community. "I thought, Oh, my people are gonna just banish me to hell. My people are gonna hate this! But actually, I have gotten more Timberland-wearing, saggy pants–drooping, tattooed-up dudes coming up to me saying, 'Man, I love that hustle! I love that character.' . . . I am fortunate."

Fortune ain't the half of it, as fans of Charlaine Harris's Sookie Stackhouse series know. Lafayette's character actually dies very early on in the books. Ball, however, had plans of his own. "[Alan] said you can't have a small southern town like Bon Temps without black people." And with a number of awards under Ellis's belt, including a Satellite Award from the International Press Academy for Best Supporting Actor in a Television Series, a Brink of Fame award from NewNowNext Awards, and an Ewwy Award for Best Supporting Actor in a Drama Series, Ball's decision to keep Lafayette around might have just as much to do with Ellis's raw talent. "[Alan] sees something nobody else does," Ellis gushes. "[H]e sees things that you don't. I mean, his intuition — he hired me, and I don't know what I did in the audition that was any good whatsoever. But, I'm certainly enjoying myself now! . . . Alan Ball is Alan Ball, and he's a god among men."

Ellis appeared in 2009's dramatic feature *The Soloist* with actors Robert Downey Jr. and Jamie Foxx, further evidence that this star is on the rise. But he's never far from home, grounded as always, and thinking about his Thornridge teachers, Tim Sweeney and Bill Kirksey. "If this moment never happens again," Ellis muses, "I hope that it will be enough to show Mr. Kirksey and Mr. Sweeney that their investment in me wasn't in vain."

ALEXANDER SKARSGÅRD (Eric Northman)

"The celebrity culture is very different in America. There are no paparazzi in Sweden, so I'm not harassed. It's a socialist country, so you shouldn't think you're special. It's not like L.A., where people drive around in their pimped-out Bentleys. In Sweden you're supposed to drive your Volvo and shop at Ikea."

– Alexander Skarsgård

"[Alexander's] very humble, extremely talented, and so freaking Mount Olympus good-looking that sometimes I just want to be him."

– Nelsan Ellis

Alexander (Johan Hjalmar) Skarsgård, born August 25, 1976, in Stockholm, Sweden, is the eldest of seven siblings. He has five younger brothers, Gustaf, Sam, Bill, and Valter — all actors — and one younger sister, Eija. His family has been called acting royalty, the Skarsgård Dynasty. His parents, My Skarsgård, a doctor, and Stellan Skarsgård, a well-known actor, divorced in 2007. Stellan Skarsgård has since remarried, and fathered another son, Ossian.

Skarsgård was seven years old when his father's friend, Allan Edwall, cast a young Alex in a film adaptation of the Swedish children's book *Ake och hans värld* (*Ake and His World*), in which Stellan Skarsgård also appeared. Watching the film, it's clear the junior Skarsgård already possessed the quiet contemplation, and intense intellect, required to portray the thousand-year-old vampire sheriff, Eric Northman.

On growing up in an acting dynasty helmed by the internationally renowned Stellan Skarsgård — whose North American film credits alone include *Breaking the Waves*, *Good Will Hunting*, *Pirates of the Caribbean*, *Mamma Mia!*, and *Angels & Demons* — Skarsgård remembers, "[My father] wasn't that big a star when I grew up . . . he was mostly a stage actor . . . I've got younger siblings, and it was different for them. They did more of the traveling around the world, being on sets and all of that exotic stuff. For me, it was running around backstage at the theater . . ."

(B. Henderson, www.alexander-skarsgardfans.com)

Pursuing an acting career at such a young age was largely his decision. "My parents never dragged me to auditions . . . Things just kind of happened, and I thought it was fun." But, by the time Skarsgård was 13, he'd decided it was time for a break. He'd become an icon for his 1989 role in *Hunden som log* (*The Dog That Smiled*), and the focus on his celebrity confused Skarsgård who was becoming increasingly self-conscious, citing that pre-teen life is already tough enough. He began to doubt if he was liked (in particular, by girls) because he was appealing, or because he was on television. He made the unseasonably mature decision to step back from the limelight.

"If I didn't quit at that time," Skarsgård says, "I would have crashed and burned, and I doubt I would be acting today."

For seven years, Skarsgård declined every role he was offered, figuring life out as he went. He distanced himself from his parents, living with friends in a small apartment, and even winding up in jail one night after a fight when he was 17. He turned his attentions to political science, and entered the Berga Naval Academies as a sergeant (patrol leader) to serve with the Swedish Navy. "I grew up in downtown Stockholm . . . I figured if I was going to do this, I wanted to do it for real and full-on, and actually physically and mentally challenge myself . . . [M]ost of the guys I was with in my platoon were kind of like Rambos, you know? I wasn't like that, at all. I knew this definitely wasn't a profession for me. I did this solely for my own reasons . . . It was kind of weird, and at times I hated it, but I'm glad I finished it."

After the military, Skarsgård considered architecture, but, in 1997, at the age of 20, he decided he was ready to take another shot at acting, so he enrolled in Marymount's theater arts program in New York City. "[L]ike most guys of that age, I was trying to figure out what to do with my life . . . Leaving acting had never had anything to do with the craft, the work, at all. It was only because I wasn't comfortable being recognized . . ."

However, alone in the city, broke, and missing his girlfriend, Skarsgård dropped out of school after six months to return home to Stockholm. "New York is a difficult city to be in as a poor student and unfortunate in love. One gets eaten." Regrettably, almost immediately after his return, he and his girlfriend ended their relationship.

In 1999, after a long departure, Skarsgård began to act again in his native Sweden, taking a role in *Happy End*, and going on to complete over 15 films, even appearing in a hospital soap opera *Vita Lögner* (*White Lies*). In 2000, he appeared in the crowd-pleaser *Vingar av Glas* (*Wings of Glass*), securing his place as a Swedish star.

In 2001, Skarsgård appeared briefly in Ben Stiller's blockbuster comedy *Zoolander* (2001), as a "really, really, ridiculously good looking" male model. This was North America's first taste of Skarsgård, whose character, Meekus (spoiler alert!) suffers an untimely demise in a gasoline fire that erupts during a spontaneous bout of orange mocha frappuccino horseplay.

If Hollywood was calling, Skarsgård wasn't ready to answer. He describes auditioning in Los Angeles as a "conveyer belt" of actors, all up for the same roles. "[T]here are, like, twenty guys there . . . that look like you, are as old as you . . ."

His decision to stay in Sweden proved the right one, and, in 2005, he appeared in the successful Swedish movie *Hundtricket* (*The Dog Trick*), a role that earned him a

(B. Henderson, www.alexander-skarsgardfans.com)

Guldbagge nomination for Best Supporting Actor. It was during this time that Skarsgård directed his first film, with friend Björne Larsson, an award-winning short, *Att Döda Ett Barn* (*To Kill a Child*). Skarsgård cast his younger brother, Valter, while his father, Stellan, contributed the voiceover. The film screened at a number of international film festivals.

Skarsgård had his big North American break in the 2007 HBO miniseries *Generation Kill*, the story of the Marines' First Recon Battalion in the earliest stages of the Iraq War in 2003. The series was based on the book by *Rolling Stone* reporter Evan Wright, who spent time in Iraq detailing firsthand accounts of military life, tensions, and distractions.

Skarsgård was cast in the lead role of Marine Sgt. Brad Colbert, known among his peers as "Iceman" for his intense focus, intellect, and, at times, apparent lack of compassion.

"There was a lot of discussion throughout the ranks about casting him," says casting director Alexa L. Fogel. "In walks this skinny guy that looked like a really tall Kurt Cobain," says Rudy Reyes, a former recon Marine sergeant who was cast to play himself in the seven-part series. He continues, "But once the cameras started rolling, Skarsgård became Colbert."

As intrigue built around Sweden's five-time sexiest man, Skarsgård started to receive international scripts. To date, he's wrapped and pro-moted the animated film *Metropia* (2009), completed *Beyond the Pole* (2009), *13* (with Mickey Rourke and Jason Statham), and *Straw Dogs* (with Kate Bosworth), a remake of Sam Pekinpah's 1971 film of the same name. Fans can enjoy Skarsgård in the music video for Lady Gaga's "Paparazzi," portraying a murderous lover.

But it's his charismatic performance as *True Blood*'s Eric Northman, sheriff of all Louisianan vampires, that has throngs of fans filling screenings of his other projects. Skarsgård read the Sookie Stackhouse novels in preparation for his role, but had no prior knowledge of the fan base leading into the series. Was he worried about the reaction to his portrayal of one of the series most popular characters? To answer like Eric, in a word, no. "I'm having a blast. [Eric] is an amazing character to play. It gives me a lot of freedom. I can do whatever I want, because who's going to tell me what a thousand-year-old Viking vampire is like, you know?"

Despite the inevitable ascent of his career, Skarsgård holds tight to the simple pleasures while showing up for the causes he believes in, notably the Tails for Whales campaign, in support of the International Fund for Animal Welfare's (IFAW) global initiative calling for stronger whale protection (www.TailsForWhales.org).

For now, television audiences can look forward to more Skarsgård for the small screen. "I enjoy everything [about *True Blood*]. Every single part of it . . . It's HBO, and it's Alan Ball. Just look at the cast, and the writing is phenomenal. I couldn't ask for a better job."

MICHELLE FORBES (Maryann Forrester)

"When someone offers you an entrance where you're standing in the middle of the road naked with a pig, you don't say no."

— Michelle Forbes

"A few bumps and bruises? A small price to pay for bliss."

— Maryann Forrester

"I love Michelle . . . [S]he's so good at that part, and she's so open and free, and she has fun . . . but she's kind of creepy. She's just a cool chick, y'know?"

— Sam Trammell

Michelle Renee Forbes Guajardo was born on January 8, 1965, in Austin, Texas. Forbes was training formally at the Performing Arts High School in Houston to be a dancer when, at 16, she vacationed in New York City and on a whim decided to audition for a film. "I started off as a ballet dancer. I knew, pretty early on, that I needed another form of expression, and it just seemed that acting, and this idea of playing pretend and telling stories, was really fascinating to me. It was a natural progression, out of the dance world and into the world of theater and cinema." While she wasn't offered the role, she did succeed in signing with the prestigious William Morris Agency, which helped the young Forbes launch into a career as a professional actor.

Many fans will recognize her instantly for roles in such cult faves as *Star Trek: The Next Generation* and *Battlestar Galactica*. She's also appeared, or had recurring roles, in some of television's most celebrated and talked-about shows: *Homicide: Life on the Street*, *24*, *Prison Break*, *In Treatment*, and *Durham County*, making Forbes one of the most familiar actors to *True Blood* audiences.

Take a ride in The Way Back Machine, and you'll get a special double dose of Forbes, who in 1987, at the age of 22, joined the cast of the daytime soap opera *Guiding Light*, portraying twins Solita and Sonni Carrera. "Every day I [had] to cry or be on edge. It gets crazy sometimes.

(Eileen Rivera, www.BiteClubShow.com)

When I got hired to do a soap, I thought I'd get to wear pretty clothes and talk about who's sleeping with whom. [We were] talking religion, sex, guilt, rejection, loyalty, greed . . . not what I would have expected at all."

Forbes left the show in 1989 after earning herself a Daytime Emmy nomination, and relocated to Los Angeles, where she appeared in a number of television guest roles before joining the cast of *Star Trek: The Next Generation* as Ensign Ro Laren (1992–1994). In 1993, she appeared in two films, the dark thriller *Kalifornia* (with David Duchovny, Brad Pitt, and Juliette Lewis) and *Love Bites: The Reluctant Vampire*, a romantic comedy with British singer and actor Adam Ant. In a highly publicized decision, Forbes chose not to reprise the role of Ro for the follow-up *Star Trek* series *Deep Space Nine*, opting to focus on a film career. "There were all sorts of rumors about why I didn't take [the *DS9* role] . . . It was, again, about wanting variety in my career . . . That's not to say I wasn't grateful for the opportunity . . . However, I had to make a choice that felt right for me, which was a difficult one, especially as a young actor being offered a steady job."

Forbes exercised her funny bone in 1994, appearing in the black comedy *Swimming with the Sharks* (with Kevin Spacey) and in a guest role on *Seinfeld*, before turning back to science fiction for John Carpenter's *Escape from L.A.* (1996) and another television guest appearance on *The Outer Limits*.

The same year, Forbes joined the police drama *Homicide: Life on the Street*, where she played chief medical examiner Julianna Cox for two years before being let go. (She reprised her role in the 2000 TV special *Homicide: The Movie*.) That same year Forbes's series *Wonderland* was pulled from the small screen only two episodes in.

Since 2000, Forbes has never been far from television audiences, appearing in a number of recurring roles on *The District*; the British TV movies *Messiah*, *Messiah 2: Vengeance*, and *Messiah: The Promise*; the critically acclaimed series *24* (2002–2003) as Lynne Kresge, the aide to the President of the United States (where she was reunited with past *Star Trek* actors, Timothy Carhart, Jude Ciccolella, Penny Johnson, and Harris Yulin); *Prison Break*; and in *Battlestar Galactica* and the TV movie *Battlestar Galactica: Razor* as Admiral Helena Cain, a role she was initially hesitant to accept. "I tend to play a lot of authoritative, strong women." She continues, "God bless them, though, for being so pursuant . . . *Galactica* is amazingly good and well written. I shudder to think I almost lost out on working with those wonderful people and on such a powerful story."

During this time, Forbes also shot an independent feature with *Angel* alum and current *Mad Men* star Vincent Kartheiser; returned to UK small screens with roles in *Holby City* and *Waking the Dead*; and appeared in guest roles on *Boston Legal* and J. J. Abrams' mega hits *Alias* and *Lost*.

It's hard to imagine that an already thriving career could take a further upswing, but in 2008 Forbes joined not one but two HBO dramas — *In Treatment*, playing the wife in a troubled marriage with Gabriel Byrne's psychotherapist character, and *True Blood*. Forbes also appeared in the second season of the psychological drama *Durham County* as Dr. Penelope Verity, a grieving mother and troubled psychotherapist, starring alongside musician and actor Hugh Dillon.

Forbes confesses that her character on *True Blood*, the sultry Maryann Forrester, came as a pleasant tonic to years of playing characters that have it rough. "*True Blood* is a very technically difficult show, and there is a lot of depth to it. It's illegal how much fun we're having . . . Even though I was tortured on the show by having to face a few fears."

Maryann's desire to ease up in life, and on ourselves, is one that inevitably carries over to the audience, something Forbes understands, especially when it comes to the sudden rise of interest in vampires in the cultural zeitgeist. And in Maryann fashion, Forbes doesn't hold her tongue when offering her explanation. "My theory is that [America has] been through eight years of nonsense and hell with the Bush administration — our economy is just in utter chaos, people are out of work, and we're stuck still in the middle of an endless war . . .There is something refreshing about being able to watch something that is fun and escapist . . . [where] the show still serves as a beautiful place for social commentary looking at injustice and compassion . . . Plus: lots of sexy people running around with no clothes on. Can't beat that, right?"

The Pleasure and Pain of Alternative Lifestyles

Vampires have been with us for so long in mainstream media that it seems they've lost much of their eerie mystique. While they may not be to everyone's taste, vampires as metaphor are as common as the girl next door archetype. They're everywhere. But some readers will still be surprised to learn that there are real people who identify with vampires, or aspects of the vampire lifestyle, to the point of calling themselves one.

What we consider alternative begins first with how we define traditional. Not every person sees, or participates, in the world in the same way. Some practices are played out in full view via a particular taste in clothing or music, and displayed at social events (like concerts or other gatherings) that cater to like-minded people. Other practices, deeply intimate, are conducted in private between consenting partners away from the public gaze.

True Blood pushes boundaries, breaking the mold of what many of us consider typical by exploring a variety of lifestyles. The series doesn't attempt to explain or apologize, and as a result over the course of each episode we're introduced to the many shades of each character as complex, rich, and utterly unique. Yet of all the lifestyles, only one is a pure fictionalization: the existence of vampires as undead creatures. The rest are very much alive. So, let's explore some of these subcultures in an effort to demystify them.

When two people love each other very, *very* much . . . kidding! This won't be The Talk.

We've already established that "vampyre" is a term often used to describe people who identify with the, for lack of a better word, theatrics of vampiretainment. Some go by "Goth," white faces, red lips, black hair, and eyeliner being some of their identifiable markings. If you're of a certain age, you probably had a few as good friends in high school, if you weren't one yourself. I'd like to put myself in that category, but, alas, my claim to fame was being the only kid *not* to get frisked at a Skinny Puppy concert. Vampyres may also go by the term "lifestylers."

Rebecca Summers runs the United Kingdom's leading vampyre society, the London Vampyre Group (LVG). Her interest in vampires began with a love of fairy tales. "*Sleeping Beauty* was one of my favorite stories," she recalls. "I remember being fascinated by her death and following resurrection. She was beautiful too — pale skin, black hair, and red lips. As I grew older I saw connections between that character and vampires in terms of death and seemingly coming back to life."

Summers says that many members of the LVG see dressing up as a natural part of their day-to-day lives, and don't consider it a costume. The group does, however, organize themed parties that allow the members to, as Summers says, "dress up over and above our usual gothic/vampyric uniform, and in some ways become another character."

Nancy Schumann is the editor of *The Chronicles*, a fanzine dedicated to promoting interest and discussion about all aspects of the Gothic, pagan, fetish, and vampyre genres. The zine's articles cover cinema, literature, music, art, and style, as well as essays and opinion pieces covering a wide range of topics such as Lilith, the Brides of Dracula, the origins of corsetry, paganism, burlesque, and book and DVD reviews, just to start. The zine boasts a diverse set of contributors: academics, cartoonists, reviewers, and performers. "What brings the LVG members together in the first place," Schumann says, "is a common interest in vampires, and everybody has their own story, their own particular interest in the subject, which helps to fill the magazine with many interesting things that are very diverse in nature but all relate to the main topic." She does note one major distinction between *The Chronicles* and mainstream fare.

"Vampire-featuring entertainment is not quite the same as a genuine interest in all things vampiric ... Much of [our] magazine's content is quite serious, looking at vampire folklore or literary analysis, which is not everybody's cup of tea."

When asked if the LVG engages in any fetishistic activities — the sexual or even spiritual gratification derived from non-sexual objects, or an excessive devotion to a particular activity — Summers suggests that depending on one's definition, an obsession or interest in vampires alone might constitute fetish. Many people into the vampyre culture are naturally drawn to fetish, "partly due to the fact that we like to dress up in leather, PVC, latex, and 'fantasy' costumes," she says. Many of the vampyre community's members are highly artistic and creative individuals. Summers elaborates, saying there are some who do take their interests to the extreme, "by indulging in a blood-drinking fetish, although this tends to be behind closed doors and not generally condoned by most groups." At its core, however, the LVG exists to provide an avenue for those who just want to meet up with friends to chat about a genre that they love and identify with.

Rebecca Summers of the London Vampyre Group. (Courtesy Rebecca Summers)

But let's back it up a bit. Did she say *blood-drinking*? This brings us to the oft-asked question: are there real vampires? And do they all drink blood? The answer to the first question is yes, self-identified vampires exist, but they're not of the undead variety. And to the latter question, the answer is no, not all, if many, "real vampires" drink blood . . . but some do, with the assistance of a consenting donor.

To break it down, the major vampire groups are: sanguinarian (sang) vampires; psychic (psy or psi) vampires; and donors who may also be vampiric, but more often claim to suffer from an overload of energy that they need to expel. "Real vampires" are mortals who have awakened to, or self-identified, a need to feed from a variety of energy sources in order to maintain physical or spiritual health. They claim to suffer from energy deficiencies that result in deep cravings. They subscribe to any number of faiths and religions, and attach significant meaning to their ritual feedings. Sure, these vampires may dislike garlic but only as a personal preference, and all will die if staked in the heart, because . . . you'd be hard-pressed to find someone who wouldn't. (And, that said, don't be staking anyone in the heart!)

By far the smallest group, a sanguinarian vampire will experience a weakened immune system and may develop pain and depression if they don't consume blood, a tablespoon or two a week, offered by one or more donor. While there are famous sangs, such as Don Henrie ("The Vampire Don") who appeared on the reality show *Mad, Mad House* as well as a number of talk shows, most prefer not to be publicly identified because they see their condition as a natural state, rather than a lifestyle. As such, they don't necessarily engage in activities such as Gothic dress and music. As to the expected question of safety, most vampires and donors are in good health and take every precaution to ensure a safe session.

Michelle Belanger, author of the bestseller *Psychic Vampire Codex* and a regular guest on A&E's *Paranormal State*, is a psychic vampire. In her youth, Belanger had multiple surgeries. She claims that feeding on psychic energies made her stronger, so much so that she's since staved off a looming bypass, having experienced a complete reversal of her symptoms.

How does a psychic vampire feed? Most draw from the ambient energies given off by large crowds. Others may draw from specific individuals in a social setting. If you ever feel suddenly drained of your energy, it's possible you could be under a psychic attack, although this practice is frowned upon within the vampire community. One-on-one feeding is more intimate, and requires a donor. Some donors experience

Alix Fox of *Bizarre* magazine pops fang at an event celebrating the UK premiere of *True Blood*. (Courtesy Alix Fox)

a sense of euphoria during a feeding. The energy itself can be tapped into via eye contact, touch, sexual intercourse, intense conversation, and even dreams. Nature is also a source of energy, in particular storms, oceans, and bright sunlight.

If this sounds completely out in left field, Belanger offers another way to look at her vampirism, suggesting that if we can open ourselves to such "'esoteric' concepts as Reiki, feng shui, and the world soul, vampirism really isn't as far-fetched as you think." She continues, "Everything must have its opposite to balance it out. For every light worker who gives energy to heal, there is one of us who must take energy for ourselves. It's yin and yang."

But do "real vampires" possess any "real" powers? And what of garlic, holy water, and sunlight? That's for the fictional vampires. Some real vampires claim to experience heightened senses, such as light sensitivity and a nocturnal sleep cycle, but they're just as willing to suggest that that could be because so many community events are held at night.

Vampire Crib Sheet

Awakening: The moment one becomes conscious of their vampirism and embraces it.

Beast: The primal nature of a frustrated vampire.

Black swan: A non-vampire who accepts the vampire lifestyle. May adopt a vampyre-fetish lifestyle.

Blood drinker: One who drinks blood, regardless of motivation.

Blood fetishist: One who drinks blood for erotic pleasure, but does not need it to sustain physical or spiritual well-being.

Blood junkie: A derogatory term for one who experiences a physical need to drink blood, known as a Sanguinarian.

Bloodletting: The act of cutting flesh to extract blood for purposes of blood play, fetishism, and feeding.

Bloodplay: The act of using blood for sexual or fetishistic scenarios.

Clinical vampirism: One who experiences an urge to drink blood. Can be satisfied by drinking their own. Also clinically known as Renfield's Syndrome, named after Dracula's insect-eating assistant in Bram Stoker's novel.

Coming out (of the coffin): Living openly as a vampire.

Coven: Groups of individuals who identify with and participate in a vampire/vampyre lifestyle.

Donor: One who offers their blood freely.

Elder: Long-time, devoted member of a vampire/vampyre community who has often contributed to the sustainability of the community.

Embrace: Roleplaying term for turning one into a vampire.

Energy signature: Each person's unique energy pattern. It's believed that vampires can recognize one another via a specific signature.

Energy vampire: One who experiences a need to feed upon the life force of others, typically the chi or psychic energy rather than blood.

Feeding: To consume pranic energy (blood) or psychic energy (emotional and elemental energy).

Hematodipsia: Strong form of hemophilia, a condition in which even the slightest wound can result in profuse hemorrhaging.

Human: Non-vampire. This term is not universally accepted in the vampire community for the suggestion that vampires are non-human. Sometimes also referred to as "mundanes."

The Hunger: Psychological and physical need to feed. Also known as the Thirst.

Hunter: One who hunts, threatens, or does actual harm to one who identifies as vampire.

Immortal: Used loosely in vampire communities to describe those who appear to escape effects of aging, disease, and injury.

Latent vampire: One who is vampire, but has not awakened.

Leech: Derogatory term used to describe vampires.

Mentor: One who makes another a vampire, or aids in his/her awakening.

Mundane: Non-vampire.

The Nephilim: Some in the vampire community believe vampires to be descendents of the Nephilim, children born of a union between an angel (Watcher) and mortal women.

Of the Blood: A vampire.

Porphyria: Medical condition often referenced as a possible source of traditional vampire myths. Those with the affliction have pale skin and are sensitive to sunlight. Severely anemic, some sufferers have been known to drink blood to relieve the cravings.

Poser: One who claims to be a vampire, but is not.

Pranic energy: Blood and sexual energy.

Primus: Vampire who founds a coven. Almost always an Elder.

Psychic energy: Emotional and elemental (of the earth) energy. The life-force of all living things.

Psychic attack: An uninvited attack perpetrated by a psi-vampire, intended to drain one's energy.

Psychic vampire: One who feeds from psychic energy (life energy) rather than blood. (Sometimes also known as psi-vampires.)

Real vampire: One who has a significant need/thirst for blood or psychic energy.

Renegade/Rogue: Vampire or donor who becomes hostile toward the community.

RPGer/Roleplayer: One who engages in roleplaying games. May be a lifestyler or have no involvement with the community.

Sanguinarian: One with a physical need and craving for blood to sustain physical and spiritual well-being.

Sanguine: Blood-drinking vampire. Also includes psi-vampires who also drink blood.

Seeker: One who seeks out vampire and vampire knowledge in an effort to become one.

Sexual vampirism: Lesser known vampirism in which one feeds from sexual energy.

Sire: Fictional term for one who turns another into a vampire.

Slayer: One who boasts about killing vampires.

Thirst: Intense need or desire to drink blood.

Turned: Fictional term for "making" a vampire.

Vamping out: Intense physical and behavioral reaction to not having fed.

Vampire: Fictional vampires, folkloric, or modern "real" vampires.

Vampire bait: Poser who desperately wants to be noticed by vampires. Typically naive and ill-informed. Also known as a Wannabe.

Vampiric community: Those who openly identify as "vampire."

Vampire magick: Used by pagan vampires.

Vampyre: Humans who identify with fictional vampires. May dress like vampires, sleep in coffins, and belong to a coven. Also known as "social vampires" or "lifestylers."

White swan: One who disapproves of vampires. Often members of Goth or fetish scene despite their distaste for the community.

However, many say that they experience psychic abilities such as enhanced empathy and clairvoyance.

Alix Fox, an editor at *Bizarre* magazine (the world's #1 alternative magazine), helped celebrate the UK launch of *True Blood* at Central London club Ruby Lo where guests were invited to partake of a "True Bloody Mary" cocktail with pasteurized pigs' blood. She's since become what she jokingly calls an "undead talking head," the person people call upon to comment on the pervasive pop culture appeal of vampires. Recognizing the humor and escapism of the vampire genre, she good-naturedly offered a recipe for her ideal vampiric cocktail, a "sinful, stubbly, not-so-smoothie that would contain a whole bottle of Ryan Reynolds, neat (i.e. naked) over ice, with a chaser of Kiefer Sutherland's platinum *Lost Boys* mullet, the juiciest segments of my favorite newfangled erotic books, and a sprinkling of Japanese vamp-themed anime. And I'd ban Stephenie Meyer's prick-teasing, purity-ring-wearing, Mormon wet-wipe wusses from being within a 10-mile radius of the bar." Now that's a cocktail!

As part of her role at *Bizarre*, Fox has also attended hardcore BDSM (bondage, discipline, sadism, masochism) events where she's seen bloodplay in action. BDSM is consensual roleplay that incorporates elements of pain and power in order to achieve sexual release. Bloodplay, or blood fetishism, is the controversial and largely underground practice of using blood to achieve arousal. While it has been known to appear in the vampire subculture, most blood fetishists do not consider themselves to be vampires.

And unless you've been actively turning away from the naughty bits, you know that *True Blood* has more than a few references to BDSM, all explored from the safe distance of our comfy couches. Welsh psychoanalyst Ernest Jones theorizes that when sexuality becomes repressed, it's replaced by "regressed" behaviors, something he calls "oral sadism," or feasting off another person. Stacey May Fowles, publisher of *Shameless* magazine, a forward-thinking magazine for young women, offers a fascinating take on the nature of Bill and Sookie's romantic relationship. Sookie is presented as an assertive woman, yet when she meets Bill it could be argued that she loses her individuality in favor of pleasing her man. In her case, that man is a vampire who, when aroused, wants desperately to feed on her.

Fowles' take on Bill's actions is different. She says, "I felt that when Bill had proven that he respected Sookie as an equal she was able to be in a more submissive role." She continues, "With any dom/sub relationship, when trust is established that opens the door for 'play.' I have often viewed Sookie as a powerful and empowered female character who used her relationship with Bill to — for lack of a better word — rest. Her individuality was intact, yet she was able to submit to a more traditional role with Bill because his respect and her trust allowed that to happen."

When asked how she reconciles the inherently violent nature of a vampire feeding off mortals, Fowles suggests, "I think that's where the escapism and fiction of pop culture entertainment comes into play . . . it provokes discussion . . . The dynamic between Sookie and Bill, the violent nature of their sexuality, and the subsequent popularity of their romance, all suggest that we can be attracted to and aroused by things we intellectually know are problematic."

Finally, when asked how as viewers we should reconcile the violent fantasy with our daily lives, Fowles suggests, "The reality of life is that we [should] negotiate safe words and have long and even boring discussions about our desires before we enact them with a partner. The fantasy of entertainment leaves those parts out . . . [Ultimately], what is really important is how we view [these scenes], whether or not we question it, and how it makes us feel." No one knows this better than *True Blood*'s creator Alan Ball. "There's definitely an erotic basis for why vampires are such powerful symbols in our psyches. You know, the fact of hard fangs penetrating skin," he says. "That was definitely a part of Charlaine's books. They're this great amalgamation of satire and horror and humor and romance novel . . . And the romance and the thrill of surrendering to a vampire is such an inherent part of it, I thought, I'm not going to shy away from that, that's the fun part."

Viral Vampires

HBO's Contagious Promos

What better way to put television viewers into the headspace of a society in which vampires are already mainstreaming than to create a pervasive media campaign that sneaks up as quietly as the undead?

Before season 1, HBO hired CampFire NYC to create a viral marketing campaign. Viral marketing capitalizes on existing social networks to increase the chances of users talking about your product in the hope of solidifying your brand through invaluable, and unpaid, word-of-mouth. An early example of viral marketing would be the "Pyramid Scheme," in which investors depend on the exponential word-of-mouth of a network of friends. Other examples include *Mystery Science Theater 3000*, which encouraged viewers to make and share copies of the show hoping to increase distribution. And Nine Inch Nails' viral campaign for the 2007 album *Year Zero* included leaving USB drives containing their music in various public places throughout Europe while they toured. In fall 2008, thousands of DVDs of the first episode of *True Blood* were handed out to attendees of the Toronto International Film Festival's annual Midnight Madness screening. Blockbuster Video also offered a free rental of the first episode in the days before the premiere.

But how did HBO plan to send out their message online? By having would-be fans follow a series of clues. Leading up to the show's premiere, HBO sent press releases to vampire enthusiasts and bloggers. Then they set up BloodCopy.com, a blog that purported to be written by a vampire to "chronicle the amazing days we live in as vampires attempt to integrate with humans." It featured viral videos; news items from Bon Temps, Louisiana; the vlog "BloodCopy Reports"; and even an invitation to contact the blog's vampire via Skype. From there, the bloggers took over, anxiously anticipating and deciphering every new post or vlog, some of which eventually featured actors from the show appearing in character.

The *True Blood* campaign deliberately set out to blur the lines between fact and fiction, creating a backstory for vampires and humans with the launch of a series of websites and ads designed for the vampire consumer or to reach out to humans. HBO launched TruBeverage.com to promote Tru Blood, a line of synthetic bottled blood for vampires, which rivaled real product sites for its innovation, complete with a blood type finder, product descriptions, and merchandise. Outdoor ads also went up for Tru Blood in select cities along with empty Tru Blood vending machines to make it appear that as if the synthetic beverage was always sold out, leading to the natural question, who drinks synthetic blood? Vampires!

HBO also launched an inclusive dating site for humans and vampires, www.lovebitten.net, as well as an anti-vampire coalition, the Fellowship of the Sun (www.fellowshipofthesun.org), a remarkably real site run by Reverend Steve Newlin and his wife, Sarah. The actors who portrayed the characters, Michael McMillian and Anna Camp, appeared in a series of vlogs called "Reflections of Light," short vignettes on everything from marriage advice to the temptations of being turned by a vampire to avoid uncertain death.

Beyond these strategies, vampire profiles began to appear at various social networking sites such as Facebook, livejournal, and YouTube. On MySpace, the profile for "Blood" was created and two videos uploaded: "Vampire Taste Test — Tru Blood vs Human," which features a vampire comparing the taste of synthetic blood to a fresh human, and "BloodCopy Exclusive — Interview with Samson the Vampire," in which Samson professes the necessity for vampires to embrace Tru

Blood and "make something" of themselves. At the 2008 Comic-Con, attendees were given a prequel comic that featured the vampire Lamar who tells readers about a synthetic drink, Tru Blood, and the possibilities for it to make things safer for his kind.

The campaign also drilled down to the mundane, airing evening weather radio reports and running "local business" ads before films in select theaters. A faux newsmagazine show also aired on HBO on Demand that featured "The Vampire Report," which covered segments from the world of vampire news, everything from cooking for humans to hate crimes.

Not everyone was a fan of the initial campaign, however. Tru Blood slogans such as "Real Blood Is for Suckers," "Friends Don't Let Friends Drink Friends," "All Flavor. No Bite," and "Because You Don't Need a Pulse to Make Hearts Race" struck deep to the core of self-identified vampires who felt the campaign was insensitive if not mocking. HBO representatives have answered those charges with the response that it's not possible to make fun of something that doesn't exist. Which would be a valid argument, if they hadn't sent follow-up press materials to known vampire covens. Was it intended to be cruel, or just a case of HBO having not done its homework?

The campaign went so far as to boast that Gawker Media had purchased the BloodCopy site. This didn't just rustle a few vampires. Even *Business Insider* was duped into reporting on the alleged merger, leading many to call into question just how far a faux marketing campaign should be allowed to go. Not to mention that it upset many of Gawker's editorial staff, who felt that much of the coverage BloodCopy enjoyed on the site equaled that of sponsored posts.

During research for his book *Vampires Today: The Truth About Modern Vampires*, author Joe Laycock learned about the marketing campaign for *True Blood*. In his article at www.religiousdispatches.com, he offered his insight into the rift between real vampires and the network by drawing the line at what he considers an elaborate ruse. Laycock's opposition is more philosophical. He states, "The real vampire community is in the strange position of experiencing an unprecedented level of media attention," he begins, "even as they are often pejoratively characterized as being unable to discern media from reality." In other words, just because fictional vampires have come out of the closet doesn't mean that those who live a vampire lifestyle want to attract the same degree of curiosity.

It was an interesting dilemma that HBO surely never planned for. In his essay, Laycock states his case clearly, concluding, "This position invokes a worldview in which reality consists only of what can be empirically proven to exist, and that anyone who believes otherwise is foolish or somehow deserves to be deceived."

Heading into season 2, HBO took their campaign straight to the mainstream, this time steering away from mystery and straight toward full assimilation of vampires living openly in society. First, they released a dual-image teaser poster, a Rubin's vase–like blood splatter that could also be seen as one figure biting another's neck, a beautifully simple yet evocative treatment. HBO also released a minute-long promotional video that featured the incomparable Bob Dylan's "Beyond Here Lies Nothin'," first showing on *Entertainment Tonight*. They launched an online interactive game for U.S. residents — "Escape the Every Day" — which had a pot of $10,000 to be used toward HBO services and more. Players navigated through scenes such as Merlotte's, Bill's house, or the graveyard, their goal to unlock and collect objects, earning points and additional chances to enter the sweepstakes. There were also chances to win instant *True Blood*–related prizes such as DVDs, T-shirts, and mugs, all no doubt by fans just chomping at the bit for season 2 to start.

They took the theme of mainstreaming even further by running a series of Digital Kitchen ads featuring real advertisers pitching product to vampires: Ecko ("Attract a Human"); Geico ("The money you could save if you were immortal"); Gillette ("Dead Sexy"); Monster.com ("When you sleep in a coffin, it's easy to think outside the box"); Harley Davidson ("Outrun the Sun"); and BMW's Mini Cooper ("Feel the Wind in Your Fangs"), which ran a combined campaign of national print, online, and out-of-home outlets. Digital ads also ran on Yahoo, CNN, AOL, HBO's *True Blood* home page, and across the show's microsites.

The counterpart to the Fellowship of the Sun was launched with the online home of the American Vampire League (www.americanvampire league.com), which exists to promote vampire rights. Designed to look and operate like a not-for-profit organization, it featured news items, an "Intolerance Watch," PSAs on the addictive dangers of V (vampire blood), vampire-friendly brands, and a downloadable rally kit.

The BloodCopy wiki was created along with Twitter accounts for the Fellowship of the Sun, the American Vampire League, BloodCopy, and Facebook fan pages for each. The *True Blood* Facebook fan page alone has over 1.23 million fans to date.

In September 2009, HBO launched a gothic-themed *True Blood* jewelry line with Udi Behr, chief designer for Love Peace and Hope, and filed a trademark registration for a possible future electronic game based on the series. And the viewer was also *finally* allowed their own taste of TruBlood in September 2009. Bottled to look the same as it does in the series, the beverage itself is a blood orange carbonated drink, manufactured by Omni Consumer Products, a company that specializes in creating products as distinct as their fictional branding.

The Pop Culture Politics
of *True Blood*

From Chaos to Repair and Mainstreaming Vampires as an LGBT Metaphor

Jason Stackhouse: A lot of Americans don't think you people deserve special rights.

Bill Compton: They're the same rights you have.

Jason Stackhouse: No, I'm just saying there's a reason things are the way they are.

Bill Compton: Yeah. It's called injustice.

"The vampire is a subversive creature in every way, and I think this accounts for much of his appeal. In an age where moralists use the fact that sex is dangerous to 'prove' that sex is bad, the vampire points out that sex has always been dangerous. These days, if you wish to make love to someone without a layer of latex separating your most sensitive membranes, it becomes necessary to ask yourself, 'Would I be willing to die a slow, lingering death for this person?' The answer may be yes – but for the vampire, it's not even an issue. He laughs in the face of safe sex, and he lives forever."

– Poppy Z. Brite, *Love in Vein*

By the time viewers had taken their first taste of HBO's *True Blood*, vampires were already among them, revealed along with their supporters and detractors in a viral marketing campaign that spanned print, electronic, and online media. Not since *The Blair Witch Project* (or much earlier in 1938 when Orson Welles ushered in a nationwide panic with the radio play *The War of the Worlds*) had audiences seen such commitment to advance buzz for a film or television series. The biggest difference, of course, was a viewer who's savvier than ever, along with a host of blogging platforms, Facebook, and Twitter acting as the tools of choice for the make-culture generation of civic journalism. It's the stuff of a marketer's dreams and nightmares: how to engage an audience so they don't call hoax before you've had a chance to roll out your campaign, and how to entertain them so they won't cry foul for flogging your product.

Enter vampires, and the accompanying fear surrounding their lifestyle, and whoever was orchestrating this extravagant production had caught our rapt attention. Some of the campaign riffed off LGBT rights (one public service announcement stopping just short of equating vampires — gays — with pedophilia), prompting some bloggers to question whether the pieces were intended to be anti-gay. These PSAS appeared to unearth the worst fears of the ultra-conservative right wing while simultaneously confirming them. Conversely, some argued the other extreme, ranging from savvy societal comment to a direct opposition to the democratization of LGBT life.

The question lingers: was it proper to satirize homophobia in absence of a larger context or an accountable creator? Even after the campaign revealed itself to be more than just a gag, there was still the question of intent. What did this all mean? And would HBO be able to sustain the excitement, not to mention intense mystery, it had awakened in a viewing public that had yet to see the show? And, who, exactly, was this show for? What audience was it trying to attract?

Not to worry, because beyond building buzz, the campaign was an ingenious precursor to the series, something that had already succeeded in encouraging viewers to suspend both belief and disbelief, straight out of the coffin. And not just mainstream viewers, but hardcore paranormal fans as well. You'd be hard-pressed to encounter a metaphor more malleable than the vampire, but fans of the genre tend to be as polarized in their opinions of what makes a "real" vampire as some in the LGBT community are about bisexuals. Which is why *True Blood* succeeds on so many levels. It takes chances, using the media to educate, entertain, and titillate. By the time Bill Compton first walks into Merlotte's, the debate of natural versus unnatural is already on the fringes. The core of the story is more akin to the Kinsey scale — there are extremes, but most of us fall somewhere in between.

Brian Juergens writes and reviews for a number of horror-themed websites, notably Camp Blood (www.campblood.org), where he also co-hosts with illustrator Andy Swist the "Blood Work" vlog, a campy recap of *True Blood* episodes. When asked how and why the horror genre and queer community intersects, he points to a recurring theme, what he notes

Brian Juergens of www.CampBlood.org senses something behind him. Duck, Brian!!! (Photo by Mark Bradley Miller)

is queer viewers' "appreciation for the uncanny, the over-the-top, and the beautifully chaotic." He continues, "A lot of queer folks grow up feeling hemmed in by a world that they don't feel that they belong to, and horror movies tend to explode society's dominant moral paradigm all over the screen. It's one of the few genres where melodrama, gorgeous excess, and life-and-death peril are visited upon normal, everyday characters, and I think those overwrought extremes lend a visually compelling and operatic escape to a lot of queer genre fans."

As to why vampires seem to be such prevalent queer icons, Juergens suggests that the easy answer would be that the undead are "sexy, horny, and operate somewhat beyond the societal restrictions of traditional heterosexuality." But he also believes that vampires have evolved alongside society's fears, coming to represent what he thinks are the internalized fears of what many queers fear meeting, if not becoming, "namely, the purely sexual being that destroys what it desires. In a world with AIDS," Juergens begins, "the fluids-obsessed sexual predator is extremely taboo, and can therefore be fascinating." He's quick to qualify that not all vampires fit this analogy, noting that vampires have been interpreted in so many ways as to be unrecognizable from one film to the next. "For instance," he says, "I don't know that the doting, neutered sparkly things from *Twilight* have much to offer queer viewers."

Where the LGBT metaphor of *True Blood* differs greatly from the LGBT community is the prevailing notion that a vampire is not born, it's made, something that should stick in the craw of any gay rights activist who has spent his or her life arguing the exact opposite: that sexual identity may evolve, but it's not something that's forced upon a person, nor can one be changed, one way or the other. Nor, to hearken back to a time where gays wondered if there was a synthetic alternative to the way LGBT people "feed." Sexual conversion camps have tried to satisfy this purpose, offering God as the tonic. Drink deep enough and you'll stave off the cravings.

That said, *True Blood* has created a world in which it's actually fun to get upset about such things. And it's by far the safest show on television to house these kind of conflicts. Alan Ball introduces hefty themes of excess and consequence, fanaticism and redemption, cult and community. It's emotional, boundary-pushing, and surprisingly spiritual, which is where most bloodshed begins.

Bringing vampires out of the coffin is a brilliant narrative device, because it introduces the notion that something can be both timeless *and* ever-changing, more or less the key to ensuring that humanity survives, and peaceably at that. Wrapped in attractive vamps and busty waitresses, there's a lot of navel-gazing to be had. On a level of pure escapism, this gives *True Blood*'s writers the chance to play on the politics of contemporary society while having fun with what Ball describes as "the terrors of intimacy." In doing so, Sookie and Bill's story isn't just girl meets vampire, a modern love story for modern times; there's plenty in the series to suggest that times have not a-changed. So *True Blood* observes traditions alongside expanding definitions of normality. (In truth, a Sookie and Bill hook-up is so conservative, it's downright monogamous. One man, one woman, for all eternity? And, she's a *virgin*, no less?)

The idea of vampires living openly in Louisiana may feel progressive, but if history is to repeat itself, any time a group "outs" itself, it's at the risk of remaining open to criticism and violence. Bill may have been around for close to two centuries, but he's not impervious to threat. In the real world, most of us can remember in our lifetimes Harvey Milk's assassination or Matthew Shepard's torture, after which he was left to die alone. So while it may seem supernatural to some to cast diversity in a range of paranormal creatures (and those who love them), this is where popular culture has the opportunity to promote innovative thought and action, such as in 1968 when *Star Trek* showed the first interracial kiss on American television between Captain Kirk (Caucasian) and Lt. Uhura (African American); in 1977 when Billy Crystal played a gay man on *Soap*; in 1991 when two women kissed on *L.A. Law*.

Is it really necessary to read politics into pure entertainment? If the answer is no, then we're left to believe that art doesn't have the power to inspire and alter when we know that not to be the case. And while even Alan Ball has referred to the storylines of *True Blood* as "lady porn," he's never shied from making statements in popular fare, which is why he draws such a diverse audience.

So, there's no doubt that *True Blood* is queer-friendly, but would Juergens go so far as to say that *True Blood* is a queer show? Absolutely, he says. "*True Blood* is as queer as they come, even if the gay characters and elements are sometimes not front-and-center." He continues, "But the show itself comes from a place that is decidedly left-of-center in its overarching moral structure . . . Everything that the show discusses, from the persecution of minorities in society to the challenges faced by an independent woman in the South to straight sexual addiction, is filtered through a queer lens . . . It's easily the queerest mass-market show since *The Golden Girls*."

Being Bad Never Felt So Good

True Blood's Opening Credits

"I'm not a fan of title sequences that parade the actors' faces . . . You're about to watch an hour of these people, so why would you need to do that?"

— Alan Ball

"We knew from the start that the best way — the only way — to create a powerful introduction was to insert ourselves into the middle of Louisiana and find out what happens — unmannered and unvarnished."

— Digital Kitchen press release

"When Mariana Klaveno was added [to the credits] . . . I had the hot girl in her underwear, but alphabetical order pushed me back to the slow motion snake strike! Nobody wants that creepy baby."

— Todd Lowe ("Terry Bellefleur")

With the first strains of Jace Everett's "Bad Things," *True Blood*'s opening sequence unfurls a sweaty montage of swamplands, sex, snakes, and sacred ritual. With not a vampire to be found, nor the familiar rotation of cast shots, Alan Ball strives to treat the supernatural as something primal rather than that which originates outside of nature. The sequence supports that, rotting roadkill and all, setting the mood for ritual and ecstasy, be it bar or baptism. It's also lustful and sticky, which works in beautifully complicated opposition to the other themes: redemption and forgiveness.

The people at Digital Kitchen are the design masterminds behind *True Blood*'s Emmy-nominated credit sequence. They've also produced the opening credits for Alan Ball's HBO series *Six Feet Under*, as well as *Dead Like Me*, *Queer as Folk*, *House M.D.*, and *Dexter*. With offices in Seattle, Chicago, Los Angeles, and Manhattan, Digital Kitchen's clients include Budweiser, Coke, Showtime, Sundance, AT&T, and Microsoft, making them one of the leading digital agencies in the U.S.

Conceptually, Digital Kitchen decided to contrast images of sex, violence, and religion to play off the idea of "the whore in the house of prayer," progressing from daylight to nighttime, when the predatory voyeuristic thrill reaches a feverish peak. The team's hope was to string the tension so tight that the viewer couldn't take anymore, arriving at an iconic image of cathartic release: the original sin washed away in the sacrament of baptism. The crew borrowed inspiration from Andrew Douglas's film *Searching for the Wrong-Eyed Jesus*, pulling from the charms of its southern surrealist cinema. *Searching for the Wrong-Eyed Jesus* follows a country singer on a road trip through the Deep South, framed by his encounters with a marginalized subculture of churches, prisons, biker bars, and coal-mines. (Some argue that Digital Kitchen borrowed a little too heavily from the film with at least one scene — the night baptism — appearing almost identical to one in the film.)

To achieve the home-movie effect of the "found" footage, the team took a four-day trip to Louisiana looking for inspiration in the smallest details. Most of the outdoor footage was shot in Louisiana, but the crew also gathered material in Chicago (the church) and Seattle (the bar scenes and writhing bodies). "There are no tried-and-true techniques used on the *True Blood* opening," says creative director Matt Mulder. "The way we decided to gather imagery was entirely new to us, and we wanted to celebrate that adventure." That adventure sometimes included jumping out of their cars the moment they saw something they thought might work, hopeful for a little extra hospitality when that "something" landed on private property. They were pleasantly surprised how often that instinct led to a whole new set of possibilities. "I saw a wrecked school bus in somebody's yard," says creative director Rama Allen, "so we knocked on the door and ended up getting approval to shoot all over his property, even inside [the owner's] home." Another shot includes a man in a rocking chair, just a good-natured fellow who invited the crew to hang out for beers. They picked up the camera, immortalizing the man in a few brief moments.

"We threw ourselves into this project literally, artistically, and physically," Allen continues, a number of the crew showing up in the credits themselves. Executive producer Mark Bayshore appears in two shots, one involving a shoving match in a bar, the other a lively dance with one of its female patrons. Bayshore's sons also appear with berries smothered all over their faces. The two weeping women deep in prayer were played by Digital Kitchen's office assistant and assistant editor. And the woman who rises from the water during a night baptism is held up by producer Morgan Henry and a line producer.

That hands-on approach also extended itself to other areas, the team's background in film apparent. "We shot everything from 16mm film to HD video," Bayshore notes. They bring athleticism to each step of the process. For instance, some of the fonts, based on hand-painted road signs, were created using an X-Acto knife and other tools (eight different typefaces in all). The effect contributes to the duality between rushed urgency and carved permanence, all in keeping with the show's overarching artistic vision that, as Bayshore says, accentuates the story, not the production. And, remarkably, while no vampires appear in the opening credits — the only nod being a roadside sign that reads, "God Hates Fangs" — the overall feel is nonetheless vampiric: death, morality, excess, escapism, an ever-present underlying fear, and rebirth.

The result is something *Newsweek* calls the "perfect amuse-bouche," original chef creations designed to thrill the taste buds and demonstrate a chef's methodology and approach to cooking. In the case of Digital Kitchen, their expressions of religious fanaticism and sexual energy are the perfect moody concoction. "The show itself," Mulder says, "is a kind of gumbo of flavors," presented teasingly. While you couldn't call the credits understated, they do leave a lot to

Recognize Lucky Liquor from the opening credits? Next time you're in Shreveport, Louisiana, be sure to stop in for a cold one. A cold brew, that is. Vamps aren't on the menu. (Eleanor Tivnan)

the imagination. And like a tasty morsel of food, you want to revisit it, uncover each pairing and preparation technique, the conflicting ingredients of religion, sex, innocence, and bloodlust working successfully in tandem rather than in opposition.

One method Digital Kitchen employed a fair bit was jump-cutting, in which frames are removed from shots to produce a purposeful visual skip, while other shot speeds were altered to play the action back at a slower rate, the impact feeling like a loss of control, both in mind and body. In a few instances, the transition effect was achieved through a process called Polaroid transfer technique. Ryan Gagnier designed these sequences. A Polaroid image was taken of the last and first frame on either side of the transition. The emulsion was then boiled away from the Polaroid backing, the image floating off like a membrane, or plastic wrap. That emulsion was filmed during this process, the final image at once raw and ethereal, bubbling up in the temptation of a sticky, tactile bond. "It immediately transports the viewer into the *True Blood* world," Alan Ball says, "where the conjured thematic images of sex, death, and religious fervor blend into a gripping crescendo. I'm enthralled every time I watch [the opening credits]."

Of course, the opening credits aren't all about the visual effects. Many people love the beginning of *True Blood* just because of that raw, raunchy song that takes us out of our own worlds and firmly plants us in the dark, mucky recesses of Bon Temps, Louisiana. Jace Everett's "Bad Things" is the perfect soundtrack to the world of *True Blood*. Jace Everett was born on January 7, 1972, in Evansville, Indiana. Growing up, he lived in Indianapolis, Carmel, and St. Louis, before moving to Fort Worth, Texas, when he was six years old. A self-taught musician, save for a few piano lessons as a child, he began to play music in his church and school before moving to Nashville, Tennessee, to attend Belmont University.

Jace Everett had two other albums under his belt, and had co-written a #1 single ("Your Man" performed by Josh Turner), when Alan Ball went cruising around iTunes in search for a placeholder song for the credit sequence for *True Blood*. He found "Bad Things," and he never found anything better. Which is meant as a compliment — the song didn't just do for what Ball needed at the time: the song came to define the show.

As all things vampiric, "Bad Things" has a past life. It was originally released on Everett's debut album *Jace Everett*. Reborn via *True Blood*, the song won a 2009 Broadcast Music Incorporated award (cable TV category), was nominated for a 2009 Scream Award for Best Scream Song of the Year, and is an integral part of the Emmy-nominated credit sequence. Everett estimates as a result of the song's success he receives approximately 10,000 visits a day to his MySpace page.

To take the vampire metaphor to its limit, Everett recognizes new life was breathed into his career with this recent success. Everett was at the point of desperation and considering a new career path when Alan Ball came calling. And when opportunity comes knocking, it's best to be prepared. He called in recording artist Chuck Prophet to co-write some songs. He says he was frustrated, but hopeful that this could be his break. With the help of Prophet, who has 12 albums of his own and has played with such artists as Kelly Willis, Aimee Mann, Warren Zevon, Lucinda Williams, and Cake, they penned close to 20 songs.

In June 2009, Everett released his third studio album *Red Revelations*, with "Bad Things" showing up anew on the track list, sweet respite after Sony Music's Nashville Epic imprint dumped Everett from the label after the Sony/BMG merger dropped 12 artists and 40 employees in one day. "[T]hat was a little shocking and threw me off for a little while," Everett told *CMT*, "but I just kept writing and wound up making a live-in-the-studio acoustic record [*Old New Borrowed Blues*] that I went and toured the UK." He was writing and booking gigs as a bass session player, playing with Trent Willmon, when the news came through that Alan Ball wanted to purchase the rights to "Bad Things." He continues, "I was able to get some things worked out to where I could begin to go make a new record ... It's definitely been a game-changer, but you know, I was in the game the whole time."

Everett was asked to perform different versions of the song, ones that were less country, ironic considering that country radio didn't get behind the song when it was first released. Ultimately, the original recording was used in the credits, prompting some to wonder if he plans to write more tunes like it. But he says he sees "Bad Things" as a novelty song, brooding and melodramatic, but also humorous, something he thinks Alan Ball picked up on when he first heard it. "[I]f you watch *True Blood*, yeah, it's about vampires, but it's also funny as hell at times. [Alan Ball] likes that black humor ... and so do I."

The inspiration for the song itself did not come, as some have speculated, from Chris Isaak's "Baby Did a Bad, Bad Thing." In an exclusive interview with the *True Blood* fan site The Vault (www.trueblood-online.com), Everett concurs there's a similar rockabilly feel, but continues to say that he wasn't aware of Isaak's song when he penned his own, likening it more to Steve Earle's "Poor Boy." He also hears a marked difference between his voice and Isaak's, saying Isaak's is much smoother, whereas his has a more "whiskey-soaked and sandpaper sound." As for the song's meaning, he goes on to explain its progression from a song of personal vengeance — Everett was owed money and fantasized about doing bad things *to* you — to realizing "*to* you" could easily be interpreted as date rape ("not good!"), to changing the lyrics to "I want to do bad things *with* you." Even with the lyric change, he knows that many people still think the song is talking about doing bad things to another person. ("I'm really a very nice boy.")

Everett considers himself to be a cross-genre artist, in perfect keeping with both Alan Ball's vision as well as Charlaine Harris's. Everett enjoys writing country, pop, blues, and even rock operatic tunes. It shows on *Red Revelations* in Everett's vocal range, hot bass lines, and soulful stories. He describes the music off the album as cinematic and hopes his instinct to play with expectations might lead to more work in film and television. He likens his approach to a chef that only makes a marinara sauce. Rather than be known for one thing, he'd rather do it all. Among his favorite artists he cites Willie Nelson, Bob Dylan, KISS, U2, Tom Waits, Bob Marley, Miles Davis, and Jay-Z, but cautions that it's unlikely anyone will ever hear those influences in his own music. That diversity, however, is in keeping with the core theme of *True Blood*; it's certain to have seeped into the infectiously catchy "Bad Things," far more sophisticated and crafted than perhaps first meets the ear, so familiar that you're singing along before the final bars have faded out.

But what many people want to know is, did Everett set out to write music that makes listeners want to get down — and nasty? Not intentionally, he says, although he can't deny the sensuality inherent in his thumping bass lines. "The truth of the matter is, when I was a kid I knew all the Michael Jackson moves. Now I'm just old and insecure . . . But I love dancing. I think it's one of the most intimate and cool things people can do together." He also has some background knowledge of how to incite passion in an audience growing up in a devoutly religious family, something he's since left behind. "But I still have this intrinsic desire to preach," he confesses, "so no matter what the song is about, you're going to get a little of the sweaty Mississippi preacher-man."

No wonder Alan Ball couldn't find another song or artist to sing in his hit series; it's almost as if Everett was born — again — to do the job.

Season 1

September–November 2008

1.01 Strange Love

Original air date: September 7, 2008
Written by: Alan Ball
Directed by: Alan Ball

Bill: Vampires often turn on those who trust them, you know. We don't have human values like you.
Sookie: Well, humans turn on those who trust them too.

Vampires have "come out of the coffin," able to subsist on a Japanese synthetic bottled blood called Tru Blood. In Bon Temps, Louisiana, Sookie Stackhouse, a telepathic waitress, meets Bill Compton, a vampire, and saves him from a pair of "vampire drainers," people who steal vampire's blood for resale.

From the opening scene, nothing is what it seems. The greasy goth in the Grabbit Kwik is not the real vampire, but the attractive professional-looking blonde talking to Bill Maher on tv? She is. From the first frame, we're prepared to see the worst that vampires can do, instead we see them restrained, even when baring fangs. In this pilot episode, Alan Ball sets up vampires as an invisible minority akin to the LGBT (Lesbian, Gay, Bisexual, Transgender/Transsexual) community. Normalizing the unknown and prejudice based in fear are two of the stronger themes, but they don't just apply to vampires. These themes resonate for us mortals, and the closets of our choosing, or those that normative society would prefer to see us locked inside, delegitimizing our voices so the struggle to "come out" is even tougher. (For instance, *True Blood* doesn't ask the question "Do vampires exist?" Yet many people would argue that homosexuality is a myth.) The world of *True Blood* may appear familiar — there's a neighborhood bar, friends who have known each other since childhood, people working hard and partying harder — but Bon Temps, Louisiana, operates more like a funhouse.

This episode succeeds in introducing us to most of the main players, giving us a solid idea of each character's personality: where they work, how they connect to one another, and, most important, where they stand on vampires, which is also a thinly veiled indication as to where they stand on *anything* that's different from them.

Gran's stove. Can't you just smell the sausage and biscuits? Hands off, Jason Stackhouse! (Jodi Ross, courtesy of The Vault www.trueblood-online.com)

Perhaps because she's a telepath, we shouldn't be surprised that Sookie Stackhouse is gleeful when Bill Compton, a vampire, enters Merlotte's. We're shown her pure joy at being around someone who is magical, even supernatural. What makes Bill different isn't something he was born with, it's something he was turned into, something that forever — in his case, forever and ever — sets him apart and makes him misunderstood as untrustworthy, something Sookie can relate to because people worry she'll penetrate their most intimate thoughts. However, she cannot hear or see Bill's thoughts, a stunning new development in the romantic life of a young virgin who has been unable to date, often knowing her suitors' next thoughts before they do.

On its simplest level, this is the main story of the episode and it is universal. Two outsiders meet, connect, and — because people typically can't will others to do things or read their minds — they engage in small talk. Since the beginning of time, and 'til the end, this is how it will go. It's only when we see them as telepath and vampire that it seems absurd.

Ball doesn't shy away from injustices, interweaving themes of race, gender, sexuality, and class throughout most of the characters. Tara and Lafayette are visible minorities, African American, at Merlotte's as employees, not as patrons. While Lafayette is prob-

The booth where it all began. Just think, Stephen Moyer warmed that seat. That's okay . . . take all the time you need. (Jodi Ross, courtesy of The Vault www.trueblood-online.com)

ably "getting" as much as Jason Stackhouse, his play is for pay, while Jason is making more to do less as the foreman of the town's road crew. Sookie and her female co-workers doll themselves up for bigger tips, while most of the men command authority via strength and prowess, resulting either in getting what they want or what they need.

The notable exception among the men is Sam, the bar's owner. We're led to think that he's as solid as they come, self-made, but also protective of Sookie and not without his edge. It works in nice contrast to his scruffy, puppy dog face, but something bubbles under his passivity in this world where nothing is as it seems.

Our introduction to Tara is priceless. Everything about her screams anti-consumerism, yet here she is working at the Super Save-A-Bunch. We just know the minute her shift ends, she rips that work vest off. She's indignant toward customers and authority figures, but equally heroic for speaking her mind, cutting that customer down into bite-sized pieces with the deadly accuracy of a sniper. We love Tara because she gets to make all the mistakes we would *if* we could. Yet as much as she puts up her walls, we know people like her: a little too smart for her own good, a bit bratty, always testing authority. She is introduced to us in the brilliant image of a young woman lazing in the middle of one of the store's displays, reading a highly critical account of the rise of

Merlotte's Bar and Grill. Interestin' folk in here. I'll have a gin and tonic, easy on the tonic. (Jodi Ross, courtesy of The Vault www.trueblood-online.com)

capitalism in times of devastation and crisis — incidentally conditions that have also been suggested as the cause for the rise in popularity of vampire entertainment.

If it feels like Tara's backstory runs deeper, it's because she isn't plucked from the pages of Charlaine Harris's books like most of the other characters. In the TV series, Alan Ball re-envisioned Tara as African American, working class, living with an abusive mother, and hung up on Jason. Much of this is changed from the books where she's Caucasian, owns a fashion store, has lost both parents, and doesn't pursue an interest in Jason. But it's a great departure that ties together a lot of elements. As Lafayette's cousin, she draws him further into the story so he isn't left on the sidelines. And because Tara is so reactionary — often to a cringe-worthy extent — Sookie ends up looking rooted when she talks to her friend or calms her down, rather than judgmental.

Let's not forget the final character we meet in this episode: SEX. Sex and all it represents is nothing Alan Ball has ever shied from. Sex is to mortals what bloodlust is to vampires. If it's a part of who we are, Alan Ball's not going to hide it. For someone like Jason, the change in times puts him at risk of becoming a minority: a straight, white, *mortal* male.

It's not all good times in Bon Temps. For some it's Armageddon, for others it's ecstasy. And historically when emotions are high, people will do what they have to in

Out back of Merlotte's Bar and Grill. Look out for drainers, Vampire Bill! Didn't your mother ever tell you not to talk to strangers? (Eleanor Tivnan)

order to save themselves, or to prosper in the confusion. The Rattrays bridge the worst of both worlds, those who drain vampires and resell their blood, an illicit yet powerful narcotic to humans.

Toward the end of this first episode, Sookie and Bill have just begun to explore the liberation that comes from knowing one another freely and without pretext. As "Strange Love" closes on Sookie being jumped in the parking lot, we're reminded that monsters live among us, often in our own backyard.

Highlight: Sookie [on Bill's self-regenerative healing capabilities]: "Shut. Up."

Nightcap: When we first meet Tara, she's reading *The Shock Doctrine: The Rise of Disaster Capitalism* by Naomi Klein, which features commentary on the economic aftermath of Hurricane Katrina, which would appeal to Tara as someone who doesn't trust that the many will ever enjoy the same riches as the few. Lynn Collins ("Dawn Green") and Carrie Preston ("Arlene Fowler") both appeared in Alan Ball's film *Towelhead*. Adele Stackhouse ("Gran") is seen reading *Last Scene Alive*, a novel by Charlaine Harris. The set in Gran's house is littered with artifacts brought in by Alan Ball and his crew.

Relationship Crypt Falls: Bill, we know you're a bit rusty with the ladies, but telling them you have a penchant for groin arteries is what we in the 21st century like to call "TMI."

Paging Dr. Creepy: Liam the Vibrating Vampire. Watching a vamp get his groove on is one thing. But watching a vamp watch me watching him get his groove on is almost too meta for me. Besides Liam, didn't anyone ever tell you to keep your eyes front? Or, from rolling back in your head? Why not switch things up and wear a blindfold?

Location, Location, Location: Merlotte's Bar & Grill exists as two sets on different studio lots. The bar's exterior sits on the Warner Brothers back lot in Burbank, California. It consists of a lagoon, roadhouse, and cabin, enclosed by trees and foliage. Nicknamed "The Jungle," it was built originally for the 1956 film *Santiago*, and has since been used as Sherwood Forest in *The Adventures of Robin Hood*, in *The Dukes of Hazzard*, *The Waltons*, *Maverick*, *Bonanza*, *Fantasy Island*, and *Private Benjamin*. The interior of the bar is an original creation by set designer Suzuki Ingerslev and sits on a sound stage at the Hollywood Center Studio, California. In season 2, the set was moved to "The Lot," also in Hollywood, California.

Suzuki Sets the Scene: Merlotte's Bar and Grill was the most challenging set for Ingerslev's team to design. With little time, they had to incorporate a number of key features, notably how each of the rooms had to stay within eyeline of one another, while creating a clear path for the director of photography to follow the characters on foot with a Steadicam, and at least 25% padding on all sides (to protect the sets and camera), including behind the bar. The set is so authentic — functioning beer taps, and all — that many who visit it have remarked that they thought it was an existing bar.

Encore: As Sookie turns back to talk to Tara while she drinks margarita, we hear "Strange Love" performed by Slim Harpo. James "Slim Harpo" Moore was born in 1924 in Baton Rouge, Louisiana, the eldest in an orphaned family. He worked as a longshoreman and began performing his style of post-war rural blues in bars under the name Harmonica Slim before circles started to call him Slim Harpo. He was known for his warm, lazy, sexual voice, and his song "I'm a King Bee" was recorded by The Rolling Stones. The Stones, along with The Pretty Things, The Yardbirds, Pink Floyd, and Them all covered Slim's songs. His biggest hit came in 1966 with "Baby, Scratch My Back" which went to #20 on the Billboard Hot 100, and was a #1 R&B hit. During the '60s, he owned a trucking business, while he continued to perform. He died unexpectedly of a heart attack in 1970 at the age of 42.

1.02   The First Taste

Original air date: September 14, 2008
Written by: Alan Ball
Directed by: Scott Winant

Bill: Humans are usually more squeamish about vampires than you are.

Sookie: Who am I to be squeamish about something out of the ordinary?

Bill rescues Sookie from the Rattrays, saving her from certain death by having her feed on his blood. Later, Bill visits with Sookie's grandmother and receives a cold welcome from Jason and Tara.

In "Strange Love," we were shown what the main characters get up to when left to their own devices. In "The First Taste," we see how some of the characters are handling all the changes in Bon Temps, who's evolving and who's having a hard time. Territory, and what it takes to hold on to it, is the major motif in this episode.

Ryan Kwanten's performance is exceptional. Jason is losing his grip and Kwanten plays it with a mix of bewilderment and quiet rage. Jason is nothing if he isn't The Man, and vampires in town cramp his style. He's sharing all his women with vampires: lovers, Sookie, and even Gran, who dresses him down in front of Bill. And if he were a vampire, he would be able to break free of the cotton scarves Dawn uses to tie him to the bed. What he loses, he tries to replace with sustenance, always refueling or self-medicating, whether he's consuming beer, food, or women. Freud might say that Jason is stuck in the oral stage. And we have yet to see where he lives.

Tara continues on a similar bender, often seen nursing a drink or a swizzle stick. She too is all but homeless, hers a home she'd prefer not to return to, where she's likely to find her mother passed out. The difference with Tara is that she knows her choices are bad. When she confesses to Jason that all they want is to be seen, it's the first time we could believe that she and Jason share something in common. They're born soldiers looking for a fight to pick because they can't get in on the real battle. It brings to mind the Martin Luther King Jr. quote "The ultimate measure of a man is not where he stands in moments of comfort and convenience, but where he stands at times of challenge and controversy." You just can't call Jason and Tara fence-sitters, but they're the blankest slates in terms of how drastically their characters could change over time. It will be interesting to see if, and how, they adapt to increased tensions.

On an institutional level, we witness two spokespeople go toe-to-toe, the Reverend Theodore Newlin of the Fellowship of the Sun Church who accuses Nan Flanagan of the American Vampire League of criminal activity. It's a good tactic. When going up against a force of nature that can't easily be eradicated, stir up public opinion and make sure every eye is upon them, driving them into the daylight, so to speak.

Bill and Sookie seem to be the only two who are prepared to divorce from tradition. Everything comes with some measure of risk, at once threatening and intoxicating. When Sookie feeds on Bill to survive, it's like first intercourse for them. It's a matter of life and death, so we're asked to suspend our disbelief that there was no

Gran's porch, where Sookie first gave Bill permission to cross her threshold. (Jodi Ross, courtesy of The Vault www.trueblood-online.com)

choice, and that drinking his blood isn't akin to a supernatural Rohypnol. Upon realizing that the regenerative powers of Bill's blood also carry irreversible consequences — Sookie's libido will spike, and Bill will be able to locate her instantly through vampire GPS — she doesn't shy away. She accepts a fate that is not only life-changing, it means she will forever be tied to Bill, the ironic flip side of one who prior to this had had no success meeting anyone.

In this episode, territory also spans time. A good example is the scene in which Bill bristles at the name of Gran's group, the Descendents of the Glorious Dead. Nothing is glorious about cold and starving boys, he argues. This scene demonstrates why vampires are such a clever narrative device. Bill is talking in the present about something he experienced in the past, but he relives it as presently as he stands in the here and now with Sookie, this person who is but a blip on Bill's timeline, listening intently.

He's an historian because he's able to talk about past events, but it's not passed-down knowledge, it's first-hand experience about something that happened over 140 years ago. Just think how much else he's seen and done since then, and how much he can educate Sookie, who's still quite naive to the ways of the world. (I'd make a model of a modern Major-General joke here, but, alas, Bill was a lieutenant.)

Conversely, Sookie's personal history is only two and half decades old. But while she may have not fought in a war, she knows how to face her battles, a timeless strength of character they share. It's also an absurdly macabre moment. Watching Bill and Sookie stroll down the lane to her car, matted in their own blood and that of each other, they appear so quaint; it's as if they stepped out of a Norman Rockwell painting. Actually more like Norman Bates, if his medium was paintball.

As Sookie and Bill learn more about one another, it's their extreme age difference that draws them closer. Who better than Bill to know what it's like to lose family, as Sookie has lost her parents; he's undead and will outlive anyone mortal he ever knows. In a moment of honest passion, they kiss, then Bill prematurely fangulates, his true nature manifesting itself against his will.

It's clear that their romance will be front and center to the show. The bigger the tension, the bigger the release. We've seen Jason's approach to sex: pure, non-committal pleasure. If sex is the most earthly gateway to temporary transcendence, then when we finally do see Bill and Sookie together it will have to be epic, otherworldly. It will have to be the best sex for *all* time.

As this episode closes, Sookie is swarmed on Bill's porch by three hungry vampires. We're left to think about how we control our territories. Do we defend them to the death, join forces, or expand our borders to accommodate newcomers and a new way of life?

In Gran's house you can see Jason's graduation picture. Aww, don't you just want to tussle his tassle? (Jodi Ross, courtesy of The Vault www.trueblood-online.com)

Highlight: Gran: "Jason, you don't need any help lookin' like a fool."
Nightcap: In the scene where Bill recounts stories of the slaves his father owned, Tara's expression is a mixture of fear, betrayal, and disbelief, as if the one thing she had, her history, has been taken from her. Rutina Wesley shines again as Tara late in the episode when Jane Bodehouse asks her to "make mama another stinger." Tara lashes back, asking Jane if she's ashamed of herself, a clear strike intended against her own mother. It's a sad, powerful moment. Anna Paquin says she was kicked approximately 80 times during the shooting of the opening scene. The "blood" she

drank from Moyer's (prosthetic) arm was a sugar-free, no carb concoction. The tabloid on Lettie Mae's coffee table reads "Angelina Adopts Vampire Baby." Because vampires don't breathe, Stephen Moyer's breaths had to be digitally removed from his exterior night shots.

Relationship Crypt Falls: Sookie, Bill is *really* old. It will surface each time he doesn't like your taste in music, finds your clothing immodest, or another man wants to be your friend. But he has been through almost seven of your lifetimes thus far. Try to keep that in mind the next time you describe the Descendents of the Glorious Dead as "mostly a bunch of old people who had family in the war."

Paging Dr. Creepy: Remember the part where Bill bit into his wrist and that flap of skin pulled back, and not in a Six Million Dollar Man kind of way? *Shudder.*

Encore: We can hear "The First Taste," performed by Fiona Apple, in the background at Gran's house when Sookie and Bill leave for their walk. "The First Taste" comes from Fiona Apple's 1996 debut album *Tidal*, known best for its Grammy Award–winning single "Criminal." Its music video gained controversy for its raw sexuality and focus on female body image. Coming from a widely artistic and musical family, Apple's influences include everything from early jazz and pop to alt-rock. She's also known for her deeply candid lyrics and intriguing arrangements, pairing such instruments as the French horn and optigan (early electronic keyboard). The video for "The First Taste" was never aired in the U.S., appearing only in France.

1.03   Mine

Original air date: September 21, 2008
Written by: Alan Ball
Directed by: John Dahl

> **Malcolm:** Honey, if we can't kill people, what's the point of being a vampire?

Sookie sees another side of Bill. Sam and Tara reach out to one another in a time of loneliness. Jason turns to Lafayette in a moment of need.

There are two main reasons why we seek community: survival (the family that plays together, stays together) or companionship.

The nest of vampires Sookie meets at Bill's home (Malcolm, Diane, and Liam) live together, under their own rules, in order to feed as often as they please. Bill warns them that there will be consequences if they flaunt their habits in front of humans. It's an interesting departure from mortal life in which to remain solitary — the life Bill has chosen for himself — would normally result in the exact opposite of a human semblance; with no community or outside stimulation, we would feed on ourselves,

Exterior view of Bill Compton's home. Who mows the lawn? (Eleanor Tivnan)

becoming less in tune with customs and social mores. However, in a vampire's world, confinement is on par with the spiritual ritual of one who abstains from mortal sin.

When Bill tells Sookie he would never feed on her, it rings untrue. He's already connected to her through blood, and now he's claimed her as his own so other vampires won't feed on her. Malcolm argues that there's no point to being a vampire if they can't kill people. His measures are sadistic, but there's something to be said about Bill fighting his true nature. Is it feeding at all that's at issue for Bill, or that he believes others feed on too many? It feels like a comment on monogamy versus polyamorous partnerships, making Bill's assertion that he will not feed on Sookie akin to a boyfriend who doesn't want to rush her first time. In one of the sappier moments of the episode, Bill tries to prove to Sookie that they both run on magic. But he makes his point when he tells her she'll never be able to be herself with a mortal man. Bill and Sookie are both the outsiders in their respective families. But what Sookie has that Bill does not is Gran, who in this episode proves even further that real investment takes patience, an open ear, and a willingness to share. We learn that Sookie's grandfather may have been telepathic.

Tara and Sam are the complete opposite of Bill and Sookie, friends with benefits, each desperate in their loneliness. Their partnership feels a bit forced, but it's a more than passable diversion from the books (in which Sam and Tara don't hook up) if it means we get to see two fine actors in the same frame. In this episode, we see Sam reveal himself as hopeless and deeply wounded. And the scene in which Tara's mother hits her — first with a Bible, then with a liquor bottle — is heartbreaking. Tara makes the choice to leave, looking to Lafayette for comfort; he offers a place to stay, medication, and weed.

Jason, too, has come in search of comfort, although his negotiations are all business. Lafayette holds the power, and in one of the more subversive scenes we've seen yet, a Caucasian male is forced to dance to supplement his need for V-juice, sexualized for profit while two African Americans look on.

Sookie finds Dawn murdered, and as the episode ends, it's every man for himself, each character having invested in something only to have something else taken in return. Bill continues to show himself to Sookie, but it's at the cost of pushing her away. Sookie follows her logic, going against every urge in her body. Tara and Sam turn to one another, one turn further from where they'd rather be. And Jason resorts to vampires' blood in order to regain his mortal manhood, another diversion from the original books. Only Lafayette seems to be safe for now. Living in relative solitude like Bill, he's devised a way to keep people coming through his door. We can't help but wonder if he's figured out the secret. No ties, no troubles. To thine own self be true.

Highlight: Lafayette: "The vamps don't take kindly to the juice dispenser."

Nightcap: In the scene in which Sookie finds Dawn dead, there's a visible pulse on her neck. The movie Jason watches briefly while flipping through the television channels is *Dracula* (1958). When Sam says he'd like Blade or Buffy to come to Marthaville, he's referencing two vampire hunters — Blade, a Marvel Comics character personified by Wesley Snipes in three film adaptations, and Buffy the Vampire Slayer, created by Joss Whedon and popularized in the long-running cult cable series of the same name (most fans pretend the movie didn't exist).

Relationship Crypt Falls: Bill, with all this talk of making Sookie yours, I recommend you listen to Simon and Garfunkel's "The 59th Street Bridge Song" from 1966. It's okay to slow down; you're moving too fast. So get some sleep, and give Sookie some space. In time, you'll get groovy, as the song goes.

Paging Dr. Creepy: It's a tie between Jason's voice modulation during the scene in which he attacks Dawn, sounding like something out of *Scream*, and the Carmen Miranda outfit he's wearing, which it's hard to believe any self-respecting vampire would be caught . . . dead . . . in.

Location, Location, Location: Dawn's cottage is part of a group of houses found in the Eagle Rock neighborhood of Los Angeles, which also includes Rene and Arlene's home, and Hoyt's home with his mother. The "cottages" are located close to the Eagle Rock Plaza mall.

Suzuki Sets the Scene: Ingerslev took a lot of inspiration for Lafayette's pad from reading the books. After she felt she had a handle on his vibe, she turned to the wardrobe department to see what direction they were thinking, in particular, how eccentric they planned to take his style. She was thrilled with the result, having a blast constructing Lafayette's home out of leopard carpeting and foil wallpaper.

Encore: "Mine" performed by Bing Crosby and Judy Garland can be heard when Sookie sneaks up on Bill and they kiss. Recorded in 1944, Judy Garland's natural charm is on display in this duet with the inimitable Bing Crosby, with whom she also partnered on the tracks "You Got Me Where You Want Me," "Connecticut," and "Yah-Ta-Ta, Yah-Ta-Ta (Talk, Talk, Talk)." Garland and Crosby were two of the originating multimedia stars, popular on both the radio and in movies, and this is the perfect backdrop to the sexual do-si-do Bill and Sookie are undertaking.

1.04 Escape from Dragon House

Original air date: September 28, 2008
Written by: Brian Buckner
Directed by: Michael Lehmann

> **Tara:** People think because we got vampires out in the open, race isn't the issue no more . . . Race may not be the hot-button issue it once was, but it's still a button you can push on people.

Jason becomes the lead suspect in another murder, and Sookie uses her gift to try to find the real killer. Bill takes Sookie to Fangtasia, a vampire bar, where she meets Eric, the bar's acerbic owner.

We really have to give it to the writers for this episode. They manage to interweave the politics of segregation into a storyline that includes Jason brewing a blister the size of a nickel from chronic masturbation. Even Bill's explanation that Fangtasia was named as such because vampires like puns — what Charles Lamb described as "a pistol let off at the ear; not a feather to tickle the intellect" — effortlessly leads directly into the scene in which Sookie and Sam are at odds over their stance on vampire rights, hearkening back to the Louisiana law of 1890, "separate but equal." *True Blood* has been referred to as pulp opera, a perfect mingling of camp, sharp satire, and serious drama. It lives up to that label in "Escape from Dragon House."

What's the missing ingredient in Merlotte's kitchen? Oh, hells yeah. It's Lafayette, the hottest dish this side of Shreveport! (Jodi Ross, courtesy of The Vault www.truebloodonline.com)

This episode focuses on choice and logic versus values and traditions. People stick to what they know in times of change, Sookie remaining the exception. She holds to her ideals, with her belief in full rights for vampires running alongside her belief in common courtesies, such as Bill learning to say sorry for someone's loss. But she's also flexible and believes, as Gran does, that God's plan will be revealed in good time, and that until that time, we can't stop being who we are or evolving into who we could be. For Sookie, that means mining others' thoughts for possible clues as to the real killer's identity.

In this episode, the experience of Sookie's telepathy is given added texture via speed changes in filming. It's particularly prevalent in Merlotte's. A vampire's approach is often sped up, as if bypassing the obstacle of time. By contrast, slowing things down around Sookie shows us the intensity of her focus, which, for her, is scary, allowing in a flood of details unfiltered. What she hears challenges both her delicate sensibilities and her core values. It's also the second opportunity the writers have taken in this episode to echo the bigotry that we as viewers recognize from our own worlds, vampires aside. ("Dead fucks, niggers, and regular folk all living together. If God wanted it like this, he'd have made us look the same.") It would seem that everyone has their demons, vampires and mortals alike.

The shift board at Merlotte's. Notice how Sookie requests days only. (Jodi Ross, courtesy of The Vault www.trueblood-online.com)

Sookie is, however, willing to settle back into tradition when it serves the situation better. We know she doesn't like the idea of Bill owning her, but when they approach Fangtasia she lets him slip his hand around her waist. When Eric shows his interest in Sookie, she herself declares that she is Bill's. By mainstreaming, Bill begins to looks normal, especially in a place that looks more like the Hard Rock Cafe than a vampire bar. When Sookie helps Eric, Pam, and Bill escape from the police raid, it's less about keeping them safe than believing it's the right thing to do. While most of Bon Temps has already declared vampires guilty, Sookie continues to believe the undead are innocent *until* proven guilty.

Tara's beliefs are similar, not to mention hilarious as demonstrated in the scene in which she storms the sheriff's station with the threat of discrimination if they can't believe a white man (Jason) and a black woman (Tara) could be together, thereby offering Jason an alibi that frees him from police custody. It's also a great scene because the writers never forget the real-life struggles, in this case, of race relations. Every chance Tara's given to sound off, we get commentary on some of the show's most poignant themes. Tara may not be evolving at the same rate as Sookie, but she's smart . . . if not always wise. Now that we know Jason kept her safe from the biggest monster in her life — her mother — it's easier to accept her dedication to him. Bud and Andy's reactions to her rant are priceless. Bud's known everyone since birth, making him more like the town godfather than a sheriff. He is detail-oriented, establishing motive from fact, but he also shows a prejudice against vampires. Andy, on the other hand, is reactive, but by acting like a cop in a movie, his imagination might make him better suited to a town whose dead don't always die.

Poor Jason. He continues to leap before he looks, and his get-out-of-jail-free cards are running low. It's as if vampires have glamoured his charms. He operates by no code or common sense. By not coming clean about OD'ing on V, his predicament gets, quite literally, larger as time passes. When the doctor drains his penis, the birth metaphor is Jason's worst nightmare come true. With Tara by his side, he's completely emasculated. That said, a lot of his character's humor is derived from his anguish. It's hard to believe anyone could get themselves into such trouble, but we all know someone like Jason: well meaning, but *really* misguided.

As the episode draws to a close, Bill has shown us that while his choices make him different from many vampires, those choices go against his true nature. When his buttons are pushed, his impulses remain the same. We also see Sam rolling through Dawn's sheets, huffing her scent like an animal. He remains at a distance, his personal loss fading out into the credits. We still don't know if his stance against vampire rights is to protect himself or those he loves. In Bon Temps, that can only mean it's a matter of time before everyone's true selves start to surface.

Highlight: Jason: "Were you listenin' to me? I got gout of the dick!"
Nightcap: The coroner's assistant, Neil Jones, is played by Kevin McHale, who plays Artie Abrams on *Glee*. Behind the bar at Fangtasia, you can see a painting of George Bush taking a bite out of the Statue of Liberty, which marks the second time a Bush has appeared on the show, the first being the mask Jason wore in "Mine" that bore the likeness of Laura Bush. And when Pam and Eric talk to one another in Swedish, Eric is saying, "Our little zoo is starting to grow." Pam responds, "I know." Young Jason has blue eyes, while older Jason has brown eyes. The writers imagine that the effects of V would probably be like a cocktail of Ecstasy, Viagra, and crystal meth.
Relationship Crypt Falls: Between telling Sookie she looked like vampire bait and making the officer pee himself, Bill's social graces need some work since he seems to think wooing an attractive young woman is all wrapped up in the insider information that old vampires dig a good pun.
Location, Location, Location: The Bon Temps Police Station is an actual jail, located in Hawthorne, California, mere blocks from the location used to film Big Patty's House of Pies, seen in episode 1.11. Fangtasia is filmed at Alex's Bar in Long Beach, California. Visit the bar's site at alexsbar.com to see inside.

Encore: "Escape from Dragon House," performed by Dengue Fever, plays as Bill and Sookie drive home from Fangtasia. Dengue Fever is an eclectic six-piece Los Angeles group that fuses Cambodian pop music and lyrics with psychedelic rock. On their album named after the track, they delve into horn-driven Ethiopian '60s and '70s pop, ideal for Bill's worldly view and in stark opposition to Sookie's girl-next-door naivete. Dengue Fever is the subject of the documentary film *Sleepwalking Through the Mekong*, which follows the band to Phnom Penh, Cambodia, in 2005, a trip home for the band's front singer Chhom Nimol. Their songs have also featured in Jim Jarmusch's film *Broken Flowers* (2005), the Showtime series *Weeds*, and *City of Ghosts*.

1.05   Sparks Fly Out

Original air date: October 5, 2008
Written by: Alexander Woo
Directed by: Daniel Minahan

> **Sam:** Sookie, you have no future with a vampire!
> **Sookie:** They don't die. I've got nothing *but* a future with one.

Bill speaks to the Descendents of the Glorious Dead. Meanwhile, Sam tries to get closer to Sookie, who makes a horrifying discovery.

With such a departure from "Escape from Dragon House," it's a wonder these episodes follow one after the other. And yet it works. The pace is much slower in "Sparks Fly Out," and the tone is more contemplative. At first, the episode appears to be about moderation: Bill tells Sookie he would have fed on, but not killed, the police officer he glamoured; Jason goes back to the V, but in smaller doses; Sookie agrees to a date with Sam, but in a public place; and Tara, acting for once in her best interest, tells Jason she wants to wait until he's sober before they act on his advances.

Ultimately, though, this show is about sad departures. The look of "Sparks Fly Out" is quite different from the others — plenty of tight frames, characters off on their own, the eerie candlelight of Lorena's cottage — allowing it to stand alone as the episode that will be remembered for the moment we saw the mortality of both Bill and Gran come to violent ends, their sparks flying out. If we had to see Gran die — and let's take a moment to exclaim how brilliant Lois Smith was in this role — better that it should be in the episode in which we also see Bill's past, something that would have been of great value to Gran. These two felt united, an immediate warmth apparent from the first time Bill visited, with Gran's support of him never waning. Early in the episode both Bill and Gran tell Sookie that she can't be afraid of what she

The Times of Bill Compton: Surviving the Deadliest War in American History

The American Civil War resulted in the deaths of 620,000 soldiers and an untold number of civilians. Following the war, three amendments were added to the Constitution – the 13th abolished slavery, the 14th created the extension of legal protection regardless of race, and the 15th abolished all racial restrictions on voting.

Fought from 1861 to 1865, the American Civil War was the result of ongoing tensions between the Northern and Southern states on issues of slavery and states' rights. The main areas of difference included the expansion of slavery (and the retention of it in states in which it already existed), the South's plummeting political power, and individual states' rights.

Following the 1860 election of Abraham Lincoln, who was against the expansion of slavery, 11 Southern states seceded and formed the Confederate States of America, also known as the Confederacy, led by Jefferson Davies. They fought against the United States, also known as the Union, which was supported by the free states in which slavery was either prohibited or had been eliminated, and the five border slave states.

Southern troops won many victories until Gettysburg and Vicksburg in 1863, when the North hit their stride, conquering the South into surrender in April 1865. On April 14, five days after the South's surrender, President Lincoln was assassinated while at a play at Ford's Theatre in Washington. John Wilkes Booth, the assassin, was killed by Union troops shortly thereafter while fleeing. Vice President Andrew Johnson rose to the seat of president.

The period that followed was called the Reconstruction, during which Union troops occupied Southern states while they reintegrated into the Union.

The following essay by Lisafemmeacadienne, a Louisianan teacher, author, linguistics specialist, and dedicated Billsbabe, originally appeared as a guest post at The Vault (www.trueblood-online.com) and evokes memories of Bill's journey home, cut short when he stopped at Lorena's for food and rest, and what his family would have suffered through in his absence.

The Reconstruction Period in Louisiana by Lisafemmeacadienne

Lavish ball gowns adorning doe-eyed maidens, fanning themselves on a sweltering Louisiana night, waiting for a dance with a suitor as minstrels play a lively waltz. Couples strolling arm in arm along a meandering bayou as the wind gently blows the Spanish moss draped from the ancient oaks.

The Antebellum period: a romanticized view of Louisiana before the Civil War. Everything changed when Louisiana seceded from the Union in 1861, and brought the War of Northern Aggression to Louisiana's rivers and bayous.

After the Civil War came Reconstruction. It was a time of division, poverty, disease, starvation, and death. The phrase "brother against brother" held true during this time, as families divided over allegiances to the Union (the U.S. government) or "The Cause" (states' rights).

After the men were released from the Louisiana Regiments, they made their way home. Some did not make it due to lack of transportation, disease, or injury. Oftentimes, these men were desperate for food, comfort, and shelter, and simply took what they needed to survive. Widows would try to coax the men to stay as they passed through; the amount of young, able-bodied men in Louisiana had significantly decreased, and a woman without the protection of a man was extremely vulnerable to the whims of passersby.

Reconstruction was a very violent time, more so than during the war itself. Families became divided over loyalties to the Union or to the Confederacy, and it was common to see public hatred and prejudice from both sides that would erupt suddenly, often with deadly results. Riots would occur with very little warning; for example, many bystanders were killed at the Cabildo Riots in New Orleans. The military and local police did what they could, but it was a very volatile, chaotic time in Louisiana's history.

As part of Louisiana's lot for successfully repelling the Union army during the war, food stores and crops were confiscated after the war for troop use, making food scarce and diets monotonous. Hot sauce was created in Louisiana due to the bland diets the survivors faced from lack of crops and livestock that were decimated in the war. The South was the breadbasket of the United States at that time, and with that depletion, the entire country was suffering from shortages, so no post-war aid was available. After slavery was abolished, there were simply not enough workers to maintain the giant plantations, and no money to pay those workers.

The lack of proper diet also brought a resurgence of disease in the area from the suppressed immune systems of Louisianans, almost doubling the current mortality rate. Epidemics, such as the dreaded Yellow Fever, became more prevalent in the state, closing down entire towns and stranding barges of supplies on the Mississippi River, the main transportation route in Louisiana. Shreveport was all but abandoned from August to December 1873, as people fled to adjoining areas to escape the scourge. Trains that finally arrived, loaded with relief supplies, were unable to come into Shreveport due to the quarantine, and many people died from lack of medicine.

Reconstruction was a dark time in Louisiana's history, but even facing wartime conditions, the people persevered, making the state a unique center of culture and commerce for the United States. Mardi Gras made a comeback during this period, as well as theater, music, and dance halls, giving a distraction from the bleak conditions.

The Treme area of New Orleans gave birth to some of the most iconic music, such as the stereotypical marching brass band playing "When the Saints Go Marchin' In."

These distractions evolved into modern-day jazz, American theater, and the Mardi Gras — celebrations that we continue to enjoy today.

doesn't understand. They are kindred folk. It's hard to imagine what Sookie, and we, will do without Gran's check-ins and comic quips, or how Bill, for that matter, will fare now that his most sincere fan is gone.

Of all people, it's a high Jason who arrives at the sage conclusion that it's "bullshit that keeps people apart." If Sam's unchecked rage makes him a guard dog, in Jason we see a penned-up puppy; he doesn't mean to get into trouble, it's just that no one's taken the time to train him. Lafayette appears to be willing, but a pusher isn't the role model Jason needs. While finding joy in earthly delights has been a good distraction, Jason is looking for deeper meaning, which is ironic in one as shallow as him. It is, however, through the transcendence of V that Jason receives meaning from Bill's speech to the DGD, that in war soldiers sought a destiny "handed down from above."

Could this be a foreshadowing of Jason's path to come? In this episode, Jason reminds us of young men with directionless futures who are recruited into the military in the hope that they'll provide for their families, find a greater purpose, or simply learn a skill that will make them valuable upon re-entry into civilian society. As Jason leans forward seeing the world anew, just behind him is Terry Bellefleur, back from the Iraq War, damaged and clearly haunted by what he's seen and done.

Bill's speech and the resulting flashbacks of how he was turned provide the episode's pulse. During his talk, he breaks a number of preconceived notions of what it means to be a vampire, placing himself in the history of Bon Temps to emerge as both orator and comrade, sharing stories of their ancestors, and as such offering the townspeople the gift of closure. With each anecdote, more of Bill's human condition reveals itself, if not in a rosy glow then in his ability to connect with humans, his goal in mainstreaming. When he's presented with the family photo, so convincing is his loss that it's hard to tell where the man ends and the vampire begins. He's as afflicted as any mortal who has lost a great love and been forced to move on.

The flashback scene in which Bill visits his home one last time is extremely powerful. The magnetic pull Lorena has on him is palpable, and we're reminded of Lafayette instructing Jason to take the vampire juice deep inside him. Lorena too is a pusher, hooking Bill in so that he can never be without her. When Lorena growls, "You are mine" as Bill feeds, we are reminded that, to Bill's mind, he wasn't claiming Sookie as his directly, he was only declaring it to others to protect her. In stark contrast to Sam, whose method of protection has only been to try to restrict Sookie's thoughts or movements, Bill has always respected Sookie's wishes.

As Bud and Andy interview Bill about the deaths of Maudette and Dawn, we can see his frustrations bubbling up. We know he has feelings about authorities. With Sookie possibly dating Sam and his family long behind him, Bill plays up his dark side, trying on for size what it feels like to be what everyone expects of him. Yet, after they leave, even the strength of a vampire cannot destroy the toaster iron he kept from Lorena's cottage, as if to suggest that his eternal fate is as unyielding and permanent as the tie to his maker.

Stephen Moyer delivers a remarkable performance in the most subtly terrifying episode this season. And we get to see more of Jim Parrack as Hoyt Fortenberry who, in his late 20s, idolizes Bill like a young boy would Evil Knievel or a monster truck driver. He thinks Bill is cool and shows signs of being the first mortal other than Gran to sympathize with vampires.

Highlight: Terry [to Bill]: "They don't understand, man. None of 'em will ever understand. You stay sharp, brother."

The fireplace in Bill Compton's home, where he spends many a pensive night reading and reflecting. (Jodi Ross, courtesy of The Vault www.trueblood-online.com)

Nightcap: In the scene where Nelsan Ellis prepares to fight the "AIDS burger" customer, he pulls off Lafayette's clip-on earrings, a detail he says he carried over from his own childhood when his sisters would take off their earrings when they prepared for trouble.

Relationship Crypt Falls: Sam's so uncomfortable in his own skin he doesn't know how to perform in situations that call for the greatest sincerity, not explosive reactions showing worse impulse control than an excitable vampire. Sookie, for her own part, accepted an invitation from a man she doesn't feel any passion for. In thinking with her head and not her heart, she may have crowded her own thoughts with so many excuses that she couldn't see from the start that if things didn't go well, Sam would lash out. And Jason, who finally sees Tara as a worthy companion, only does so through the filtered lens of V, the beer goggles of Bon Temps. Not a great night for lovers in *True Blood*.

Paging Dr. Creepy: You know when you're shredding a carrot and it gets near the end and you chip a bit of your nail on the grater? That's how I feel every time a vampire rips his wrist open, or, in this case, slits her own neck so that a dying mortal can feed. It's never like the movies in which the person simply clamps his or her mouth over the open wound, barely slipping a drop. In *True Blood*, it's like a molten lava chocolate fountain, their tongues darting around like a kid trying to catch snowflakes on the first day of winter.

Location, Location, Location: Crawdad's Restaurant (where Sookie and Sam have their date) is actually a Mexican restaurant called Poncho's Place, located in the small town of Piru, California, just blocks from the location used for the Descendants of the Glorious Dead meeting. That was filmed in a real church, the United Methodist Church, built in 1888 by Piru's founder David C. Cook. The church contains a pipe organ built during the Civil War in 1862.

Encore: When Jason talks to Tara at Merlotte's, we hear "Sparks Fly Out," performed by Paul Burch. Burch started his career in Nashville in the early '90s singing in honky-tonk bars, and catching the eye of such notables as Marianne Faithfull and Chet Atkins. In 2003, he released his fourth album *Fool For Love*, which featured guest appearances by Mark Knopfler, Tim O'Brien, and Ralph Stanley. His songs have appeared in several film and television shows, such as *The Appalachians*, *The Rookie*, and *A History of Violence*. "Sparks Fly Out" is a playful tune, an ideal backdrop to Jason's attempt to woo jaded Tara. He strokes her, claiming he can feel sparks along the length of her arm. Anyone else and it would be creepy, but it's intense because as surely as we believe Jason thinks he's experiencing an effervescent sensation, we, the viewers, know how Tara feels about him, and that on just about any other day of the week she would have jumped at the chance to be his Pop Rocks.

1.06   Cold Ground

Original air date: October 12, 2008
Written by: Raelle Tucker
Directed by: Nick Gomez

Sookie [to Bill]: Do it; I want you to.

In the aftermath of Gran's death, Sookie seeks refuge from the voices in her head. Jason struggles with withdrawal from V-juice. Tara and Sam turn to one another again in search for something real. And Tara's mother asks for her help.

With Gran gone, Sookie takes the final step, walking through darkness into new life as Bill's partner. After listening to Sam tell her what she should do these past few episodes, it comes as great relief to us when Sookie finally acts of her own accord. Guided by heart and conscience, she goes into the unknown. As she prepares herself for Bill, she's calm, controlled, and completely alone, no voices to influence or dissuade her — so certain, in fact, that it's not until she bursts from her house that Bill senses her emotion. When she tells him she wants him to bite (read: penetrate) her, she gives as much of herself to him and she's ready to take back in personal pleasure.

Gran's pantry. (Jodi Ross, courtesy of The Vault www.trueblood-online.com)

The Stackhouse family photo collage, given to Gran as a birthday present from Jason and Sookie. (Jodi Ross, courtesy of The Vault www.trueblood-online.com)

The aftermath of Gran's brutal death was a last straw for Sookie. Tradition would have bound her to a selfish brother, an abusive uncle, a community that would rather see her dead, and a man who can't give her an inch to breathe in. Sookie creates a chosen family for herself, a troupe of loners and outsiders who take only what they need, and offer only what they can in return.

Anna Paquin is a revelation in the scene in which Sookie eats Gran's pie. It's similar to the final moments of *Six Feet Under* in which we're asked to witness how each character will die. In kind, we watch Sookie systematically feed herself in an act of ritual closure. It's a nod back to the day Gran found Sookie mowing the lawn, unsure of how she wanted to proceed with Bill. Gran insisted Sookie eat, but not because she was hungry, the implication being that life will move on with or without you, no matter what you do. So as simple as it is, you'd best have food in your belly. We're also reminded of what Lafayette said, that people can taste the love you put into your food. Sookie continues to eat, having her last, silent, heart-to-heart with Gran at the kitchen table. She shares with no one, no pieces parceled off like on her date with Sam after the DGD meeting. We'll also grieve the loss of Sookie's connection to her past, with so many of Gran's stories delivered in that kitchen. By digesting "Gran's pie," Sookie fuels herself for the next battle, and takes back her home as the new matriarch.

While Tara's blood ties are strong enough to draw her back to her mother, it's because she'd be adrift otherwise. She returns to her family home the way an abused lover returns to her mate in the hope that the honeymoon will last, or that if she pours herself into their healing it will pay itself forward. Adina Porter infuses so much terror, shame, and hypocrisy into her performance of Lettie Mae that we pity her, going back and forth between understanding Tara's choice to be estranged from her and judging Tara for leaving a sick mother to her own devices. When Tara decides to return home, embracing her mother on the couch, it's almost as if for Tara to survive this stretch, she'll have to keep her mother close . . . like an enemy.

Meanwhile, Jason delves deeper into self-abuse and isolation, stuck inside his own desperate ramblings as if he's been buried alive with his own thoughts. It's as if he's finally shuttered himself into casual sex, unable to connect to anyone or anything without V. His transformation into an addict is complete. He's stuck in mortal purgatory.

While Sookie and Bill's first sex scene is kept at a modest distance, we are offered a little release when Tara, bless her, kicks the entire town out of Sookie's house. Lafayette is the most sober we've seen him, his campy performance toned down, but he still delivers his signature witticisms as well as serving up some of this episode's most spot-on observations.

Fan Sarah Napier catches up with Todd Lowe (Terry Bellefleur) on a day off from Merlotte's. Mmm, I bet he smells like fried catfish. Tasty! (Sarah Napier)

As the episode draws to a close, it feels at last that one thing is certain: Bill and Sookie's affection for one another. Apart, however, their worlds remain as different as night and day. Bill cannot protect her during the daylight, and there's a serial killer on the loose who knows the victims well enough that he can kill them in their homes without having to break and enter. And while Sookie is now formally Bill's, Sam will no doubt continue to mark his territory whenever the opportunity allows.

Highlight: Lafayette [about Maxine Fortenberry]: "I mean, if she talked any more shit she'd be shaped like a toilet."

Nightcap: Alan Ball refers to this episode as "the hate sandwich," because the director and director of photography didn't get along, and neither was considered a good fit for the show. After reshoots and editing, he feels they produced a strong show. On the lighter side, Tara and Sam drink Steam Whistle in Tara's motel room. Steam Whistle is not available outside of Ontario, Alberta, and British Columbia, Canada. (This author lives in the city in which it's brewed! It's delicious. Get some!) And it's interesting to wonder why Bud and Andy haven't considered that if Bill really wanted to mess with their investigation he could just glamour them into thinking he was never a suspect.

Tribute: Todd Lowe (Terry Bellefleur)

"Nobody ever listens to me, but they should."

– Terry Bellefleur

Terry Bellefleur is deceptively simple. His intense personality and uncensored speech make it easy for people to dismiss him. But what makes him one of the most loveable characters on *True Blood* is that by the time we meet Terry for the first time, he's already embedded into the lives of the other Bon Temps citizens. We don't write him off because the other characters we love seem to care deeply about his good will and intentions.

This is in no small part attributed to the respect Todd Lowe brings to his portrayal of Terry, forged in a desire to pay tribute to war vets who suffer from post traumatic stress disorder (PTSD). "[W]hen I was in high school a few of us would go to this glorious VFW hall and play bingo," he says. "[M]y friends and I got cornered by this intense Vietnam tunnel rat; you know, the guys that go into tunnels searching out bombs? He literally had four big ol' high school boys pinned to the trunk of my car without ever touching us, he was that intense. . . . So, I always think of that guy. I feel like I have to do it right because of the responsibility to the veterans . . ."

I'll confess, though, watching Lowe makes me pine at times for *Gilmore Girls*. When he first appeared on-screen I screamed, "Zach!" followed immediately with ". . . is hairy!"

Where you've seen Todd Lowe: *Gilmore Girls*, *The Princess Diaries*, *Without a Trace*, *Navy NCIS*, playing with Pilbilly Knights, his L.A.-based country-rock band (www.myspace.com/pilbillyknightsmusic)

Location, Location, Location: Bill Compton's house was actually a Confederate head-quarters during the Civil War that was turned into a makeshift hospital.

Encore: "Cold Ground," performed by Rusty Truck, plays during the end credits. Truck's connections served him well, employing help from such friends as Jakob Dylan, Lenny Kravitz, Sheryl Crow, Gillian Welch, David Rawlings, and Willie Nelson. His first album, *Broken Promises*, is a confluence of country, rock 'n' roll, blues, and easy-listening. Cat Power's "Half of You" plays in the scene before, an apt and moody ballad about wanting to have all of a person, appropriate for Bill and Sookie's first love scene. But as Sookie is making love for the first time, Jason is having sex for the umpteenth time, and Tara and Sam head deeper into their friendship-with-benefits arrangement. Not everyone's bed is warm above this cold ground.

1.07 Burning House of Love

Original air date: October 19, 2008
Written by: Chris Offutt
Directed by: Marcos Siega

Lafayette: It ain't possible to live unless you crossin' somebody's line.

Bill settles a score from Sookie's painful past. Jason meets an exotic new woman. Tara takes her mother to exorcize her demon.

Considering this is the episode we've been waiting for ever since the opening credits first rolled — Bill and Sookie finally do bad things! — it isn't the strongest one of the season. To start, we don't get to bask in the afterglow of Sookie's first time having sex with a man, not to mention being fed on, before it's tainted by Sookie's

The Bon Temps swamp, where vampires go to heal telepathic waitresses and bar owners streak in the early dawn. (Jen Bark)

Powell's Gas Station where Jason and Amy make small talk before going back to his place to get existential. (Jen Bark)

confession that her Uncle Bartlett had sordid thoughts about her as a child. As a story-line, it feels inserted and rushed, all but unnecessary for the amount of time the uncle remains in the show. It's already been established that Sookie hasn't been romantic with a man because she would be able to hear his thoughts. Not until Gran's funeral had there been anything to suggest Sookie was affected for any other reason.

Bill is also robbed of the chance to vocalize what it meant for him to be with Sookie. They've each worked so hard to come to this place, it would have been nice to spend more time watching them connect as friends as well as lovers. We believe now that Bill truly cares for Sookie. While they can't sleep in the same bed, he makes himself vulnerable by showing her where he rests during the day.

The character of Uncle Bartlett does serve the purpose of showing that Bill would do anything for Sookie. Unlike his defensive response against anyone who threatens him or Sookie, killing Sookie's uncle is a premeditated act. And while we can find his thoughts unsettling, the law judges people based on action, not thought. Sookie wouldn't endorse her uncle's murder any more than Bill's war comrade, seen in Bill's DGD flashback, condoned Bill wanting to put a wounded boy out of his misery. All

As you can see from this picture of the beautiful Adina Porter, she undergoes quite a transformation to become Lettie Mae. (KH1/Keystone Photos)

told, the writers might have handled this story more delicately. As it is, it takes away from the immensity of Sookie's ultimate choice to offer herself to Bill.

This episode does deliver one of the finest performances of the season by Adina Porter. In lesser hands, Lettie Mae's addiction and exorcism would be comical. We have every reason to believe that her demon is an alcohol-induced hallucination, or, at the very least, an elaborate hoax to get Tara back in her life. But we want so badly for Tara to get her mother back that we, too, begin to believe, if not in the demon itself, then in the hope that there's a cure for what ails her. Rutina Wesley's usual anger is absent from these scenes, replaced with a new complexity and lack of control. It's rare to see Tara without words, or the answer. Tara *always* has the answer.

Jason's addiction storyline is weaker than Lettie Mae's. And while the writers had the good sense to let the worst of Lettie Mae's struggle peak in one episode, we'll have to watch Jason suffer a while longer, a shame when Ryan Kwanten has shown he's capable of a much wider range. His journey is more bearable with the addition of Lizzy Caplan in a guest role as Amy Burley, a nomad who subscribes to Nietzsche's concept of nihilism where nothing is real and everything is permitted. When contrasted against Miss Jeanette's chanting and crone stones (her teachings having been around centuries longer), Amy's modern pharmacology of cutting V-juice with aspirin seems more manufactured than organic. What they share in common is that they're both dealers, doling out measured promises of transcendence. For Lettie Mae, the path to joy is to rid herself first of the demon. Jason hasn't gone deep enough to acknowledge his demons, so his medicating is more like a Band-Aid than a cure.

While it's harder to put a face to joy than misery, it is a bit disappointing to see *True Blood*'s vision of transcendence is nothing more than a Lucky Charms com-

mercial, and Jason's "communion" with Amy marks the first time that nudity has
started to feel gratuitous, which may not have been the case if the opening scene
with Bill and Sookie had been allowed to play out longer, making Jason and Amy's
a natural bookend.

The episode ends with the possibility that Bill has been burned along with a nest
of vampires. When he leaves Merlotte's with Malcolm, Diane, and Liam, Sookie misses
Bill's attempts to communicate with her. Confused and betrayed, Sookie has no one
to turn to when it appears that her lover could be dead.

With the exception of Lettie Mae's storyline and the opportunity it gave Rutina
Wesley to play down Tara's anger, giving us a glimpse at her younger, scared self,

"Burning House of Love" is a bit heavy-handed. It talks at us a lot without leaving enough to the imagination.

Highlight: Arlene: "Suppose she gets pregnant. How in the world can she nurse a baby with fangs?"

Nightcap: The stones that are used in Miss Jeanette's exorcism belong to the show's writer Chris Offutt, who started collecting stones with holes in them as a child. The shot of the possum hissing was the only one caught on film. Possums play dead when they're actually scared. And did you catch Andy's ring tone? That's the theme from *Hawaii Five-0*!

Location, Location, Location: The gas station where Jason and Amy stop before going back to his place to do V is Powell's Grocery in Doyline, Louisiana, just east of Shreveport, Louisiana. The lake on which Andy and Terry are fishing when they see Sam streak through the woods is located in Doyline, Louisiana. It's Lake Bistineau in the Lake Bistineau State Park. Interestingly, Sam Trammell's father's family is from Doyline. "I have 13 relatives buried in the cemetery . . . I moved to West Virginia, New York, went to school in Rhode Island, California, and here I am shooting a scene for an HBO series on this land I used to go to as a kid. It was so circular."

Encore: When Sam tries to kick Malcolm, Diane, and Liam out of Merlotte's, we hear "Burning House of Love," performed by The Knitters. The Knitters formed in 1982, made up of a true patchwork of musicians from other bands: X, The Blasters, and The Red Devils. Their first album consisted mainly of traditional and cover songs, leaning heavily on folk and rockabilly influences. Over 20 years later, in 2005, the group reformed to release *The Modern Sounds of The Knitters*, including the track "Burning House of Love." John Doe is probably the most recognizable member of the band, having also acted in such films and television series as *Roswell*, *Road House*, *Boogie Nights*, *The Good Girl*, *Gypsy 83*, and *Pure Country*. (Of additional interest, in *The Bodyguard*, it's Doe's version of Whitney Houston's massive hit "I Will Always Love You" that plays on the jukebox in the scene in which Kevin Costner and Whitney Houston dance. It's extremely rare to find now.) "Burning House of Love" is barely audible in the scene, lost under bar noise and the thoughts of its patrons. Regardless, it's right there under our noses, telling us that a house will be burned down in revenge. It's a sneaky move as well as a nod to how hopeless Bill and Sookie are when she can't hear his thoughts; his multiple attempts to send her a message that he's not leaving with Malcolm and his crew of his own volition but is trying to protect Sookie, are completely lost on her.

1.08   The Fourth Man in the Fire

Original air date: October 26, 2008

Written by: Alexander Woo
Directed by: Michael Lehmann

Sookie: I had this crazy dream this morning. We were sitting, eating breakfast, and
all of a sudden the sunlight set you on fire.
Bill: It wouldn't happen quite that way. The sunlight would severely weaken me and
eventually, of course, I would die. But I wouldn't burst into flames. Not right away,
at least.

*Jason's girlfriend shows her dark side. Lafayette visits the vampire who supplies his V-
juice. And Sookie uses her powers to help Eric catch a thief.*

If anyone ever tries to say that *True Blood* is just a show "about vampires," direct
them to this episode, which beautifully explores the complexities of interpersonal
relationships, vampire or otherwise. In the last episode, Miss Jeanette told Lettie Mae
that her demon was gone and that she belonged to herself. This episode carries that
over to ask, what if you want to belong to another? Do you relinquish your needs to
satisfy theirs? And if the ends appear futile or the means unjustifiable, do you still take
the journey?

Sookie and Bill are supernatural outsiders who can be themselves with one
another. But as they get closer, she realizes they'll never wake up beside one another,
never eat together, and she'll live in fear that if he's ever caught in sunshine, he'll
perish. These aren't just simple pleasures, they're the rituals of most intimate relationships, which is why she dreamed about Bill bursting into flames while she ate
breakfast. What hope of success do they have if they can't share the simplest of things,
the way Sookie once shared a piece of pie with Sam? When Rene and Arlene get
engaged it just points to the larger struggles Sookie and Bill will continue to face,
unable to legally marry even if they're perfectly matched, exceptions noted.

When Sookie and Bill help Eric uncover the identity of the person who's been
stealing from Fangtasia, Bill and Sookie's relationship evolves into a business partnership, Sookie tied to Bill, hence tied to Eric. While Sam may not be the answer, we still
find ourselves asking if there isn't another nice boy out there who can accept Sookie
for who she is. We make sacrifices for the ones we love, so it makes sense that Sookie
would choose to help Bill and his "family." But is it possible that Sookie is using Bill as
a surrogate for Gran? Remember, Sookie told Tara that she went to Bill when no one
was there for her after Gran's death. Save for a quick flash of her grandmother's blood
on the floor, we haven't seen Sookie fully digest the murder. She could be searching for
the same distraction as Sam and Tara, something to take her mind off life for awhile.
If so, is the high she gets from sex and him feeding on her that much different from

Jason using V-juice to reach a place of peace and clarity? Or Lettie Mae using religion to reach a place of God? Or, for that matter, Eddie using Lafayette to reach a place of self-acceptance?

Sookie flaunts her relationship with Bill, putting her work aside to gossip in detail about what it's like to be with him, also forgetting she'd offered to babysit for Arlene. She's in love, and happy, and so should be able to talk about their relationship. But as Bill warned Malcolm, if they flaunt their ways, there will be consequences. Some humans are out to kill vamps, and at least one more is out to kill fangbangers, which makes them both targets. For all Sookie has sacrificed, Bill can't be there for her all the time, even if he wants to. Her choice to be with him brings her comfort but it takes away her safety.

Jason and Amy want to connect to something primal. Amy shows Jason his world anew, things he's taken for granted. But she's soon revealed to be a spin doctor, placing herself higher on the food chain than anything else. Though she told Jason he was wise, she ultimately uses him only for his brawn, convincing him to help kidnap Lafayette's blood buddy, Eddie, a vampire who exchanges his V-juice for sex and companionship.

Eddie offers us a chance to see another side of Lafayette that's less playful. We know he's complicated, but now we can see he's also manipulative. In the last episode, he told Sookie that people need to cross lines in order to live, but that for him that line ends with blood. As she walked away, he called her a skank. When Jason tried to take some V, he kicked him out, calling him a bitch as he watched him walk away. He's not attracted to Eddie but it's a means to an end. If we look back, it becomes clearer that Lafayette makes his way seeking people on the down-low, servicing closeted, self-loathing senators, vampires, and addicts. He's the thing they want. He's attractive, out, and, by all appearances, trustworthy if only because he keeps all their secrets. He may have a conscience. He asks Eddie why he doesn't try the bars, risking his source, but he's ultimately a dealer who takes advantage of people who aren't strong enough to belong to themselves. He may be a self-made man, but sooner than later, we all have someone to answer to.

Sam and Tara are loners who have given up on fitting in. Their way out is sex, but Tara is unable to connect, and is always the first to leave. When her mother makes her breakfast, Tara's face dissolves into such an expression of gratitude, it's as if she's a child again — trusting, safe, and enjoying the simple pleasures. So it's a nice twist that after being raised by a reluctant alcoholic Tara would take the first "step" toward recognizing she is powerless and that her life has become unmanageable, voluntarily seeking out Miss Jeanette.

Heading into future episodes, the groundwork laid here is sure to draw repercussions. The characters are more estranged from one another than ever, but it gives

Tribute: Carrie Preston (Arlene Fowler)

> "She's street smart. You know what I mean? She's a single mother and she's a survivor. She speaks her mind . . . I grew up with women like that, so I just wanted to honor those women."
> – Carrie Preston on playing Arlene Fowler

Arlene Fowler is the co-worker you take for granted because she does the job so well that you neglect to acknowledge how hard the work is. And it's easy to look at some of her life choices and wonder how much of the bad stuff is of her own design, so you miss the chance to help make her life a bit easier, leaving her to do everything for everyone.

This is due, in large part, to chameleon actor Carrie Preston, utterly unrecognizable once she's in costume and character. Preston delivers Arlene's lines with the rapid-fire afterthought of a mother and ex-wife who isn't accustomed to being heard when she speaks. She uses her outdoor voice, always to the point, sometimes shockingly. She's the workhorse with little trust in sentimentality, who holds her cards close to her chest, making her just as complicated and layered as any of the non-human, or "enhanced" humans, in Bon Temps.

Where you've seen Carrie Preston: *My Best Friend's Wedding, Sex and the City, The Stepford Wives, Transamerica, Arrested Development, Law & Order, Lost, Desperate Housewives, Doubt, Duplicity, Private Practice,* and on the arm of her husband Michael Emerson, best known as Ben Linus on *Lost*

us the chance to see a broader range from all of the actors, and more screen time for Lizzy Caplan as Amy Burley (even though that storyline is the weakest) and the fearless Stephen Root as Eddie.

Highlight: Sam [about an alligator head Terry offers to him]: "We'll put it over the bar. Drunks like talkin' to the animals."

Nightcap: For the scene in which Bill Compton's hand comes out of the dirt to grab Sookie, Stephen Moyer had to sit in a box underground that was covered in plastic. When it came time, he had to punch through the plastic. Much has been said about the sex scene. In the books, the rough sex is not played down. Stephen Moyer has been widely quoted as calling it rape during one interview, something that most believe was an unfortunate choice of wording. But even Alan Ball has described it as a "major lady porn/vampire seduction fantasy."

Location, Location, Location: The vampire's nest that was set on fire *was* located in the Ledbetter Heights neighborhood in Shreveport, Louisiana. Rumored to have been a brothel at one time, the scene caused a local controversy over whether the building had historical value. (We know who won.) The building had been scheduled for demolition when the production bought it for $100. Alan Ball says, "It may have been historical at some point, but for years it had been a crack house." The location itself is also blocks from a series of other buildings seen in the show's opening credits, notably Lucky Liquor.

Encore: "The Fourth Man in the Fire," performed by Johnny Cash, plays as Jason and Amy wait outside Eddie's house. The song was written by Arthur Smith, and covered by Johnny Cash on his live storyteller album *Strawberry Cake*. Smith was a textile mill worker who became well known for his instrumental compositions, including the now infamous banjo duet "Dueling Banjos" heard in the film *Deliverance* (1972). "The Fourth Man in the Fire" tells the story of the fiery furnace from the Book of Daniel in the Old Testament. In it, three men — Shadrach, Meshach, and Azariah — refuse to bow to the self-erected statue of King Nebuchadnezzar. He condemns them to death, ordering the furnace to be heated seven times hotter in response to the men's conviction that they will be saved. They are thrown in the fire where Nebuchadnezzar witnesses them walking through the flames along with a fourth man "like a son of the gods." They emerge unscathed, upon which Nebuchadnezzar addresses them as "servants of the Most High God." The song is an apt companion to an episode in which it's revealed that Bill did not perish in the vamps' nest fire, saved by Sookie's urgent phone messages, rather than supernatural strength or intuition. It also partners extremely well with Amy's increasingly obvious personal agenda and vampirish, soul-sucking influence over Jason. In the Old Testament story, it's the soldiers who raise the heat of the furnace who ultimately die. How much closer can Jason get to the flames before he's the one who makes the ultimate sacrifice? And who is watching over him?

1.09   Plaisir D'Amour

Original air date: November 2, 2008
Written by: Brian Buckner
Directed by: Anthony M. Hemingway

> **Eddie:** Comes a point in life when you realize everything you know about yourself, it's all just conditioning. It's the rare man who truly knows who he is.

Bill breaks vampire law to protect Sookie. Jason and Amy resort to drastic measures to get V-juice. Tara visits Miss Jeanette. And Bill turns to Sam to watch over Sookie.

This episode might be more aptly titled "The Measure of a Man," double entendre intended. Breaking vampire law, Bill kills another vampire to protect Sookie. As he leaves with Eric for the tribunal, he asks Sam to watch over Sookie. Sam, having just given Tara money for an exorcism, steps up to the task. Jason, meanwhile, gets life lessons from Eddie, the vampire he's holding hostage in his basement.

Yet it's the women of the show who drive these plot points. Sookie has chosen to be with Bill, and accepts her fate. While she was displeased to be at Fangtasia under duress, she was the one who set the terms of negotiation and has never flinched from Bill's side since committing to him. Tara accepts Sam's money, but continues to set the pace of their relationship. Sam cares for Tara, but doesn't have much to lose by offering her money. It's a kind but ultimately selfish act; we give because it makes us feel good to do so. And Amy, who orchestrated Eddie's kidnapping, endlessly informs, if not controls, Jason's every move, not to mention being a surrogate-sister to Sookie.

While the men take action, it's in *reaction* to their circumstances. They haven't created the world in which they live so much as they're stuck responding to it, the possible exception being Sam whose world is entirely manufactured. But that's not to say it's genuine. Bill defends Sookie because he must. They're targets. If the threat was eradicated, his nights would be filled with reading and Wii. Sam is so intensely private and loyal that when he sees a damsel in distress he immediately falls into companion mode. Jason, even when he knows that something isn't quite right, still allows others to fill in the gaps for him, assuming whatever role he's offered.

When Jason is with Amy, it's like he's the kidnapped sympathizing with his kidnapper. But even without the ability to glamour, Eddie has found a window into Jason and is quietly pulling the shades back to reveal Amy's true nature. Eddie's take on the world isn't lost on Jason. Jason didn't have a father around to raise him, and Eddie, as unlikely a candidate, is able to speak firsthand, both as a newly out gay male and as a newly turned vampire, about what it means to break with conventions and be the man you always thought you could be. While Jason has always been one to leap, it's not without a fair degree of certainty that he'll get what he wants. Eddie, on the other hand, has not gotten what he wants, but he does know who he is.

In this episode, everyone feels a bit as if they're coming off a high or suffering from side effects. As Eddie says, there comes a time when you realize that conventions have defined you. Who are you without them? If you don't know — you snap. Sookie snaps at Andy, understandably frustrated, but, regardless, an out of character moment. Jason snaps at Rene for drilling into a tree root, then snaps at Hoyt for using his high school nickname. Earlier, Tara snapped at Sam for coming to her to try and work things out. Sookie's homestead is a crime scene. Jason's under the influence of a powerful personality, someone who wants to change the way he thinks, acts, and eats. The woman who once terrorized Tara is now healthier than her.

It's hard to believe in an episode that features an exploding vampire and a psychedelic sex scene, that the most memorable thing is Jason's talk with Eddie, Tara's conversation with Miss Jeanette, or Lettie Mae's observation that only white men bring flowers when they want sex because black men don't grovel. The viewer doesn't need bells and whistles to stay immersed in these stories. The best visual effect of this show was Pam's expression when she reached into Sookie's bra to retrieve a piece of Longshadow. This show always works best when it knows what it truly is.

With Bill's departure for tribunal, and Sookie waking up to find a naked Sam on her bed, it doesn't look like things will become any more certain any time soon. How long can Sookie hold on to blind faith?

Highlight: Eric: "Humans. Honestly Bill, I don't know what you see in them."

Nightcap: Patrick Gallagher, who plays Chow, can also be seen in *Glee* as the football coach, Ken Tanaka. When Sookie spots the dog (Sam) following her, she names it Dean. Sam and Dean are the names of the lead characters in *Supernatural*, a favorite show of some of the cast members.

Paging Dr. Creepy: Ginger, Fangtasia's human waitress, is involved in both of this episode's gory moments. Ginger Part One: puking after Longshadow is staked . . . just not what I wanted to see in that moment. Ginger Part Two: cleaning Longshadow off the floor to accompanying noises of what sounded like an octopus being pried from the linoleum.

Location, Location, Location: Lettie Mae's residence is a home in Los Angeles, located north of downtown, just east of Dodger Stadium.

Encore: When Jason and Amy transport Eddie back to Jason's house, we hear "Plaisir d'Amour" performed by Joan Baez. *The joys of love last but a moment. The grief of love lasts a lifetime.* "Plaisir d'Amour" is a French love song dating back more than 200 years. Composed by Johann Scwartzendorf, the lyrics are taken from the poem "Célestine" by Jean de Florian, and the final orchestral version was arranged by Hector Berlioz. The song is known in English as "The Joys of Love." Joan Baez recorded her version for her second studio album in 1961. It's also been covered by Brigitte Bardot, Marianne Faithfull, Nana Mouskouri, Emmylou Harris, Andrea Bocelli, Nick Drake, and Charlotte Church, among many others. The song is played for ironic effect in this scene, Jason starting to show his concern (bordering on fear) for Amy's non-humane actions against Eddie the Vampire. Jason has always been lead by the hand of strong women, but none of his impulsive actions to date match premeditated violence against another. If, in fact, "the joys of love last but a moment," so does the high of V-juice when compared against a life of remorse.

1.10 I Don't Wanna Know

Original air date: November 9, 2008
Written by: Chris Offutt
Directed by: Scott Winant

> **Sam:** Must be nice to come from such an old family.
> **Terry:** All families are old, Sam. Some just keep better records.

Sam reveals his true identity to Sookie. Tara learns the truth about Miss Jeanette. And Bill accepts his punishment for killing another vampire.

The last few episodes have provided a platform for some of the supporting cast to take center stage, in particular Adina Porter, Nelsan Ellis, and Alexander Skarsgård.

While some of the plot points of late have left me wanting — Jason's V addiction has been overplayed — with this episode, we're back on track!

Stephen Root turns in another fine performance as Eddie. His scenes with Amy and Jason are some of my favorite this season. He reserves what energy he has to pay forward the tutelage he couldn't offer his own son. Jason is Eddie's chance to be a maker.

As viewers, we need Eddie. He can speak in a way the others can't because they're too close to their situations. They're literally boxed in. Sam lives in a trailer. Tara lives in crowded house with her mother. Bill sleeps underground. Lafayette's house is littered with cameras. Sookie's world is infringed upon by others' thoughts and feelings. And Jason, in his own way, is trapped inside a body so tight, only the sweat can get out. As an outsider in life, and in death, Eddie's view of the world is narrated from the sidelines, not as a participant but as a voyeur. And because he's a vampire, his logic isn't clouded by the emotions and traits affecting everyone else: frustration (Sookie), resentment (Tara), selfishness (Amy), delusion (Maxine), suffering (Sam), or, in a rare vampire exception, martyrdom (Bill). Whether it was a conscious decision to make Eddie tempered and compassionate like Gran, his demeanor is a haunting likeness, kind in a way that Jason respects and responds to.

For these, and other reasons — notably, Sam coming out as a shifter, and Sookie's reluctance to forgive him for not telling her earlier — this episode has more LGBT ties than most. Eddie's newly vampire, so it's not centuries of living that have made him wise. When he was turned, he took with him the lessons he learned from not being out to himself or his family. Eddie's a moderate vampire, but he's an iconic gay male. Sure, he's not what the popular media trumpets as the ideal (see Jason), but he's more in keeping with the message and reality of gay/vampire rights, that it's less about lifestyle and all about changing assumptions of what you presumed to be straight/human, in the first place. Jason, for instance, is an attractive, young, able-bodied, white male with more privilege than most, but he's still not fulfilled because he doesn't know who he is.

Sam is similar, but because he's finally come out as a shifter, he's more like Eddie than Jason for having carried a secret most of his life, something that becomes invisible again the moment he shifts back into human form, the way a vampire's fangs retract. In Sam's case, however, he can lose grip on his secret when he falls asleep, his guard let down at his most vulnerable. As a child, his adopted family refused to see him for who he was, abandoning him rather than kicking him out. As Sookie awakes to find Sam naked on her bed, he's seen, but immediately mistaken for a pervert. (Poor Sam! Is it any wonder some people find it easier just to stay in the closet?)

After a few episodes of striking out with Sookie, Sam may have found his in. He's already gone on the record as saying that he wouldn't change a thing about Sookie.

He's kind, he can eat and go out in daylight, and, like Arlene says about Rene, he's there. With Bill gone indefinitely, and Sookie scared for her life, could companionship suffice? Sam's already been a pushover once for Sookie, and again with Tara. It would be a shame to see him go down that road again.

Sookie's still coming into her own. She may feel betrayed by Sam, but she lost out on the only chance she had to accept him when he needed her to the most. Had she responded to Sam's vulnerability — as Bill did to hers when he said that Sookie's tragedy and beauty was in not knowing just how different she really is — Sam would have gotten the affirmation he's been waiting for his whole life: that he's not a freak. Just as a gay person is not defined by their sexuality, Sam is not defined solely by his ability to shift, nor is Sookie defined solely by her abilities as a telepath. If anything, she seems hell-bent on defining herself as a human who dates a vampire. Like Terry, back from the war, Sookie's erratic behavior is in keeping with someone who's suffered a terrible shock and is looking to burst out of the closet, break it down, and burn it in a heap.

On the flip side, Amy is a human who shares more in common with the worst we've come to know in vampires. She's a full-blown narcissist, a soul-sucking, emotional vampire who drains the positive energy from people around her. You love someone? She loves someone more. You like to eat? She only eats organic. You don't want to die? She helped Guatemalans build an irrigation system. She's infuriating!

Jason is malleable, so she shifts her message to whatever will make him most susceptible to her wishes. Like Jessica, the "cow" Bill is forced to turn to repay the life he took to protect Sookie, Amy sees Jason as further down the food chain, and therefore expendable. Below even a cow is Eddie, because he's not alive. Amy is the character you love to hate. And that's good. We should want to hate Amy. She stakes Eddie rather than let Jason succeed. R.I.P. Eddie. Like Gran, you left us too soon.

Miss Jeanette, however, is surprisingly hard to hate. "You think knowing the answers will save you," she tells Tara. This hearkens back to the night Bill begged Sookie to see that just because she understands the mechanics of her body she doesn't have an explanation as to why she lives and breathes, even as he's dead and walking among the living. It's these random bits of philosophy that stick with us long after an episode ends, and the *True Blood* writers excel in this area. For example, we know Miss Jeanette is a con, there's no doubt about that. But we can't underestimate blind faith and the power one has to control their own destiny. While she may not be a healer, she does facilitate change. The Twelve Steps won't keep an alcoholic sober. It's the individual's choice not to drink that will. It may not be hocus pocus, but individual conviction is no less magical, a faith everyone can believe in.

There's blind faith and there's blind drunk. As Tara steps off her mother's wagon, wasted, belligerent, and scared, she swerves off the road to avoid hitting a naked woman and a pig. We know there are other shifters and they need an animal to imprint. But in a small town where everyone knows everyone else, this woman is a visitor. Who is she, and who has she come to see?

Highlight: Amy: "Don't you dare get morally superior on me. I am an organic vegan, and my carbon footprint is miniscule."

Nightcap: More Hoyt! He's so precious, we could make a drinking game out of how many times he tells someone he's sorry. First, he wants to be Bill. Then he wants to be Jason. Then he wants to be Rene. He wants to be his own man, but he's switching role models the way a child flips through television channels. Though Sookie is shocked to learn that werewolves exist, Anna Paquin played one in *Trick 'r Treat* (2009). When Sookie is being stalked inside Merlotte's she flashes to the killer's thoughts and sees a woman, played by Stacie Rippy, who guest-starred in *The Class*, a show in which Lizzy Caplan (Amy Burley) was a regular. When the senator arrives, Lafayette is watching *The Bad and the Beautiful* (1952) with Kirk Douglas and Lana Turner, an appropriate selection for two reasons: the film itself is about the toll professional ambitions take on our personal lives, and Lana Turner, who was married eight times (something that might appeal to Lafayette's playboy persona), epitomized the idea that suffering and glamour went hand-in-hand. The musician playing throughout the engagement party is C. C. Adcock, born in Lafayette, Louisiana, and known for his cajun, zydeco, electric blues, and swamp pop–influenced sound.

Relationship Crypt Falls: Amy, if our parents wanted us to know they really flushed our hamsters down the toilet, they wouldn't tell us they'd "been set free to roam in the fields." You drove a plank into Jason's pet. I don't think we have to tell you, it left a mark.

Paging Dr. Creepy: The sight of a vampire having his fangs pulled out by the root made me shudder. Because we know those roots are probably about, what, 125 years old?

Location, Location, Location: Bill's junkyard trial was shot on — wait for it! — yes, a real junkyard. One of these days, we'll hear the sordid details of the poor set designer who had to create a scrap heap from scratch. This one, however, is very much real and located at Aadlen Bros. Auto Wrecking in Sun Valley, California, a small city in San Fernando Valley just south of the Golden State Freeway. The yard has also been used for a number of films and television series, including *The Running Man*, *Escape from L.A.*, *The A-Team*, *Beverly Hills 90210*, and *Dexter*. Visit them online at aadlenbros.com. Miss Jeanette's day job location actually is a pharmacy of the same name, DeSoto's Pharmacy. It's also located in San Fernando Valley in Canoga Park, California, in a small shopping center northwest of Universal Studios Hollywood. Inside customers can enjoy drinks from an old-fashioned soda fountain while they wait for their prescriptions.

Encore: "I Don't Wanna Know," performed by Dr. John, plays during the end credits. Malcolm John "Mac" Rebennack Jr. (born 1940), known Dr. John, is a five-time Grammy Award–winning singer/songwriter, pianist, and guitarist. His music fuses blues, pop, jazz, zydeco, boogie woogie, and rock 'n' roll. Born in New Orleans, Louisiana, his career as a guitarist halted when he suffered a gunshot wound to his hand defending a bandmate. Finding his way to the piano, he became a revered session musician, and, in the late '60s, started to tour extensively with his own band, known for their extravagant stage shows that incorporated aspects of voodoo ritual. In the mid-'70s, Dr. John began his foray into New Orleans funk, and in 2008 was inducted into the Louisiana Music Hall of Fame. Dr. John's "I Don't Wanna Know" nicely bookends a show that began with Sookie discovering something that would change the way she viewed the world, and ended with Bill having to face the reality of his own world. In this episode, characters are forced to witness things they'd rather not, or they weren't ready to face, violently transporting them from the reality they once knew into another one entirely. Sam's secret revealed, he can no longer hide who he is from Sookie. Tara learns Miss Jeanette's real identity, but her convictions are tested once again later in the evening when she sees the naked woman and pig. Meanwhile, there's no mistaking what Jason's been party to when Amy stakes Eddie. It's right under Jason's nose, if not all over his face. Even Sookie, unready to face Sam's true identity, is forced to move past it when she stumbles upon the Bon Temps killer in Merlotte's, his past murders rushing into her head. It takes a tribunal to force Bill back into his true nature as a vampire. Each scenario sets the stage for the inevitable. All are shocking, but none are a surprise. The more we change . . .

1.11   To Love Is to Bury

Original air date: November 16, 2008
Written by: Nancy Oliver
Directed by: Nancy Oliver

> **Sookie [to Bill]:** I rescind your invitation!

Bill fulfills his punishment, turning a young woman with surprising results. Jason suffers another loss. Sam and Sookie grow closer. And when Tara's mother kicks her out, a mysterious woman steps in to help.

This episode sets up everything we'll need for one doozy of a season finale! Pam supervising Bill as he prepares Jessica's "grave" is a personal favorite, funny but not crass; absurd but not surreal. Yet it's two vampires arguing the ethics of turning innocents while one digs a grave for the limp body beside him. It could be farcical but it's

Big Patty's Pie House is Chip's Restaurant in real life. Come for the eggs, stay for the ambience. Crime-solving tips are extra. (Gary Wayne/www.seeing-stars.com)

as real as it gets for vampires. This is the day-to-day of how vampires are made, and the scene is carried out like a married couple bickering while washing dishes. It all comes down to Pam's commanding presence. Until now, she's rested on the sidelines, but we finally get to see the Pam who knows how to get down to business. How can a sentient person disagree with Bill's logic that everyone will turn against Jessica after she becomes a vampire? Yet Pam waves his comments off as if he's a petulant child, rising to the occasion in pumps no less, tipping Jessica's body into the grave like a bored teenager who's grown tired of tipping cows. Pam's character is the sleeper of the series. She seethes with sexuality and sin.

With all that Sookie and Bill have been through, it was a tremendous shock when she rescinded Bill's invitation to enter her home. We know that he would have stayed in a coffin for five years if it meant he didn't have to turn Jessica. When he was given no choice he performed the task. Bill likes to think he's different from other vampires, but he still holds to all their laws, only working around them when there's no one there to hold him accountable.

While it would mean death, we haven't yet seen Bill choose Sookie over his own peril. It *could* be argued that after 173 years one might make room for someone else in one's life, but vampires seem to think they own the patent on life span. To paraphrase Malcolm, what's the point of being a human if you can't fall in love with people?

Which is a long way of saying that, for once, the idea of Sam and Sookie getting together is not only reasonable, but appetizing. They had breakfast together. A nice, sunny, daytime breakfast with food. As viewers, had we not forgotten how many of our favorite film and television scenes revolve around food, a banquet, or a hot dog stand? We haven't seen Gran's kitchen sparkle with sunshine and conversation in some time, and it was a welcome alternative to dark, muddy intercourse in a graveyard, no matter how impulsive and sexy it was. When Sookie's life ends, she wants to be able to look back and see evidence of a life lived, not a life avoided. She doesn't outright choose Sam, though. She chooses Sookie. Sookie belongs to . . . Sookie.

Tribute: Deborah Ann Woll (Jessica Hamby)

> "[Deborah] is absolutely extraordinary . . . I'm sure if Bill had dreamed of a way to get his children back, it wouldn't have been in the form of a bratty or virginal psychopathic daughter. That's one of the great things about Alan. He doesn't give his characters what they want. He creates conflict."
>
> – Stephen Moyer

Beauty *and* a geek: how can you not love Deborah Ann Woll? She's a gamer who watches *Mystery Science Theater* and showed up at the 2009 Comic-Con early so she could visit panels before appearing on her own! "One of the wonderful aspects of Comic-Con is that it provides the opportunity for groups of people who may feel ostracized from so-called normal society to come together and feel part of a nonjudgmental community," she said.

Deborah brings this empathy to her portrayal of Jessica Hamby, a precocious 17-year-old from a strict, conservative household who Bill is forced to sire as punishment for killing another vampire. Jessica appears from the trunk of a car, her perfect porcelain skin offset by long, strawberry-blonde hair. She's young and innocent . . . until she discovers her newfound freedom, and Bill finds himself with a strong-headed spitfire in his charge.

Deborah Ann Woll, for all the surly, sassy, sexy life you inject into Jessica Hamby, I give you tin Hershey bars out of tin.

Where you've seen Deborah Ann Woll: *ER, CSI, My Name Is Earl, The Mentalist, Law & Order: Special Victims Unit*

This episode mercifully brings to an end Jason's V addiction, by far the weakest storyline of the season. It also provides one of the best shots of the season, drawing Lizzy Caplan's guest role to a close on a sunny, rainy day, with Jason lifting her into the sky — a sad and poignant departure. Jason's confession to the murders of Amy, Maudette, and Dawn may well be the stupidest thing he's done yet, but with no family to bail him out, or Tara to idolize him, he makes a choice. While he doesn't know why or how, he places blind faith in the certainty that he must be a murderer. We know it's Rene, which, looking back over the season, was hidden so well that it came as a surprise. It had to be a human with casual access to all the victims, but not enough clues were dropped along the way to make this a real whodunit.

Beyond that, there are more questions than ever, and new characters we can look forward to getting to know better, in particular, Deborah Ann Woll as Jessica Hamby and Michelle Forbes as Maryann Forrester. Jessica is the perfect tonic to Bill's straight-edge demeanor. She's fresh, fun, and bratty in a way we wish Sookie would be from time to time. Even though Bill pawns Jessica off on Eric, next season promises to show us Bill hot under the collar as a proud new papa. Maryann Forrester is a mystery. We've learned not to judge a book by its cover, so it's fair to assume that she's at least hiding something. She possesses far too many worldly goods to be a social worker. And why the interest in Tara? As viewers, we're torn between wanting something good for Tara and anticipating the worst.

I'm not sure what to make of Lafayette going to confront the Senator. In the past few episodes, Lafayette's flamboyant nature has been drastically toned down in favor of something harder. In some scenes, he feels like a thug. If there's a bigger story there, it's not being revealed. At this point in the series, we don't need Lafayette to remind us that there are hypocrites and bigots in the world. With no tie to a larger narrative, it just feels like the writers used Lafayette as a politically correct ambassador.

This was a procedural episode, filled with lots of fun dialogue, facts, and recaps. But it works on an emotional level because the actors commit so fully to the personal investment of their characters, leaving lots of potential for the season 1 finale to satisfy, thrill, and surprise us.

Highlight: Tara: "I'm an excellent driver. But you cannot prepare for a naked lady and a hog in the middle of the road!"

Nightcap: Writer/director Nancy Oliver lived in the South for 20 years, and has known Alan Ball since college. Their relationship turned professional when they first worked together on *Six Feet Under*. Jessica's emergence from the ground is Oliver's homage to Asian horror films, in which "they always have long-haired ghosts coming out from strange places." She asked Deborah Ann Woll (Jessica Hamby) to think of an animal sound she could make, and Deborah said she would try a whale.

Relationship Crypt Falls: When it comes to Bill knowing when Sookie is in a heightened state of emotion, it remains unclear how he discerns the difference between Sookie in danger and Sookie in flagrante delicto. If he can't distinguish the two, then he showed up at Sookie's house thinking she was being attacked, likely by the fangbanger killer. If he can, then his jealousy has cost him the one thing he could do better than any other, protect Sookie from the inevitable attack.

Paging Dr. Creepy: I've about had my fill of vampire slop. My stomach is pretty strong, but when Amy poured the contents of Eddie into the garbage disposal, I made a little wish that the next creature to expire would have fed only on tinsel and pixie dust.

Location, Location, Location: A few blocks from the location used for the Bon Temps Police Station, the scene inside Big Patty's Pie House was shot at Chip's Restaurant in Hawthorne, California, close to the Los Angeles International Airport. It was built in 1955 and is still open for business, serving fluffy scrambled eggs and creamy grits.

Encore: As Jason and Amy reconcile over dinner, they listen to "To Love Is to Bury," performed by the Cowboy Junkies. The band formed in Toronto in 1985, and three of four of them are siblings. "To Love Is to Bury" is from their 1988 album *The Trinity Sessions* recorded in 1987 at Church of the Holy Trinity, using just one microphone. The album includes a mix of originals and covers, the most notable being their take on The Velvet Underground's "Sweet Jane," which Lou Reed once called the best cover of the song he'd ever heard. The album also produced the haunting track "Blue Moon Revisited (Song for Elvis)," which combines the original with a new song by the band. It's arguable whether or not Amy knew enough about love to trust what she felt for Jason, but his love for her was genuine if naive. It's likely that without pharma-psychedelic assistance, they could have connected just as strongly. This song sets up their final hyper-sexualized romp, less sensuous than playful; unfortunately, the only trip during which their inevitable disconnect meant that Jason wouldn't wake in time to save her.

1.12   You'll Be the Death of Me

Original air date: November 23, 2008
Written by: Raelle Tucker
Directed by: Alan Ball

Maryann [to Tara]: Maybe life had just cleared out all the things that weren't working for you. Now you've got room to rebuild, decide exactly what you want your life to look like, and make that happen.

Sookie discovers the identity of the killer, putting herself in harm's way. Jason finds new salvation in an anti-vampire church. Tara embraces Maryann's teachings. And Bill risks his very existence to save Sookie.

Now that's a season finale! One door closes; several others open. The writers have given us more than enough to keep ourselves busy with anticipation for the next season, but have also tied up enough loose ends that we can go back to the beginning to critique their methods. We've earned it! There's a lot of escapism in *True Blood*, but it makes you work. It's smart, sexy, and subversive, its finger on the pulse, as it were, of contemporary politics. It's hard to believe with an ensemble cast this size that we covered so much territory in only 12 episodes.

There are some flaws in the season finale. Let's get those out of the way. We know that Sookie can elect to stay out of people's thoughts. But as people get angry or emotional, their thoughts get odder. So it's difficult to believe that once Rene knows she's close to identifying him as the killer she wouldn't be hit with a torrent of his feelings and images. Eventually, she does, and it's such a powerful experience that he feels her in his head, another trait of her telepathy we haven't seen before. Showing us the other deaths as if Sookie is seeing them is effective, but it's ultimately a procedural device, a convenience that gets us caught up on what he's done and to whom. Mere minutes later, Rene lies dead with his head severed from his body. It's a satisfying death, sure, but it all comes to a very sudden conclusion. There's a quote by Alfred Hitchcock, "There is no terror in the bang, only in the anticipation of it." The anguish/joy of possessing information that the protagonist doesn't have is how the story unfolds from that point on, watching a character inadvertently dig herself into a deeper grave. We don't get that pleasure, because it's over almost as soon as it begins.

Similarly, Sookie and Sam are beaten and choked into unconsciousness, so their sudden (in Sookie's case, downright frisky) revival seems unlikely. And while it's been established that Bill wouldn't die immediately upon being in the sunshine, his eyes bake over. He appears to be a goner. When he emerges on Sookie's doorstep, completely healed, there's no explained passage of time. Did she just bury him and walk away? How long was he buried? A day? A week? It's important, because we've already seen them reunite twice, one with dirty, raunchy results, the next met with a cold shoulder. In the last episode, Bill was gone for relatively no time and Sookie almost hooked up with Sam. In this episode, she all but tells Sam that she loves him. These would be small details if major plot points didn't hinge on Sookie's choice of mate. Time, and how it passes, is the very foundation of how Sookie and Bill relate to one another. She's impetuous and wants to set everything to her clock; he has all the time in the world and follows ancient lore. Even John Cusack came armed with a ghetto blaster. Bill arrives with his tail between his legs and kisses her boo-boos less like a

Maryann Forrester's mansion. Hm . . . it looks so tame in the daylight. (Lindsay Blake, www.IamNotaStalker.com)

lover than a father. It felt as if at that point it had become a foregone conclusion to the writers that Bill and Sookie would end up together. But I'd argue that the viewer wouldn't have minded a little more anticipation.

Nitpicking out of the way — when do we do it if not during the finale? — in the second act, things start to get clearer as the scene is set for what we can expect from season 2. In the Sookie Stackhouse novels Lafayette is killed off, so when we see that leg dangling from the back seat of Andy's car, toe nails all painted up, it appears at first glance that Alan Ball has chosen a similar fate. We have, however, seen that leg before . . .

In the here and now, Bill's rebirth is akin to a sustainable agricultural process known as slash-and-char, in which bio matter is cut down and charred, its ashes mingling with the soil to mysteriously regenerate itself. What would Amy make of that? Whether it's Bill's miraculous healing, or Jason's miraculous saving, the rest of the finale is about the choices we make, or are forced to, when we're handed the opportunity to rise from the ashes. Will we stay rooted? Or will we pick up and settle elsewhere?

As Arlene said, just because we think we know someone, doesn't mean they are who they say there are. Jason is recruited into the Fellowship of the Sun, believing, like many young soldiers, that questionable actions will be justified if done in the name of a greater good. This was perhaps foreshadowed by Eddie's sentiment that we're all conditioned. And if this isn't an accident waiting to happen, *what is*? While Jason joins a congregation of sheep, Tara believes she's finally taking a leadership role in her life, yet her every move is monitored by Maryann, a powerful shifter, and her mute house servant. Both Jason and Tara are so distracted by the bright, shiny comfort of happy faces and an abundance of love and community that they fail to see what we do — that they're, once again, under the influence, this time of people far more persuasive than Amy and Miss Jeanette combined.

Now that Sookie and Bill are together, and Tara and Sam are done like dinner, could there be new love in Bon Temps? Hoyt asks if Bill might know of any female vampires just as Jessica returns to the roost, feistier than before and ready to make things hard for Daddy. Jessica is a creation of the *True Blood* writers, not a carry-over from the books. With her around, the writers will have to work hard to make Sookie more mature in season 2, a transformation that began when she started wearing her hair down, and now in a tussled do. Jessica's character commands a lot of attention, but she's such a revelation, from her youth to her playfulness to what she brings out as Bill, a surprise as a father figure. There's a lot of material to mine from their relationship.

As we round out the season, we're given some takeaways to remind us how art imitates life. We've been given a chance to escape, but Alan Ball doesn't shy from showing us the ugly truths of our real world, offering us the tools to help build a better one. Notably, he doesn't pander to us. Like Gran or Eddie, he gives us the choice, asking only that we see things for what they truly are. For instance, Rene doesn't just beat Sookie and Sam; he bashes them. It's an all-out hate crime. And while Alan Ball has been flexible with his mythology, the idea of letting vampires construct their own myths in order to protect themselves mirrors the LGBT community perfectly, especially closeted gays and lesbians who still build narratives into their day-to-day lives to control how they are perceived. We are delivered a hopeful message, though, vampire-human marriages becoming legal in Vermont, the first state to legalize same-sex civil unions. Vampires: 1. Haters: 0.

Highlight: Terry [to Arlene]: "Your hair's like a sunset after a bomb went off. Pretty."
Nightcap: The painting behind Tara's bed in Maryann's home is *La Grande Odalisque*. Painted in 1814 by Jean Auguste Dominique Ingres, it depicts a concubine. Critics saw Ingres as a rebel, favoring sensuality over anatomical realism. When Sookie's doorbell

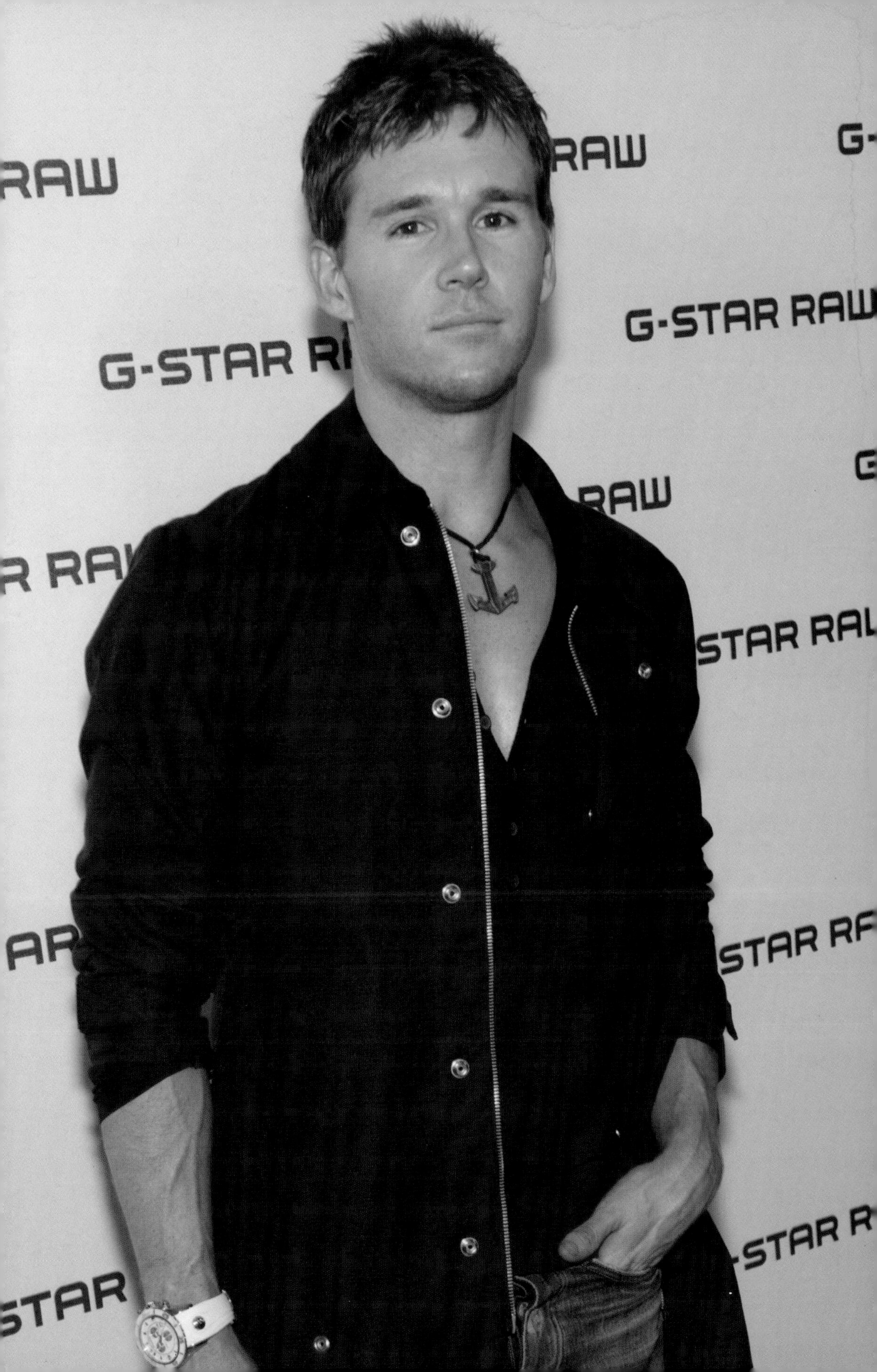
G-STAR RAW

Tribute: Michael Raymond-James (Rene Lenier)

"I said, 'What's a Cajun dialect?' You know, there's
not a lot of that in Detroit [where I'm from]."
— Michael Raymond-James on his
audition for *True Blood*

When Michael Raymond-James immerses himself in a role, he leaves no
stone unturned, going so far as to hire his own dialect coach to help
create Rene's Cajun accent. Hoping to find someone with "gumbo in their
DNA," he met Errol Guidry II, the man responsible for the authentic accent
of another fictional murderer, Eduard Delacroix (played by Michael Jeter) in
The Green Mile (1999). The two worked closely on each script, inserting
French phrasing into Rene's dialogue for effect. (Cajuns are descendants
of French-speaking settlers from Acadia and eastern Quebec.)

The result is a performance that had viewers leaning forward more often
than not to ask, "What did he just say?" It may also be a large part of the
reason we didn't see what was right under our noses — that Rene was a
psychotic killer who would go to any length to obtain the intimate access
he'd need to get close to his victims while staying off the radar as a
suspect, someone whose morals are so out of joint that he'll stop at nothing
to embed himself in the hearts and lives of people who came to love him
most. Which makes Rene Lenier one of those villains we love to hate.

Where you've seen Michael Raymond-James: *CSI, Boston Legal, Medium, Black
Snake Moan, ER, Cold Case, Lie to Me, Moonlight Serenade, Terriers*

rings, she's watching *The Little Princess* (1939) starring Shirley Temple, possibly an
inside joke as the film was originally based on a novel but introduced a number of new
characters and storylines when adapted to the screen, not unlike Alan Ball's adaptation of Charlaine Harris's novels. The novel was entitled *A Little Princess* (1904)
written by Frances Hodgson Burnett, and told the story of an orphaned girl at a
boarding school who takes up with a number of friends considered "undesirable" by
the school's standards. She develops a rich fantasy world, all the while learning that
her friends are now her family, and that she's not alone in the world, as Sookie (and
Jason) would have felt after Gran died. As Eric drops Jessica off at Bill's house he says,
"*O du ljuva frihet*" as he leaves, which is Swedish for "Oh sweet freedom."

Relationship Crypt Falls: Can we really blame Sam for being so upset that Bill's back? He needs to cool off a lot, but he'd finally won Sookie and most of the audience over with his sincerity. Sookie doesn't seem to care that he's mad, having settled on her choice of Bill. But Sam isn't as loyal a friend as his pet dog. He's said that it's hard to shift into the model of another human because they're too complex; he's barely used to being inside his own skin.

Paging Dr. Creepy: Severing Rene's head from his spinal column was pretty gross, as was Bill's charred skin receding back from his face. But it's Maryann's shimmering that gets my vote this episode. The effect of her vibrating like Liam (seen in a reprise of his sex scene with Maudette) upset both my mind and body. All told, very effective, even if I got the tummy grumbles.

Encore: "You'll Be the Death of Me," performed by Johnny Winter, is heard when Sam asks Tara if she knows the whereabouts of Lafayette. Johnny Winter is an American blues guitarist and singer, a born-and-raised Texan, who began his recording career when he was 15. Even though the town in which he was raised, Beaumont, was home to some of the worst race riots in Texan history, Winter, an albino, never felt uneasy about visiting black neighborhoods to listen to, and play, music. For over 30 years, he's been leaving his thumbprint on blues, turning it into a mixture of country and southern rock. "You'll Be the Death of Me" (*A Lone Star Kind of Day*, 1991) plays in the background at Merlotte's after the news report on vampire-human marriages. Sam makes a comment about the specialized engagement party he could throw for Sookie and Bill, replete with vampire wedding band and decorations. It's harsh, but we can't help but feel for him. He's revealed himself to Sookie, stayed by her side night and day, while Bill's only option when he does emerge from the shadows is to sizzle up in the sunshine. Throughout season 1, any association between Bill and Sookie has lead to harm's way for one of them. By further association, their love continues to threaten those around them.

An Exclusive Interview with *True Blood*'s Kristin Bauer (Pam Ravenscroft)

From the moment Pam Ravenscroft greeted Bill and Sookie at the entrance of Fangtasia, I was hooked. Not only was Pam the sexiest bouncer on television, she oozed distaste for Bill's mainstreaming lifestyle. While I've never lacked pride for Bill's choices, Pam has always been quick to demonstrate what an uncensored vampire lives like. Coupled with fantastic comic timing and the most adorable kinship with Eric this side of Joey Tribbiani and Chandler Bing, Bart Simpson and Millhouse Van Houten, or Paris Hilton and whomever will put up with her, Pam is my gal.

Behind every good character is an even better actor, so Kristin Bauer must be top drawer. After surfing her personal site, I became even more intrigued. A passionate artist, advocate, and romantic partner, acting is a large part of her life, but it's not all of it. I contacted Kristin, who responded with enthusiasm for this book and the opportunity to connect with her fans.

Tell us a bit about how you come to acting, and what, in particular, you like about working in television?

I started acting just to pay the bills and support my drawing and painting habit. But as time went on, the acting took over. I love all acting really but the fun aspect of TV is the speed of it. I started in live comedy television, and still enjoy a faster pace. That and that I usually get to sleep in my own bed at night as there's less travel.

It seems like the role was meant for you. Could you see playing anyone else on the show? A surly Tara or exotic Maryann?

I think I'm just Pam. And I really couldn't see any other character differently now either. Everyone is so good! And meeting Charlaine Harris was so much fun for me! To meet the Pam creator – my maker – was a real treat. It was just a joy.

Well, your scenes with Alexander Skarsgård are among my favorites. Pam really shines in those. I couldn't see another pairing being as well timed as the two of you, frankly. It's hard to believe you weren't cast together.

I guess we're just that good! I'm kidding! But I am happy that it comes across that way. We have gotten to be friends and I think that helps. Also these casting folks and producers are all visionaries, so maybe they saw something, or maybe it's a happy accident. Either way, I'm really lucky.

Do you have any interest in the paranormal outside the series?

Oh, yes. I am a sci-fi *Trek* lover. The paranormal, the spiritual, it thrills me. Life without it would be sadly limited to only what one can prove in a lab and that's a really banal, neutered, unloving way to view life for me. And, also, just not the whole beautiful story.

And now you're working with a visionary who sees things that most don't, Alan Ball. I went into mourning after *Six Feet Under* wrapped. Were you a fan of his work?

There is a passage in *American Beauty* that still takes my breath away. "I guess I could be pretty pissed off about what happened to me, but it's hard to stay mad when there's so much beauty in the world. Sometimes I feel like I'm seeing it all at once, and it's too much, my heart fills up like a balloon that's about to burst, and then I remember to relax, and stop trying to hold on to it, and then it flows through me like rain and I can't feel anything but gratitude for every single moment of my stupid little life. You have no idea what I'm talking about, I'm sure. But don't worry, you will someday."

What's it like to work around that energy?

It's a fun, professional, kind set with a group that works so hard to bring this show to the viewers. The actors are the only ones you see, but the crew is impressive. Take our costume designer, Audrey Fisher. Without her clothes, there is no Pam. She helps me be Pam, period. Then it's just more crazy outfits, great shoes, great dialogue, some laughs, and some gore.

So the answer to the age-old question — do the clothes make the vamp, or does the vamp make the clothes — is Audrey Fisher. Got it! In what ways are you nothing like Pam?

Pam is over the human race, whereas I still have hope that we can do better.

And if you got to see Pam do something completely outlandish, what would it be? Horrific, hilarious, musical à la *Buffy*?

I feel like I've gotten to do all of that! Except, thank god, the musical part. But I think I'll leave Pam's future to the great writers and just show up and try to do their words justice.

Kristin Bauer glamours the consumer in a charitable campaign between IFAW and Lush. (Courtesy Kristin Bauer; photo by Larry DiMarzio)

Have you watched any scenes from the show and thought, "Man, I'd really like to take a crack at that?"

Yes! Alex made ripping bodies apart look pretty fun, even though it's probably not as easy as it looks.

I wanted to go back and ask you about your artwork. When did you start painting?

I've been drawing and painting since junior high. That was what I went to college for, in fact. It's a great solace for me, a wonderful escape, and contrast to the hectic life of acting. Art is solo, whereas acting is a huge team effort. I paint whenever I can. It's always there for me.

Your husband, Abri van Straten, is a musician. What's it like sharing a household with another artist?

It's really wonderful because we get each other! We have complete understanding. And I also love his music; that's also very lucky. Can you imagine if I didn't? But for me to hear his classical guitar style and that voice in my house is a dream. It's why I hunted him down! As for challenges, it's just the usual ones like, "Honey, can you put your socks in the hamper?"

Abri also helps you practice the Swedish dialogue in your scenes.

It's funny! Another bizarre aspect of acting for a living. But Abri's first language was Afrikaans, and his grandparents were Swedish, so it is much more familiar to him. Some Afrikaans words are even the same as in Swedish. He's a big help; I always panic when I have Swedish lines!

When you encounter fans of *True Blood*, do they mention things they'd like to see for Pam?

They usually ask me about my pumps. And the writers did such a great job on Pam's dialogue, it's memorable, which is fun.

A number of the show's metaphors are quite political and progressive. Does it affect how you play the role, knowing that it has social impact?

For me, the best part of acting is the doing of it on the set, on the day; then, it is over for me. I create it, like a painting, and then it leaves my control and goes to live on with someone else. I try to forget about it. So, any future Pam ideas excite me and also make me nervous as a performer because my mind jumps to wanting to do the writing justice. As far as social impact, that's not something I can control, what the reaction is, whether good or bad, helpful or offensive. I appreciate immensely being part of a show that is more than meets the eye, that has many layers and deals with timeless concepts of acceptance and, ultimately, tolerance and kindness as we all must share this floating ball called Earth. How we can do that better is a big concern of mine in my life. But as far as playing Pam, I just want to do a good job and I hope that comes across. The larger concepts, the writing that comes before, and the reactions that come after I do my part, are not really my province. My job as an actor is a tiny part in the middle, and that is plenty!

Which leads us to your causes, which you're vocally passionate about. I've included links at the end of this interview for those who would like to get involved, as well.

There are way too many causes that need our help. I try to do what I can in my everyday life. I am not one of the heroes like the Sea Shepherd Conservation Society, but I can pay attention to who I support when I grocery shop; I can buy recycled paper products; I can buy natural laundry detergent and be nice to our oceans; I can buy free-range meat and rescue my pets. We are more powerful than we can know. Every company does everything they do to get our dollars. We pay their mortgage, so let's be powerful when we shop. Corporations need us! Right now I am working with IFAW (International Fund for Animal Welfare) on a "Tails for Whales" campaign to help whales from going extinct from unnecessary and preventable deaths like being run over by a ship. IFAW and I are working with LUSH stores to support this project. We need photos of people making the "whale tail" and to shop at LUSH! Both fun and easy!

Is there one question that you wish people would ask you, but don't?

How do I get my hair so shiny? Just kidding! I do have all kinds of thoughts, rants, opinions, though, that I'm beginning to be so bold as to share with the world on my website. I'd love for people to visit.

For more information on Kristin Bauer,
check out the following websites:

Kristin Bauer: www.kristinbauer.com
Abri van Straten: www.abrivanstraten.com
Sea Shepherd Conservation Society: www.seashepherd.org
IFAW: www.ifaw.org
Tails for Whales: www.tailsforwhales.org

Online Fandom

The Internet and Beyond

Before I put one word into this book, I'd taken to Twitter, Facebook, the HBO *True Blood* wiki, and iTunes to connect with people who lend their time and resources to the discussion and promotion of *True Blood*. What do they all share in common, beyond a love for this series? They're all online, creating platforms that other fans flock to for everything from celebrity news to behind-the-scenes coverage to historical lore to images of favorite cast members to, in one case, their all-but-naked likenesses in the form of some of the coolest printable dress-up dolls since the Ziegfeld Girls. In short, *True Blood* fans are creative, passionate, and dedicated.

For a one-stop-shopping *True Blood* experience, fans of the shows can visit the HBO *True Blood* wiki. A wiki is a collaborative website that focuses on one topic and is run by its users. In the case of *True Blood*, the HBO wiki is for the fans, powered by the fans. There are images, videos, chats, fan fiction, and places for "Truebies" — fans of the series — to connect, as well as "Bookies" — those who prefer Charlaine Harris's books. The discussion threads drill down into each episode, the characters, and, of course, the ties each of us have to Bill Compton or Eric Northman.

This is where web admin "Dallas" met a number of other self-professed fans, people who have since become close friends. They've even traveled together. Out of this new camaraderie, Dallas launched the highly popular "Loving True Blood in Dallas" (www.lovingtrueblood indallas.com) and subsequent "Talk Blood" radio show, taking to the podcasting airwaves after every *True Blood* broadcast to rehash and react to that night's episode. She's also produced themed shows such as "It's a Man's World," which focused on the men who love Sookie and *True Blood* and featured an international broadcast during which she interviewed Sookie fans live via Skype from Spain, Peru, Israel, Sweden, and Australia.

Along the way, Dallas has had a few sweet surprises, such as when "Bad Things" singer/songwriter Jace Everett dialed in to declare himself a long-time listener, first-time caller. And her regular guests and co-hosts keep fans coming back for more, including Twitterverse celebrity roleplayer @SookieBonTemps, Mark Blankenship of the *Huffington Post*, and Brian Juergens and Andy Swist from the high-larious *True Blood* vlog "Blood Work." The show has become so popular that Dallas and her team have never been able to take all the calls on any given night.

Lynn Fu and Eileen Rivera also run a blog and radio show, but their approach is a little more intimate. "Bite Club Show: Wine. Women. Fangs." (www.biteclubshow.com) began as a three-person operation, with the two hosts joined by a technical producer. They created a podcast out of shared enthusiasm, something that fans have described as like listening to a late-night conversation with your friends. Part of that has to do with the show's inclusive approach to vampire-entertainment. "We found a lot of podcasts existed specifically for *Twilight* and a few for *True Blood*," Fu says. "Since we love both, it's only appropriate to include them. Also this gives us an opportunity to expand and discuss old or upcoming shows and movies such as *The Vampire Diaries*, *Daybreakers*, and *Buffy the Vampire Slayer*."

The "wine" portion of the show was originally intended to keep the hosts' nerves at bay. "Both of us are used to producing and coordinating shows, not being the voice of them," Rivera explains. But the idea quickly evolved into wine reviews, and a way to introduce new and affordable wine suggestions to their listeners. "All of our wines have been red," Rivera continues, "with the exception of one chardonnay named 'Bella.'"

Michael McMillian (Steve Newlin looks different with his hair down!) with Bite Club Show co-host Lynn Fu and Alexander Skarsgård. (Photo by Eileen Rivera, courtesy of Lynn Fu, www.BiteClubShow.com)

By far one of the most successful *True Blood* fan sites is maintained by someone who didn't have an initial interest in *True Blood* or vampires. But when Shadaliza Monterosa, Mistress of The Vault at www.trueblood-online.com, learned that Alan Ball was attached to the show, she had a change of heart. She decided to start a website with the goal of being the preeminent fan site of the show rather than the novels, citing, "[The series] was original, exciting, humorous, and sexy. It was initially the romance between Sookie and Bill that drew me in, but it was the intriguing storylines and multi-layered characters that got me completely hooked."

Boasting exclusive interviews with cast members Jim Parrack, Kristin Bauer, Michael McMillian, Deborah Ann Woll, and Carrie Preston as well as a host of integral behind-the-scenes players (composer Nathan Barr, music supervisor Gary Calamar, writer/producer

Shadaliza Monterosa, Mistress of The Vault at www.trueblood-online.com, models a fang-watering bottle of Tru Blood. (Shadaliza Monterosa)

Raelle Tucker, and Jace Everett), Monterosa has fans visiting The Vault from more than 192 countries on a regular basis. "I am Dutch and live in Italy," Monterosa says, "so that makes it all a very international mixture." The universal flair is a good mix for such an international cast and a series that broadcasts in over 40 countries. "The Vault started as a one-woman project," she says. "Now I have a whole network of people who provide me with information, including my co-admin Lynnpd, the message board connected to The Vault (www.StephenMoyer.yuku.com), HBO, several publicists, random strangers, good old Google, Twitter, and Facebook."

Then there are those who are quite content to focus all their attentions on what many fans see as the defining debate of *True Blood* and the Sookie Stackhouse novels: Bill versus Eric. Shannon of Billsbelles Blog (@BillsBelles, billsbelles.wordpress.com) and Misty (@sbookclub) of Viking Wenches (@VikingWenches, www.vikingwenches.com) are two such women. "I, for one, love the geeky side of Bill," Shannon says.

"The computer-using, alien-movie-watching Bill. . . . As for the rest of the Belles, most enjoy the southern gentleman . . . [although] we have also collectively come to the conclusion that Bill, underneath it all, is the true bad boy."

BillsBelles spend most of their time on Twitter, interacting with the roleplayer @VampireBill. "There are several thousand people following him," Shannon explains of the competition to catch his eye. "[But] he knows who is loyal to him . . . The two of us have long running jokes and conversations [and he] has been known to 'pop fang' once in a while if one of us says something he finds particularly intriguing." It's nary a night that the Belles aren't checking in on one another on Twitter, sharing jokes, or toasting to the end of a long week, their connection played out to anyone following their daily travails, almost always peppered with a sly flirtation with their favorite vampire.

"Loyal to our Viking, wenches through and through" is the motto of Misty's Viking Wenches, and from the books to the screen, they're Team Eric all the way. "Eric is just so true to himself," Misty begins. "He never wavers in his desires . . . [and] Alexander Skarsgård is a perfect Eric, incredibly sexy with a hint of a softer side." When asked if she hopes to see Sookie end up with Eric, Misty says no, explaining, "Personally, I want Sookie to end up with someone she can have a normal life with. Kids, football games, and a big family around her. . . . Besides, I want Eric all to myself."

But beyond her role of head wench, Misty also administrates the online Sookie's Book Club (ssbookclub.wordpress.com). With over a thousand people following them on Twitter, the club meets in a chat room every Sunday evening to discuss Charlaine Harris's novels, detail by detail. They have a newsletter, fan fiction, and recommended reading lists, all working to create one of the most dedicated and regular online gatherings of readers. "We discuss two chapters a week," Misty says. "I usually start with a recap and we go over the plot, characters, and our favorite lines." Belles and Wenches are both welcome, and Misty has her "sheriffs" on hand for when things get out of control.

Beyond the awesome ability of the internet to gather people together to have these conversations is its ability to host them after the fact. Each chat is posted on the blog for members who couldn't attend, so they never have to feel left out. "We have a great community," Misty boasts. "Viking Wenches, BillsBelles, a Man Wench. We have vampire lovers of all shapes and sizes. Shifters, weres, fairies, and teacups. The book club accepts all. We get along really well and are ready to defend our vamp-of-choice like a pack of wolves."

Doug Knipe may well be the lone wolf in this pack as one of the men Dallas invited to appear on her show about the men who love Sookie. A rabid fan of urban fantasy (UF) and paranormal romance (PNR), Doug Knipe is the proprietor of www.SciFiGuy.ca, winner of the Best Speculative Fiction Blog for the 2009 Bloggers Appreciation Week. Sci Fi Guy is a powerhouse of commentary, community, and connectivity. It offers book reviews, news, and opinions on UF, PNR, and science fiction and fantasy (SFF), along with an incredible array of interviews, giveaways, and vlog guest appearances by authors. Knipe cites the likes of Anita Blake, Harry Dresden, Sookie Stackhouse, and Rachel Morgan as his first forays into the urban fantasy and paranormal genres. "Coupled with all manner of supernatural entities and imaginative world-building," Knipe says, "I find the genre always has something new and exciting to offer."

Originally Sci Fi Guy was born out of a desire to host a dialogue with other SFF readers, but as he reviewed more and more UF/PNR titles, he came to know that community better, and branched out to include interviews and overall coverage of the scene, a move that drew an incredible and engaged group of people right to his virtual doorstep. "Everyone participates — the writers, fellow bloggers, and readers," he gushes. "They are amazingly friendly — almost family — smart and well read across many genres. The majority are women with a smattering of men. Guys still don't seem to have embraced UF but they'll come around."

When asked to sum up his feelings on the books versus the series, Knipe says it's like comparing apples to oranges. "I love the books for the smart, funny, sharp, and observant inner dialogue that makes Sookie real and the stories compelling. *True Blood*'s focus," he continues, "is broader, more of an ensemble, but it explores the same fasci-

True Blood fans flew from all over the United States to party it up at Alex's Bar (a.k.a. Fangtasia) in Long Beach, California. (B. Henderson www.alexander-skarsgardfans.com)

nating and unique world that Harris created and I watch it to see how it can surprise me."

Like many North Americans, Barbara Henderson wasn't aware of Alexander Skarsgård before *True Blood*, but quickly took notice, especially after the success of *Generation Kill*. One night, she was posting on one of HBO's community forums when fans started to bemoan a lack of online coverage for Skarsgård. Henderson decided to take things into her own hands and created Alexander-Skarsgardfans.com saying, "I felt it was time to help others learn about the mysterious Swede. Also, since Eric was one of my favorite characters from the Sookie Stackhouse novels, it just made sense to spend time on the website for his character." The result is certainly one of the handsomest blogs on the internet, chock-full of bright and beautiful images of Skarsgård. It also has an active chat room and forums for fans to gather in.

But Henderson's value to the *True Blood* community, as well as most of the others mentioned here, extends to when she takes her adoration offline. A great number of the images contained in this book were graciously donated by fans and bloggers who traveled far and wide to snap some pics of the people and places that bring them so much joy. One such shot is of Henderson and her friends, a group of women who flew in from different directions, all to sip some drinks and sing karaoke at Alex's Bar, which stands in for Fangtasia. It's a good example of the cyclical nature of social media — each world, online and off, feeds into the other.

Of course, to be a fan doesn't mean you have to like everything. In fact, some fans are quite critical of *True Blood*. Few demonstrate this quite like Simba of Blood Bonds (www.bloodbondsblog.com), whose voice drills down through the saccharine like a stake to the heart. She's smart, crass, and never beats around the bush. One of her beefs was with the portrayal of women in season 2. "They were all pretty much pigeonholed into the madonna or whore category. They were either simpering after men, or if they were strong, they were pretty much evil." She continues, "The worst part was having Sookie as heroine degraded to doing nothing when she was abducted. It's 2009, not 1950. The damsel in distress is just not working anymore."

In fact, Simba is so set in her convictions that she initiated a letter-writing campaign to respond to what she saw as an archetypal white hat/black hat divide between Bill and Eric, a not-uncommon complaint among many fans of books, and something that would have been impossible to mobilize in an era before blogging and online community. Simba explains, "I'm really against the oversimplification of Bill and Eric . . . My natural reaction is to rebel against it . . . They're using the characters as mouthpieces [and] I prefer characters with depth and complexity."

All this energy ultimately comes from a place of passion, and Simba is also quick to celebrate the show's successes along with the other reviewers for the site (such as Lil who also maintains Blood Bond's Twitter and Facebook presence). "I love seeing the world [Alan Ball's] built around sets, costumes, and props, and watching the actors bring the characters to life," she says. "What I've loved most, though, is all the people I've met online who are fans of both the books and series, great for a lit freak/nerd like me." Hence, the focus of Blood Bonds, which Simba says has more to do with providing viewpoints and analysis rather than news or spoilers.

And, finally, there are bloggers who could in most respects be considered autodidacts for the amount of information they collect on vampire-entertainment and mythology. One such individual is Aspasia Bissas. Always "drawn to the darker side of the spectrum," Bissas maintains Blood Lines (bloodtyping.blogspot.com) a mélange of reviews, commentary, and recaps. Her *True Blood* episode guides rival those of professional publications. "I'm a collector of useless information, so I'd say my knowledge of vampire lore is fairly extensive," something she brings to each entry. "The thing with the older mythologies, though, is that they don't exactly resemble our modern idea of a vampire," she continues. "I don't think even the most devoted vampire fan would want to hang out with *lamiae* or Malaysia's intestine-trailing *penanggalang*."

While the internet appears to have all its bases covered with content and engagement, what do you do if you're a complete newbie to online communities? FanBase offers an option for those who want it all, want it now, and want it in one place. With the launch of "I <3 Bon Temps" (www.ilovebontemps.com), FanBase believes they've created the first social site for fans of *True Blood*. It includes forums, groups, personal profiles, and user blogs alongside filming news, games, contests, and giveaways. "We saw a real opportunity to connect Truebies from all of the *True Blood* online communities," a FanBase representative says, "from the official HBO site, the *True Blood* wiki, Facebook, and Twitter." Indeed, visitors can do almost anything from the site. But it's most attractive feature by far has to be the ability for users to change the theme of the page. "This feature allows visitors to switch the design of site to their favorite character: Bill, Sookie, Eric, Pam, or Lafayette, with room to grow to incorporate a completely different homepage with content geared towards that character."

By now it should be apparent that the two things each of these hosts and admins have in common is a desire to start a conversation and the wherewithal to know that while never before has it been so easy to produce, prepare, and promote online content, it takes far more work to keep it running. And with so many destinations to choose from, rather than look at one another as competition, they showcase what they enjoy most, in some cases drawing a hard line between what they will or won't include on their sites. "I don't post gossipy stuff on the blog, or Hollywood stalker-type photos of the actors," Dallas says. "[My visitors] read and discuss about vampires, vampire books, and other vampire TV shows and movies . . . [And] I just don't take sides of 'Team Eric' or 'Team Bill' . . . I really think you miss a lot when you let something like that color your viewing/reading experience."

One fan who takes the whole show in is Jenny Robinson. Robinson doesn't have a Stephen Moyer or Alexander Skarsgård blog, nor does she write about her love of PNR or the Sookie Stackhouse novels. However, she's an expert fan, a mega fan. I came to know Robinson from Twitter when my feed suddenly filled with the live tweets of a woman in attendance at the "Inside the Writers' Room: *True Blood*" panel at the Paley Center for Media. I contacted her at first because I wanted to thank her for sharing with followers across the world what she was able to experience firsthand. But when I asked her why she loved the show, she sent back an email bursting with so much personality and a particular love of music that I asked her for an interview, proving that even tiny 140 character tweets can reach from one stranger to the next. Out of these serendipitous encounters, the most amazing stories unfurl.

A frequent visitor to Alex's Bar (Fangtasia) before *True Blood* started using it as a location, Robinson loves live music, and comes from a lineage that groomed her to appreciate the flavor of *True Blood*'s soundtrack. "With my parents being from Kentucky, the music on *True Blood* hits the bones," she begins. "My 'folks' are actually my grandparents who adopted me when I was super young. My pops was born in 1927, and Ma was born in 1938. They definitely come from different times."

Robinson recalls car trips, children crammed into a Chevy van for days accompanied by Johnny Cash, Willie Nelson, Hank Williams, and Waylon Jennings. "Every time I hear the Grand Ole Opry, I remember those road trips, or music playing from my uncle's house while rain

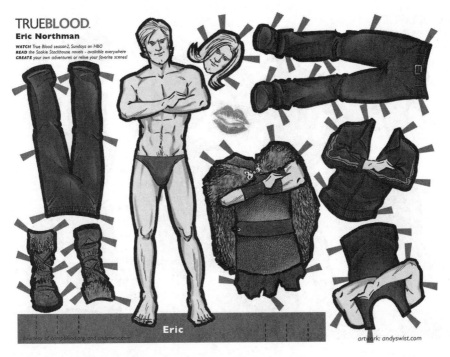

Who do I want to play with today? Viking Eric? Sporty Eric? Racerback Eric? Maybe . . .
Undies Eric! (Andy Swist)

poured down, the steam coming up from the hills. I hear this in *True Blood*. There's a different music vibe in the South." It was Robinson's email that bolstered me on to do research into each of the episode's title songs, her love of music urging me to find the next neat fact, or something unique to connect meaning between the song and the show's themes. "*True Blood*'s music takes me back to memories of super hot humid Kentucky summers . . . Music sets the theme. Someone whose soundtrack is Slayer is definitely in a different place than that of Loretta Lynn." (If you're curious, visit www.RebeccaWilcott.com to see the song list Robinson created for her own personalized *True Blood* soundtrack.)

If you're reading this and still trying to wrap your head around why a community would spend so much time online, imagine the online *True Blood* fan community as a big bar. Every time you sign into a chat room, or log in to Twitter, it's like you've pulled up a stool with no plans

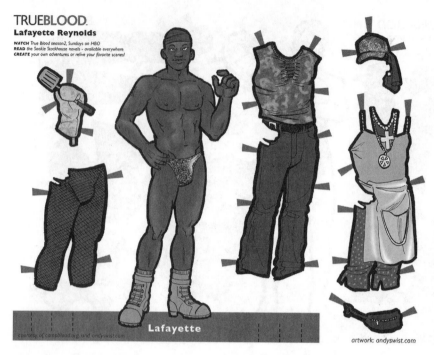

TRUEBLOOD.
Lafayette Reynolds
WATCH *True Blood season 2*, Sundays on HBO
READ the *Sookie Stackhouse novels* - available everywhere
CREATE your own adventures or relive your favorite scenes!

courtesy of campblood.org and andyswist.com

Lafayette

artwork: andyswist.com

Ooh, child! Dress Lafayette up in your love! Find more True Blood paper dolls at
www.AndySwist.com. (Andy Swist)

for the night and it's only a matter of time before someone like Andy Swist shows up and you realize you just haven't seen everything. Swist (of the aforementioned "Blood Work" vlog) is the mastermind behind the *True Blood* dress-up paper dolls found at www.AndySwist.com. The dolls each come with more than one change of clothing and props, their default wardrobe designed to show off their fine (or imagined) physiques.

Swist's clients include DC Comics, Tommy Hilfiger, DKNY, and UGG, among others. When asked to explain the genesis of his *True Blood* character dress-up paper dolls, he replies, "[B]eyond their physical appeal, I love how everyone dresses. It's not surprising to find bedazzled baby tees, Viking battle gear, high fashion couture, and civil war uniforms in a single episode!" Swist launched an online contest to promote the dolls and asked people to take pictures of them in the workplace. He also surfed the internet to find his dolls had been downloaded to places as far-reaching as Brazil and Hungary. The success of the dolls lies, in part, in their disposability. Feasibly, people can keep downloading them and dressing them up in new and exciting ways, which taps into the playful fantasy of online roleplaying. If you can't be Eric, you can at least prop him up on your nightstand.

Does Swist find his dolls particularly camp? "I find the overt sexuality of the vampires in *True Blood* to be a prime source of camp. A vampire's fangs protrude when aroused, their blood makes humans robust and sexual, and sex with a vampire is said to be the best in the world. Drawing them in their underwear as dolls just makes them more ridiculous and fun." But if he were to unplug from the online world and escape to nothing more than a pad and paper, what would his perfect vampire look like? "Vampire Bill's bedroom eyes and brooding good looks," he starts. "Eric Northman's fashionable and sensible slicked hairdo; Drake's formidable physique from *Blade: Trinity*; a pair of sexy red briefs based on Vampirella's costume; Nosferatu's menacing and long, claw-like fingers are a must (so you know he's dangerous); and Morbius, the living vampire's bat-like wings stretching from elbow to waist because they are so cool. Yup, I think that would do nicely."

Season 2
June–September 2009

2.01   Nothing But the Blood
Original air date: June 14, 2009
Written by: Alexander Woo
Directed by: Daniel Minahan

Maryann [to Tara]: If you took care of yourself for once, instead of protecting [Lettie Mae], she'd still be your mother, and you'd just be happier.

Sookie learns that Bill's been keeping secrets. Bon Temps hasn't seen its last murder. Sam comes face-to-face with a part of his past. And Lafayette re-emerges jailed in Fangtasia's basement.

If season 1 shone a light into the darkness to find what lurks there, season 2 drags us kicking and screaming into the light where it's no safer, and it's far more complicated. Most of last season was spent acclimatizing to the characters and their idiosyncrasies, what makes them human or . . . mostly human. This season seems set to challenge the inhumanity and hypocrisies of the people and institutions right under our noses, where consequence is no longer a boundary in the unapologetic pursuit of personal salvation and ecstasy. If last season was about acceptance, season 2 is about taking what's owed to us.

Many of the characters have suffered harsh punishment in the name of playing by their own rules: Lafayette is not dead but, by putting himself so many steps ahead of social mores, he's fallen generations behind, literally shackled like a slave in Fangtasia's basement with Royce, the Merlotte's "AIDS burger" customer, by his side. There's also a lot of confession in this episode. Lafayette is forced to listen to Royce tell him that he accepted sexual favours from another boy when he was young, something that above ground would have no doubt given Lafayette pleasure and leverage. In the basement, he's stripped of his personality, his lost clothing as much a part of his armor as his sharp tongue.

Bill's and Sookie's confessions that they love each other come under duress. Bill doesn't tell Sookie he turned Jessica as punishment for saving her or that he killed Uncle Bartlett until he's confronted on both counts. His apology gets in the way of this climactic moment when they both finally admit their love for one another. What is new, however, is that when they make love, Sookie is presented to us as a woman who knows what she wants. She's a sexual being, her body placed toward the camera. Their connection is less about Bill's need to feed and more about mutual pleasure. When he bites her, Sookie's face fills the frame, her own blood smeared across her lips. Apart, they are different from their communities, but together they are one and the same. As a couple, they show us what they can do when their forces are combined. However, as a doting father and passionate lover, Bill is almost too good to be true in this episode. It's possible that the writers are making a conscious effort to differentiate him from Eric, who is clearly devoid of compassion as he tears Royce limb from limb in a monstrous display.

Renewal seems to be another theme this season, second chances and what we choose to do with them. In particular focus are the methods we use to rear our children. Bill steps into his guardian role reluctantly, but with commitment. Jessica will be reckless if she isn't shown boundaries. He wishes only to arm her with what she needs to keep herself,

The foyer in Bill Compton's home. (Jodi Ross, courtesy of The Vault www.trueblood-online.com)

and others, from harm: essentially her own code. Lettie Mae, meanwhile, abandons Tara, leaving her with no option but to do what she must to survive. With little money and no education to get herself ahead, Tara must consider Maryann the coolest mother on the block, if not a little overwhelming. The irony of Lettie Mae's condition, however, is that she's merely traded in one addiction for another, booze for Jesus, anything to keep her from having to be accountable to others. Maryann woos Tara with luxuries, intoxicants, and an exotic intellect that embraces sensuality and the belief that we are not so separate from our gods. She also helps foster Tara's attraction to Eggs, a flawed but deeply kind man that Tara may be able to trust.

Jason takes another big step on his path out of darkness as he prepares to join the Light of Day Institute run by Reverend Steve Newlin, son of the murdered Reverend

A photo in Bill Compton's home, presumably of his Civil War bride. (Jodi Ross, courtesy of The Vault www.trueblood-online.com)

Theodore Newlin of the Fellowship of the Sun. By attending the leadership conference, Jason will become a child of the Lord and a soldier for God, believing that religion is bigger than hate. The hypocrisy of this is revealed in Steve's statement to Nan Flanagan of the AVL (American Vampire League), that by having no concept of life, vampires have no difficulty killing. However, it's not the killing the church is opposed to, but that it's not done in the name of anything. Vampires are godless creatures. Jason is simple, but he's driven purely by purpose at this point. Point him toward a target and he will satisfy his mission. Amen.

Sam is the least likely to come into the light any time soon, least of all now that he's officially out of the running for Sookie's affections, the only person who saw him for who he is. If he does step further out of the closet, it won't be of his own volition but Maryann's. When he broke into her house as a young man, she devoured him sexually, assuming a pose similar to the bird lady statue in her living room. Sam experiences the same fear upon seeing Maryann again for the first time since he was a youngster as Sookie did upon seeing her Uncle Bartlett at Gran's funeral.

It's hard to take your eyes off Michelle Forbes. She already owns the role, inciting panic in a glance. Her house is littered with animal statues and effigies, two horns adorning her mantle like sculptures. In her backyard, Maryann has a large painting of the Greek god Pan and his human lover. Pan was known largely for his love of music, and his ability to incite arousal or panic, depending on his objectives. As the season proceeds, we'll begin to see stronger ties between mythology and the characters.

It promises to be the season of Gods versus Man, mischief versus morality, and revolution versus religion. That's an awful lot on one plate, but offers something for everyone. Order up, indeed!

Highlight: Jason: "I can't help it, Sook, I loved [Amy]. And when you love someone, you gotta love it all. Otherwise, it ain't love."

Nightcap: Maryann and Sam own similar horse's heads. Maryann's is life-sized and on display in her home, whereas Sam's is much smaller, tucked away in his office. Stephen Moyer shaved his chest for season 2. To prepare for her role as Maryann Forrester, Michelle Forbes watched Ken Russell films and channeled '80s artist Lydia Lunch. Cindy Jackson (www.cjackson sculpture.com), who sculpted the replica "Bird Lady" for this episode, had less than three days to create three copies of the sculpture. Working under a tight deadline was no challenge for the artist, who has also designed toys for Happy Meals (*The Simpsons*, the Yoshi toys, and the *Hercules* toys, just to

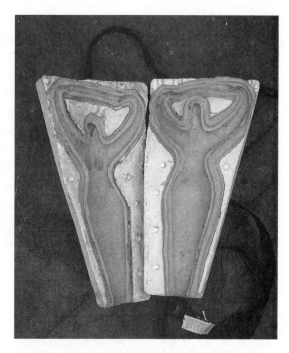

The molds sculptor Cindy Jackson used to create The Bird Lady replica, which Sam takes from Maryann's home. (Cindy Jackson)

name a few). However, it was a first for her to complete the project from her kitchen, her studio having just been demolished by a wayward driver!

Paging Dr. Creepy: Miss Jeanette's dead body, with its gaping chest wound and terrified expression, looks like something out of Madame Tussaud's Wax Museum, or a taxidermy specimen, her carcass re-stuffed and displayed for posterity.

Location, Location, Location: South of Pasadena, California, Maryann's mansion is located close to the Huntington Library and Gardens, the Santa Anita Racecourse, and the L.A. Arboretum, all popular filming destinations.

Suzuki Sets the Scene: This episode's script called for a primitive piece of art, like a dancing girl. Ingerslev's team went to the internet for inspiration, perusing Mycenaean, Etruscan, and Minoan influences in particular. They stumbled on the Bird Lady, an existing Egyptian sculpture found in the Brooklyn Museum, at once modern and primitive. The crew felt it best represented Maryann's nature, reflected in the many scenes where she's shown arms raised over head, communing with her god.

Encore: During the end credits we hear "Nothing But the Blood (Of Jesus)," performed by Randy Travis, which is an actual church hymn. In 1989, the United

Methodist Church made changes to the 962-page *United Methodist Hymnal* to modernize the text. Changes include altering masculine pronouns to gender-neutral pronouns, although all references to God as "Master," "Father," and "King" remained as is. The line "white as snow" was changed to "bright as snow" to remove any connection between race and sin, and the suggestion that white is pure, while black is not. While *True Blood*, overall, doesn't delve deeply into race politics, this episode provides the image of a captured and humiliated black man in chains who watches as Eric dismembers another man, limb from limb. Nothing is as pure as it seems. Maryann's oasis is shrouded in a cloud of pot smoke; the Newlin's message of hope is wrapped in self-agenda; the one person who knows Sam best is the one person he's most terrified of; Uncle Bartlett's money paves (or pays) Jason's way into a community of bigots; and the reciprocal flow between Sookie and Bill may connect them deeper to one another, but it's at the risk of severing all other ties to family, friendship, and community.

2.02   Keep This Party Going

Original air date: June 21, 2009
Written by: Brian Buckner
Directed by: Michael Lehmann

> **Maryann:** [to Daphne] [Y]ou care about doing a good job. Now you just keep on caring, and one day you'll be the best at what you do. That's my advice.

Sookie and Bill argue over how to "raise" Jessica. Jason excels at the Light of Day Institute. Maryann casts a spell over the customers at Merlotte's.

To paraphrase Bill, the characters are caught in the grip of overwhelming transformation, doing what they can to get back to their humanity. And every step of the way, there's another challenge or person putting up roadblocks. The writers toss us a bone when Bill and Sookie say they shouldn't get used to fighting so they don't become "one of those couples" — they don't want us to wonder why they bother with one another — yet we had to know that their trials wouldn't be over.

Eric is shown as truly monstrous, his strength and psychotic focus further dividing him from humanity and even Bill as one of his own kind. Similarly, at the shinier, happier Light of Day Institute, Steve Newlin's maniacal optimism presents the perfect companion to Eric's mission of self-preservation. Their hair says it all. They're the two most coiffed characters in the show — they don't groom to blend in. They've each been chosen to watch over their flock, enforce the rules, and recruit anyone who could help their cause. (Eric needs Sookie and the Newlins need Jason.)

Even the taxidermy knows how to party at Merlotte's. (Jodi Ross, courtesy of The Vault www.trueblood-online.com)

By comparison, Bill looks like a garden-variety, middle-of-the-road conservative. While he tries to remember Jessica is not just a new vampire but also a teenaged girl, Sookie steps in as a surrogate caregiver, talking Jessica through her first experience of crying blood as if it's her first period. She's literally going through "the change," not just physically but emotionally. When she attacks her father, it's not simple revenge but symbolic of a young woman who is tired of being defined by others' perceptions of her. Bill arrives in time, glamouring Jessica's younger sister, Eden, into inviting him in, a reminder to Jessica that while he may not be her father, he is a patriarch of sorts, able to make the rules wherever he goes because of his powers. When Bill tells Eden (named after a place of peace and bliss) that he can make the worst of it go away, we know that he's planning to glamour her. But Bill will have to learn what every parent must eventually: that we can't protect our children from everything forever.

However, in Eric's home, Fangtasia, Bill's influence is barely felt. The scene in which Bill is caught between Sookie and Eric (deciding whether or not she'll go to Dallas to help retrieve Godric, Sheriff of Area Nine) is further evidence of his struggle to come out of the coffin and stay out. He's more often than not caught between a rock and a hard place. By trying to refuse Eric's bid to have Sookie travel to Dallas, Bill thwarts Sookie's ability to arrive at her own decisions independently. However, if he concedes to Eric, he is following a code he believes to be outdated. This struggle is what we love about Bill — not to mention how amusing it is to watch Bill and Sookie all but exchange roles in each other's worlds (he as caregiver and her as supernatural hero) — but by challenging Eric's authority, Bill risks attracting the ire of his Sheriff, a vampire who doesn't care for humans' personal politics.

Tara is also struggling to figure out what she needs and where she stands in her newfound family. In her case she's not used to taking without giving. Even though she doesn't trust Maryann's generosity, she's directionless. Eggs believes you have to say what you want, out loud. Moving in with Sookie would allow them to reconnect as family, but it's still not the independence she's seeking. Maryann knows Tara wasn't raised with any guidance, using any doubts Tara may have to control her with ease. That shot of Maryann leaning against the bar is incredible. She just has to look at Tara and the girl is incapable of speech. *Tara.* That's quite a party trick.

Instead of Tara's caustic nature from season 1, we get a chance to see her in more understated scenes — notably with Eggs and Sookie — and it shows just how bright and thoughtful she really is. Before, she deserved good things but didn't know how to ask for, or appreciate, them. Now that she can, she has good reason to question Maryann's motivation, but it's at the risk of losing every comfort she's never had. Her scene with Sookie shows just how far they've each come. They're mature women compared to the beginning of season 1, each deciding what's best for herself. It's also nice to see Rutina Wesley continue to play a range outside of reactive anger.

Nelsan Ellis also delivers a powerful performance. Lafayette, the man with a plan, is humiliated and broken. In his fight to survive, he bargains, prepared to cheat death by asking to be turned, which would enslave him to Eric for eternity.

The chain around Lafayette's neck is akin to Jason's Light of Day ring of honesty, requiring them to speak the truth if they know what's best for them. However, Lafayette learns that there's no guaranteed reward for spilling everything he knows. And as Jason wrestles with guilt and flashbacks of Eddie being staked, will he share his past in order to cleanse his sins? He hasn't been a winner in a long time. Jason's story in particular could be seen as a metaphor for religious organizations that boast their ability to "de-homosexualize" gays and lesbians. To reveal his true nature would be to risk his new community, purpose, and to give the upper hand to Luke, his Andy-like nemesis.

As Sookie listens in on Maryann's thoughts she hears a foreign language. Maryann is focused on the word "bacchus," the Greek god Dionysus. Dionysus inspires people into states of ecstasy, engaging all impulses, especially sexual. In this state, they lose self-control, often hunting down and devouring the flesh of animals and humans alike. Miss Jeanette was missing her heart, and Maryann proves to be ravenous at

Merlotte's. Is she the killer, or is the killer one of her minions? As the entire bar, save for Sam, writhes to music, her ability to persuade any human to do her bidding opens up most of the town as possible suspects. As Jane Bodehouse's eyes black over, we remember some of Miss Jeanette's last words to Tara before her exorcism, that the eyes are the windows to the soul. We remember the little girl who came from the woods, her eyes also blackened over. What we took to be hallucination now seems more real. In which case, we have to ask, did Tara really kill a child?

Another big episode with big implications for the characters. Father figures, or lack thereof, will be an ongoing theme this season. Most of the main characters are father-less: Sookie, Jason, Sam, Tara, Eggs. And while we've heard that Lafayette has a mother, there's been no mention of his father. Vampire Bill may well be the only present father figure, guardianship so forced upon him that Jessica's very conception was played out in full view of the tribunal like they were at a tailgate party.

Highlight: Lafayette: "I'm a survivor first, capitalist second, and a whole bunch of shit after that. But a hooker dead last. So if I've got even a Jew at an Al Qaida pep rally's shot at getting my black ass up out of this motherfucker, I'm taking it!"

Nightcap: Daphne is Merlotte's bumbling new waitress. In Greek mythology, Daphne is a river nymph who was turned into a laurel tree by her mother, Gaia, to escape Apollo's unwanted advances. He created a crown out of her leaves and branches. In season 1, Amy told Jason about Gaia on the night they met.

Relationship Crypt Falls: Sookie, Sookie, Sookie. You meant well, but taking Jessica to see her parents is kind of like that aunt who gets her sister's kid drunk on coolers. In hindsight, wasn't such a bright idea. And how is lying to Bill any better than him lying to you? *Tsk, tsk.*

Paging Dr. Creepy: Lafayette is no stranger to personal grooming. He works out, primps, and waxes. While he isn't afraid to get his hands dirty, we know that he has his limits, notably with blood. Taking Eddie's blood was a sterile, spiritual act, performed with respect and care, but he drew the line at letting Eddie feed on him. Even without that backstory, the sight of Lafayette in the basement, trying to grab Royce's leg is upsetting enough, his bare feet wrapped up in bloody tendons, eventually pulling the metal pin from bone with his teeth. But the shudder-inducing moment comes just before that, when Lafayette breaks through the cartilage, digging his hand inside like it's a lobster tail.

Encore: "Keep This Party Going," performed by The B-52s, plays during the dance party at Merlotte's. Go to church on Sunday. Party on Monday. And every other day of the week. This isn't the first song one might expect to find on the Merlotte's jukebox, but Alan Ball is a big fan of the band, and it tells us everything we need to know about Maryann's energy and influence over Merlotte's patrons, who seem powerless to keep themselves from giving in to a good time. Sam knows the score, but is unable to do anything. The B-52s are perhaps best known for their joyfully subversive pop and it's what makes this track off their album *Funplex* the ideal choice. Because while "Love Shack" would have been just as appropriate thematically speaking, mainstream approval has all but stripped it of its raunch factor. Behind the beehive hairstyles, wildly patterned jackets, and go-go drum beats, The B-52s are the alternative band that infiltrated the ranks of mainstream radio. They're our man on the inside, with "Keep This Party Going" adopted as Maryann's sugarcoated anthem of scandal and debauchery.

2.03   Scratches

Original air date: June 28, 2009
Written by: Raelle Tucker
Directed by: Scott Winant

Sookie: The more open my mind gets, the more evil I see.

Sookie is attacked by a mysterious creature, and Bill is forced to ask Eric for help. Jessica and Hoyt meet. Tara starts to question Maryann's motives.

"Hating evil is loving good." To survive, Steve Newlin says we need hate. In the war against evil incarnate — vampires — Jason comes up against his first challenge: Steve's wife, Sarah. Jason has had no shortage of forthright women in his life, so when Sarah divulges that she was once a vampire sympathizer he has every reason to believe that she's a kindred spirit. This purging is also easier to accept than the dream Jason had about a naked Eddie gearing up to feed on him. However, Sarah's a parasite who draws her energy from sheltering herself in others, taking more than she offers in return. Sarah tells Jason that everything about a vampire down to their blood is seduction, yet she employs her own seething sexuality in a way that will soon start to suck energy from Jason, especially as he commits deeper to abstinence and a pure lifestyle.

Sookie is attacked by a half-human/half-creature that looks like the Minotaur. In Greek mythology, the Minotaur was eventually killed by Theseus, who battled foes that subscribed to primitive religious and social order. Could there be a Theseus among the citizens of Bon Temps, willing to take on a creature so mysterious that even Eric hasn't heard of it? Sookie's wounds are parasitic. The scratches are intended to weaken her, allowing the hunter to reserve his energy while his victim perishes, making it ultimately easier for the creature to complete its task. We get a good idea of what that might be when we see Carl and Maryann preparing a soup containing organs, later fed to guests of Maryann's backyard party. What could the purpose of this be, other than to enjoy the feeling of manipulation that comes from feeding people one of their own?

That only a few of Maryann's guests' eyes have blackened suggests that some individuals are either more prone to influence than others, or less inhibited to cross the divide between humans and gods. It appears the adage is true, that dancing leads to sex. But to what end? Who is Maryann and why is she in Bon Temps?

The storyline with Eggs and Tara is at a standstill. As Tara starts to clue in that things are not right in Maryann's world, leaving the party to go up to bed isn't the answer — getting as far from that house as possible is. In the books, Eggs's part is much smaller, so his storyline with Tara sometimes feels as forced as Amy's with Jason from season 1. It's not the most enthralling writing, perhaps because the sexual tension and debauchery are a distraction from real character development.

If there was a doctor in Bon Temps, somebody would have something to say about all the fried items on Merlotte's menu. It's not the vampires killing the citizens! (Jodi Ross, courtesy of The Vault www.trueblood-online.com)

Bill continues to straddle (or confuse?) his own line between good and evil, even after he sees what Eric has done to Lafayette while held in captivity. Bill has seen and possibly done far worse, so anything about Eric that is less than evil is a kindness. While Sookie sees mostly good in Bill, she knows there's darkness. By the end of this episode, he appears to have come closer to understanding what she needs — a simple shoulder touch — and what it takes to support her, which is standing by her side while she negotiates with Eric the terms of her trip to Dallas to help find Godric.

However, yet again Sookie's acceptance forgives Bill's completely out-of-check anger earlier in the episode when he accused her of undermining his authority by taking Jessica to see her parents. It was a mistake, but in that moment, Sookie had every good reason to get out of the car — although leaving an enraged Bill alone with

Tribute: Kristin Bauer (Pam Ravenscroft)

> "If it were multiple choice, choice A would be
> Sookie; choice B would be [Fangtasia waitress]
> Ginger; choice C would be Jessica. I would go all
> the way down to the multiple choice Z where it says
> 'Everyone' and pick that one! I could see Pam with
> anybody and everybody . . ."
>
> — Kristin Bauer on possible female love
> interests in season 3

Some say that behind every great man there's a great woman. Others say that a woman needs a man like a fish needs a bicycle. I'd say that Pam Ravenscroft is her own man, and needs only what she takes. She is, however, devoted to her maker, Eric, and works alongside him in any capacity that he wishes: co-owner of Fangtasia, henchman, and one-time lover. To dismiss Pam as subservient to Eric would be to underestimate her abilities (which are so fine-tuned she simply doesn't raise a finger unless she knows she'll find the pulse) and Eric's choice in partners for all immortality. Yet, as Eric would throw himself on the cross for Godric, so too would Pam for Eric. In her case, she'd more likely saunter toward it, arrange herself upon it, apply one last coat of lipstick, and make sure her pumps are fitting snugly before allowing death to commence.

In their portrayals of Eric and Pam, Alexander Skarsgård and Kristin Bauer fall into the rhythm of sibling rivalry, something slightly absurd like out of a Wes Anderson film, eccentric, witty, and bored with, if not disappointed in, (eternal) life. *The Royal Tenenbaums* with a killer fashion sense.

Kristin Bauer, I would lay my coat across the swamp lands to keep your Betsey Johnsons clean.

Where you've seen Kristin Bauer: *Seinfeld, Romy and Michele's High School Reunion, That's Life, CSI, Desperate Housewives, Dirty Sexy Money, Boston Legal, Bones, Private Practice, Three Rivers*

Photos of cast and crew are cleverly tacked on the wall behind Merlotte's bar. (Jodi Ross, courtesy of The Vault www.trueblood-online.com)

Jessica wasn't very nice — where, of course, she gets attacked. It seems that any time Sookie decides what's good for herself she gets attacked or, at the very least, makes herself vulnerable. The Rattrays, Rene, now this. The writers risk sending the message to young women that if they're planning to return to their men after a fight, then best not to bother making a fuss in the first place because they'll just get beaten, battered, or scratched. And Bill calling Sookie a child combined with the reality that she practically is one compared to his 173 years, not to mention how he's had to feed her a few times now to keep her alive, comes dangerously close to infantilization. Sookie has grown up so much, and it's time we should be seeing her as flawed without being reduced to an adolescent.

Now that the Greek mythology is dropping like nymphs (Daphne), Terry is starting to resemble Cassandra the prophet whose gift is also accompanied by a great deal of pain and frustration. She could see the future, but was cursed in that no one would believe a word she said, something that's echoed in Terry's post traumatic stress disorder. He's seen things, and a result appears to be even more sensitive to those around him, a cross he bears with a lot of discomfort. In one version of the myth, Cassandra has a deeper understanding of animal behavior rather than an ability to see the future, a trait that would make Terry's relationship with Sam so much more compelling. It's like he can smell the fear on Sam when it appears he's packing up to leave town. "Remind me never to get stuck in a foxhole with ya. Coward." Like most prophets, Terry isn't appreciated in his own town. And what a perfect character to inhabit this trait, a human for whom the line between good and evil is already supremely shaky.

As for Sam, his coat has lost some of its sheen. But Daphne, who got a whole lot more interesting this episode, managing to approach Sam without his detection, looks to shake things up. When we see the scratches on her back, we have to wonder how she healed. If she'd been saved by vampires, there'd be no trace of the wounds. Does the creature kill only some victims, and save others? If so, for what purpose? Also, Daphne's likeness to Sookie of yore is striking, so it seems all but certain that Sam will give her more than a passing glance. After both Tara and Sookie rejected him, he could use some fun, and Daphne seems willing to provide it.

The scene in which Jessica and Hoyt meet for the first time is a highlight. Sometimes, it's like the universe plops people down in front of us for all right reasons. For the first time, we feel worthy and desirable. That's the PG-rated version, anyway. When Hoyt asks if Jessica is "hungry," his question piques a host of possibilities while she swoons over the pumping jugular in his neck, his blood coursing to a tipping point. Earlier, Eggs told Tara he's always felt that if he was good at something it must be a waste of time. For Hoyt (and Jessica while she was human), being nice is the thing he does best, yet it hasn't won him any girlfriends and his mother talks down to him. He spends most of his time apologizing. But it would take a truly nice guy to see Jessica for who she is and not try to change her. It's been inferred that Hoyt might be a virgin, so if in fact he's been holding out for the right girl, he may have been waiting a long time, but it won't have been a waste.

Back at the Compton compound, Jessica pops fang, a wonderful comment on how women get turned on too, and Hoyt says exactly the right thing, that it's natural. Bill, in typical form, walks in on them, and tosses Jessica across the room, showing he's just as susceptible to erratic impulses as any new vampire or emotionally wrought human.

Highlight: Hoyt: "You should try the chicken-fried steak. It's like a chicken and a steak got together and made a baby. It's a delicious, crispy baby."

Nightcap: More Pam! Just the cocky swivel of her hips is enough to rival Lafayette for his sharp tongue and sexual charms. While she's often lazy, she will do the job, be it overseeing Bill to make sure he finishes turning Jessica, or searching the woods for evidence of the creature that attacked Sookie. She does things with style, getting dirty if she has to. (But, Pam, we think you like it.) Before *True Blood*, Raelle Tucker, who penned this episode, was a writer and executive story editor for *Supernatural*, CW's

Tribute: Jim Parrack (Hoyt Fortenberry)

"As outrageous as it sounds to have, you know, a
newly turned vampire fall in love with a 28-year-old
guy who lives with his mother, it seems like it's one
of the more grounded storylines."

— Jim Parrack

I know there are a lot of "Bill and Sookie Forever" fans out there, and that
many of you list the scene in which they meet for the first time in Merlotte's
among your favorites. But, I'll confess, if I owned His and Her mugs, one
would bear the image of Hoyt Fortenberry, the other adorned with
Jessica's soft curls. For me, the scene in which they meet for the first time
in Merlotte's is my personal pick for the sweetest, most playfully seductive
scene so far. Oh, all hands are on the table, all right, but this ain't no
innocent meet 'n' greet. Hoyt and Jessica are not only both virgins: they're
each seeking a partner whose interests and skill sets match the other's,
something that in most societies requires a trip to a niche bar, or an
anonymous online profile.

But Bon Temps has been awakened to the reality of consensual adult
situations and Merlotte's is like those small-town gay bars, come-as-you-
are watering holes where patrons inevitably learn to accept things out of
the norm because there's simply nowhere else to go. Why not take the risk
and do exactly as you feel? That's what I saw when Hoyt and Jessica first
sat across from one another and realized they were among their own kind.

And all that talk of chicken and steak coming together to make a delicious,
crispy baby . . . Until that point, a chicken-fried steak likely was the most
orgasmic experience Hoyt had ever had, certainly in public. Their love is
sweet and romantic because *they* are sweet and romantic. And it's their
honesty with themselves and each other that makes my heart soar.

Where you've seen Jim Parrack: *Monk, Annapolis, ER, CSI, Grey's Anatomy,
Criminal Minds, Supernatural*

series about two brothers who hunt evil monsters. Dr. Ludwig is played by Marcia de
Rousse, a little person who's a medium, healer, and animal communicator. In the
scene where Eric asks Pam and Chow to search the woods for the creature that

attacked Sookie, Eric says, "*Du hörde vad jag sa*" which means "You heard what I said." The Fangtasia T-shirt Sookie wears reads, "Life Begins at Night." On the back it lists the address at 44 Industrial Drive, Shreveport, LA. The lagoon Sam swims in is actually only waist high. He had to crouch during filming to make it look as if it was much deeper.

Relationship Crypt Falls: Bill, that's a neat trick you have getting Jessica to do things as her maker. Nothing against setting boundaries, but try a little tenderness. You yell an awful lot at the women in your life. Mind you, they're feisty. But if you crossed Eric, you know he could snap you like a twig and would have the authority to do so. You don't respect him, so much as fear him and respect the vampire order. When it comes to Jessica, don't abuse your authority. It's true, you have a lot on your plate, but don't become one of those dads who always chooses work over family. Work/life balance, Bill. There must be a happy medium between controlling Jessica's every move in order to ensure the preservation of your kind and giving the kid a room of her own.

Paging Dr. Creepy: Credit must be given to the sound editors on this show. More often than not, something that is moderately creepy becomes gut wrenching with the addition of an effect. Dr. Ludwig digging her finger into Sookie's wounds is compounded greatly with the inclusion of a foley effect that sounds like a mixture of toothpaste being strangled through a piping bag lined with battery acid.

Suzuki Sets the Scene: While the interior and exterior of an existing house was used for Maryann's mansion, Ingerslev's team did a lot to affect the mood of the location, bringing in new patio furniture, plants, countless flowers, and, notably, the Pan mural beside the pool. Based on a sculpture Alan Ball found from the Roman Empire, the female human figure was modified to resemble Maryann.

Encore: During the end credits we hear "Scratches," performed by Debbie Davies. Davies is a blues performer. She's been the featured guitarist in Maggie Mayall and the Cadillacs, Fingers Taylor and the Ladyfinger Revue, and The Icebreakers. Aside from her solo career, Davies has worked with artists such as Tommy Shannon, Chris Layton, Coco Montoya, J. Geils, and Duke Robillard. "Scratches" appears on her 1998 album *Round Every Corner*. Taken literally, it's a nod to one of the episode's most dramatic plot points, Sookie's attack. But it's also a playful and upbeat reprieve from the relationship drama of Bill and Sookie, replaced by the hopefulness of Hoyt and Jessica; not to mention what we as viewers now know about vampire sex. Taken to the other limits, "Scratches" acknowledges what many have been noting since the series began: the not-so-subtle connection between violence and pleasure. (All that's missing is a safe word.)

2.04   Shake and Fingerpop

Original air date: July 12, 2009
Written by: Alan Ball
Directed by: Michael Lehmann

> **Jason [upon being pranked]:** Vampires are not a joke! There's a war goin' on
> and you're either on the dark side or you're on the side of the light.
> And there ain't no in between.

Bill, Sookie, and Jessica take a trip to Dallas to help find Godric but are greeted by an unexpected visitor. Jason becomes a Soldier of the Sun and moves into the Newlins' house. Maryann throws Tara a surprise birthday party. And Daphne shares a secret with Sam.

Since Jason has been on the losing side, he's gone from golden god to the kid who got sand kicked in his face with Luke as his bully. When his bunk house plays a practical joke on him, he retaliates with fear, violence, and a script he learned from listening to Steve Newlin. Does he believe what he's saying, or is he just clinging to whatever will keep him safe, out of harm's way, and in the favor of those in a position to take care of him? In the absence of true self-confidence, Jason wants

The foyer of Gran's house, featuring family photos of Sookie, Jason, and who we assume to be their parents. (Jodi Ross, courtesy of The Vault www.trueblood-online.com)

someone to please. Until it's Sarah Newlin, her husband will have to do. He takes a jaunt with Steve to shoot up fake vampires, like a father and son at the batting cage. Around the dinner table, Steve tells Jason that he's needed, asking him to become a Soldier of the Sun.

The theme of self-loathing is stronger in some characters than others. Andy is still off the wagon, avoiding his home life. Jason is lost, and appears only to thrive in a state of adrenalin. When left with his own thoughts, he's less clear, such as when Luke suggests that he only became a Soldier to keep Sarah Newlin entertained. And self-hatred has always been apparent in Tara who, after finally gathering the strength to leave Maryann's, finds herself alone on her birthday, and lets Maryann into Sookie's home to throw a raucous party. More music. More booze. More investment in seeing Tara and Eggs together. As Tara and Eggs consummate their relationship, the only two people at the party high on each other but nothing else are Sam and Daphne, impervious to Maryann's influence. Which means Daphne is not human.

Sookie finally calls Bill on hating vampires after he treats Jessica like a predator for bringing Hoyt to their home. In keeping with the LGBT themes of the show, Bill explains that when he was made vampire he didn't have the option to mainstream. Vampires were outlaws, akin to gays and lesbians trying to find one another in secret bars, often passing as the opposite gender so they could be seen together in public. Bill envies Jessica, knowing she'll have it easier for being able to live openly, even if she has some growing up to do.

It's been a while since we had an episode as fun as this one, a nice break from the darker shows of late. Sookie's travel dress to Dallas is a ray of yellow sunshine in the dead of night. Jessica's coffin prat fall is hilarious! Deborah Ann Woll has really hit her stride as Jessica, finding just the right intersection between naughty rebel and liberated teenager. Even the scene in which Bill and Sookie learn that the Fellowship of the Sun sent Leon to capture them at the airport is lighthearted, written to show Bill's evolution as a sentient being as much as for exposition. Eric is back to his sultry self, offering his blood to Lafayette so he can track someone Sookie cares about, something he finds curious. Could Eric be evolving? Is it all business for this 1,000-year-old vampire, or can you teach an old dog new tricks? But more important, Lafayette is back, and with a kick in his step, no less!

Soon enough, it will be back to business. If Godric, twice as old as Eric, and the oldest vampire in the new world, can be captured by the Fellowship of the Sun, then all vampires are vulnerable, a cost of coming out of the coffin. Jason will have to man up, but will it be for his God or for mortal sins of the flesh with Sarah Newlin? And as the episode closes, after 25 years alone in her own head, Sookie meets another telepath, Barry the Bellboy.

Tribute: Anna Camp (Sarah Newlin)

> "I think [the writers] did a good job of showing that Sarah is not just this spiteful power-hungry woman . . . she's definitely hurt and lost and looking for answers."
>
> – Anna Camp

Anna Camp lights up the small screen every time she appears as Sarah Newlin, the somewhat hapless wife of Reverend Steve Newlin, leader of the Fellowship of the Sun Church. While Steve is calculated in his measures, Sarah is a genuine blind follower, having given herself over to faith to the same degree that Jason Stackhouse salutes his awesome manhood.

But if you really want to see Anna's blinding light shine bright, you must watch her in the *Reflections of Light* videos produced by the Fellowship of the Sun, where Sarah's hair is high, and so is she, on love for her main men, God and Steve. Camp's portrayal of Sarah's spiritual devotion and pursuit of all things glorious is nothing less than the ecstasy Maryann Forrester pursues. The bruises may be fewer, but both women are vessels over which another entity has authority, and they know how to move those vessels. (See Sarah's finger-lickin' BBQ dance scene in "Shake and Fingerpop.")

Anna Camp, I present you with all the pudding in the world, and a side of BBQ sauce thrown in for good measure, so you can get on with the real business of breaking Sarah out of her shell!

Where you've seen Anna Camp: *Glee, The Office, Cashmere Mafia, Numb3rs*

Highlight: Sookie [on mini liquor bottles]: "I've always loved these; they're like booze for dolls! They gave me ten!"

Nightcap: At Sookie's, Tara watches the Pamplona bull-run on television, a sly tip to the "bull-man" that's killing people in Bon Temps. The airline Bill, Sookie, and Jessica take to Dallas is called Anubis, named after an Egyptian god associated with mummification and protecting the dead as they prepare for the afterlife. When Eric comes to Lafayette's window, Lafayette's watching *Jason and the Argonauts* (1963), which features a sequence of reanimated skeletons. (This effect was originated in *The 7th Voyage of*

Sinbad (1958), which is perhaps why it's erroneously reported in places that it's *The 7th Voyage of Sinbad* playing on the television.) In the film, Jason is a legendary Greek hero. It's possible the Greek Jason is a reference to Jason Stackhouse's assertion that he's in a war, and he's ready to fight. When Bill and Sookie check into the Hotel Carmilla, Sookie suggests refering to Jessica as his ward, she the Dick Grayson (Robin) to his Bruce Wayne (Batman). The films playing on the hotel pay-per-view adult channel are *Intercourse with the Vampire, His First Fangbang*, and *Co-Ed Chowdown*.

Relationship Crypt Falls: Bill, you really need to pick up a copy of Don Miguel Ruiz's book *The Four Agreements*. The first agreement — "Be Impeccable With Your Word" — will help you keep a lid on it in situations where you feel challenged as Jessica's maker, and serve to remind you that what you say will be imprinted upon her for eternity, not just until she's 18 and moves out of the manor. You're lucky to have such a smart and kind progeny. And if that doesn't work, give yourself a time out. Sleep on it, and come back fresh the next dusk.

Paging Dr. Creepy: To the woman shoveling dirt into her mouth at Tara's birthday party: you missed the cake table. First, close your mouth while you eat. Second, while communing with nature is a beautiful thing, all of Bon Temps has communed in that very spot. Three, pesticides are the leading cause of gum disease in people who *eat dirt*. In conclusion, the next time you feel the need to feast rabidly, reach out for a handful of celery. It protects your teeth by producing saliva that neutralizes the bacteria in your mouth, lessening the chance of cavities. You'll have a whiter smile, and your dentist will love you!

Encore: As Sam comes to Tara's birthday party, we hear "Shake and Fingerpop," performed by Junior Walker. Walker started his career in his early teens in the late 1940s, his signature wailing saxophone style garnering the attention of Motown Records; he signed with their Soul imprint in the early '60s. His sound is also immediately recognizable to fans of Foreigner's smash hit "Urgent." Inducted into the Rhythm and Blues Foundation in 1995, Walker died the same year. The saxophone really is the star of this "Shake and Fingerpop." It's impossible to hear it and not picture Rutina Wesley breaking it down, showing off a sliver of what she had to do for *How She Move*. And with Walker's sax reigning supreme, I can't hear the instrument in a show with vampires and not think about another rowdy group party piped in by Tim Cappello on "I Still Believe" in *The Lost Boys*.

2.05   Never Let Me Go

Original air date: July 19, 2009
Written by: Nancy Oliver
Directed by: John Dahl

Sam: [to Daphne] You're a . . .

Daphne: . . . a shapeshifter, and damn proud of it!

In Dallas, Sookie gets to know another telepath. At the Light of Day Institute, Jason receives a reward. Eric reflects on the moment he was turned.

Despite all the time Bill spends proclaiming he's a vampire, Jessica's a vampire, Eric's a vampire, we're all vampires, he's lost that edge that made him most intriguing from the earliest episodes of season 1. While Sookie and Bill have hit their stride in bed, the rest of us still need pillow talk. The underlying menace is gone, replaced with an existential brooding that he feels compelled to protect those he cannot control, relying on Sookie to make him feel like a man. And as their sex is tied to his feeding, it won't be long before that's just another domestic duty. Forcing monogamy on a vampire seems almost ludicrous, even if it sustains our sense of a romantic ideal. Conversely, a large part of this show's success is precisely because it taps into alternative lifestyles. Bill and Sookie's relationships does, however, work well in opposition to the crude orgies Maryann induces, further supporting that vampires are not entirely unlike humans in their pursuit of lasting companionship. In that sense, monogamy is the more alternative lifestyle on a show where few have had ease finding and keeping a mate who isn't a killer, closeted shifter, or murder victim. Still, why waste the best metaphors in favor of showing us something we can get in any other soap opera? This isn't *The Munsters*.

In fact, most of the colorful traits of our most treasured characters have been muted, or mutated. We wouldn't expect Lafayette to bounce back quickly from what he's been through, but he's infused with Eric's blood. Sookie waxed poetic about sausage after she'd gotten a taste of Bill. Showing the effects of Eric on Lafayette would have been both organic to the storyline and a forgivable way to help Lafayette move past his hostage experience, knowing that at any moment Eric can haunt Lafayette like one of Terry's insurgents.

Eric has no choice but to stay on his best behavior or Sookie won't help him find Godric. We know now that Godric is his maker, but we hope his agreeability (if that's what we can call it) won't come at the sacrifice of never seeing him tear a human limb-from-limb again, a completely shock-and-awe spectacle. In his human life, he was clearly a hero, a lover of food, wine, and women. As a vampire, he's offered more of life, but he's physically incapable of savoring it. He's a businessman but he appears to be going gooey for Sookie. He wanted to feed her when she needed healing after her attack. And he's got his eye on her via Lafayette. But if Sookie isn't with Bill, it would be nice to see her on her own. Eric and Sookie are far more interesting right now as sparring mates. To add another vampire-human union into the mix (other than

Sam's desk at Merlotte's, home of tidy paperwork and compartmentalized emotions.
(Jodi Ross, courtesy of The Vault www.trueblood-online.com)

Jessica and Hoyt, who are adorable) would be to turn every vehicle in a race film into a hybrid, a wise choice for the environment but you can't go off-roading in an electric car. Leave our bad boys alone for a bit.

Sam has found his Alpha male, and a playmate! No more whiny puppy! Part of Sam's lonesomeness stems from the fact that he's never been able to ask anyone about their shifting experience. Acceptance is nice, but it's not the same as connecting with someone you don't have to explain yourself to. For every gay or lesbian who comes out of the closet, there are as many stories of what it feels like to think they are "the only one" until they meet someone else who's like them. Once that euphoria subsides, we're all just people again, no more or less the same as Bill and Eric. But that initial contact confirms everything you'd hoped for up until that moment: that you're normal.

Sookie experiences the same liberation with Barry the Bellboy, but comes up against a roadblock when Barry doesn't want anything to do with her. It's like seeing someone in a gay bar, then having them deny the whole thing the next day. Sookie says they need to stay together. Do we come out for ourselves, or for others? Vampires coming out of the coffin has shown there's no certainty of safety in numbers. But without visibility progress can't be made. The writers continue to find convincing and interesting ways to interweave these politics into the storylines.

Jessica and Jason remain two of the only characters to evolve in interesting ways alongside their storylines. While the vamps and humans decide between annihilating one another a little or a lot, it's Jessica's and Jason's subtle expressions of joy and hesitation that are the most revolutionary. Their sexuality is innocent — Jessica as a virgin, and Jason as a born-again virgin. Jason's leadership camp, in particular, has brought out the best his character has to offer: heart, brawn, humor, and a child-like sense of wonder. When Steve Newlin shows him the church's weapons stockpile, we can see Jason struggling between the implications of the church endorsing violence and the excitement of a young boy on Christmas morning.

As for our bad girls, let's see Maryann's cards on the table. Even her exotic spreads are starting to pale. She's consumed every saucy bit of Tara, replacing her with a quivering mess of gelatin. Sitting outside Merlotte's, Maryann experiences what appears to be orgasmic release for having incited a backlash against Tara, intended to set her up to accept not the family she wants, but the only one she has: Eggs and Maryann. When Tara comes home, Maryann sits at the kitchen table as Gran did, waiting up for Sookie. She's reading *Heartsick* by Chelsea Cain, a novel about a cop and his obsession with a serial killer who lets him live. If Maryann is the killer, the torture she inflicts on her victims is a series of crushing blows to their egos. And who is Eggs? No one can be that consistently oblivious to Maryann's methods. She keeps him on a short leash, but one night on his own, and he'd be doing keg stands at the local frat house.

But it's as Bill and Sookie make love that a new bad girl comes to town: Bill's maker, Lorena, returns, barely recognizable from season 1. I smell a cat fight!

Highlight: Sarah [to Jason]: "Let me reward you. Let me help you find your way back to joy."

Nightcap: Hoyt's cell phone ring is "When the Saints Go Marching In." Ashley Jones (Daphne Landry) shot her episodes while appearing on *The Bold and the Beautiful* as physician-cum-designer Bridget Forrester Marone often going with little to no sleep between shifts. She also had a no-nudity clause in her contract even though the casting call expressed a preference for it. It resulted in a hot silhouetted seduction scene, leaving something to the imagination. It was refreshing to go back into the darkness, away from the light. The Dallas hotel that Bill and Sookie check in to is the Hotel Carmilla, a reference to the 1872 vampire classic *Carmilla*, written by Sheridan Le Fanu, and the basis for films such as *Vampyr — Der Traum* (1932), *Et mourir de plaisir* (1960), *La cripta e l'incubo* (1964), *Carmilla* (1999), and *Carmilla* (2010). Le Fanu's *Carmilla* pre-dates Bram Stoker's *Dracula* by 25 years and is considered the original prototype for female and lesbian vampires, so it's a fitting name for the hotel, especially as it pertains to Lorena. In season 1, we saw evidence of her as a strong, sexual woman. At the end of this episode, it's clear she's just as potent as ever, popping fang at the sound of Bill making love to another woman.

Relationship Crypt Falls: Bill and Sookie's constant need to check in with each other is not only a buzz kill, it's as if they're practicing attachment parenting, hoping that if they connect deeply enough, especially in bed, they'll become more attune to one another, never wanting for anything because all their needs will be provided for. Bill is looking more and more like a father figure to Sookie every day, uncomfortable given her past with Uncle Bartlett.

Paging Dr. Creepy: In the books, Godric is a teenager. It's unclear how old he's meant to be in the series. Regardless, the sight of his face covered in blood is something to behold. Hearkening back to the young boys in the opening credits whose mouths are smeared in strawberries, he looks vicious, large, and in charge, a boy who had a life of killing forced upon him. He's enigmatic but still a child, his innocence taken just as Sookie's and Jason's was.

Location, Location, Location: The Hotel Carmilla scenes were shot in West Hollywood at the Sofitel Hotel on Beverly Boulevard, across from the Beverly Center Mall, northeast of Rodeo Drive (in Beverly Hills). Gunther Zweimuller, GM of Sofitel L.A., had this to say: "Shooting took two separate days, 18 hours one day and 24 hours the following week. It was a huge hit with guests of the hotel. They got to see Anna Paquin up close, some even brushing shoulders with her while passing to enjoy dinner in the Simon L.A. restaurant (which remained open during filming as did the rest of the hotel). *True Blood* was a wonderful match for us. Filming went smoothly and our employees and guests had a great time with the cast and crew." Visit Sofitel L.A. online at www.sofitel.com.

Suzuki Sets the Scene: When it came time to create a hotel for vampires, Ingerslev opted for the luxury and feel of an upscale resort. It retains the dramatic nature of the mythical vampire: sophisticated, brooding, seductive. The most challenging aspect of shooting these scenes was working in an existing hotel with real paying guests. As for the individual rooms, Bill and Sookie's suite was built from the ground up, and reused as Eric's room. Jessica's and Jason's rooms were also the same set, redressed to suit the needs of each. The corridors, as well, were built from scratch.

Encore: "Never Let Me Go," performed by Katie Webster, plays during the end credits. Born in 1936, Katie Webster is widely accepted as one of the most important blues artists of her generation. A boogie-woogie pianist and regular session musician, she played with Otis Redding until his death in 1967. She found fame of her own in the '80s when she recorded "The Swamp Boogie Queen," with featured performances by Bonnie Raitt and Robert Cray. She was also known for her blend of swamp-pop, bayou blues, and gospel soul. "Webster can say more about the pain of betrayal with one low, sad growl and more about the joy of fighting back against cruel life with one teasing roll of her eyes, than most could write in a book," wrote a reporter in the *Boston Globe*. In 1993, Webster suffered a stroke, leaving her with only partial use of her left hand and almost blind. She continued to play until she was forced to call it a day. She died in 1999 from heart failure. "Never Let Me Go" plays as a strange and voluptuous vampire approaches Bill and Sookie's hotel room. The song talks about a couple having just one last night in each other's embrace, knowing that the end of their relationship is inevitable. The singer urges her lover not to think of tomorrow, and to just hold her instead. In this episode, the characters give themselves over to new possibilities, relinquishing power and trust to virtual strangers in the hope that it will pay out in answers, security, and even love. In doing so they make themselves vulnerable, especially in the case of Sookie, who has found someone she can open up to about her telepathy in Barry the Bellboy. Sam flirts with Daphne, signaling a willingness to move past his feelings for Sookie. Tara is tempted to accept Eggs and Maryann as her new family. And Jason, whose actions come with the most obvious consequences, gives in to Sarah Newlin, who convinces him that his hard spiritual work deserves a reward. It's as if each character had been working to a future they can no longer see because nothing is as it once was. So if only just for now, they're forgetting about tomorrow to focus on the moment. Nothing seems to come without consequence, but for a few brief moments we believe as the characters do that it might be worth the risk.

2.06   Hard-Hearted Hannah

Original air date: July 26, 2009
Written by: Brian Buckner
Directed by: Michael Lehmann

> **Sookie [to Hugo]:** I don't just hear the hateful things that people say, I hear the things that are so hateful that hateful people don't even want to say them out loud.
> Don't you worry about me, I have plenty of material to work with.

Sookie infiltrates the Fellowship of the Sun to find Godric. Bill's past with his maker is revealed. And Jason falls further under Sarah Newlin's influence.

The last episode closed with Bill in bed with Sookie. He called her a "girl," and she corrected him: "woman." This episode begins with a lady of the sanguineous night calling Eric "baby." He tosses her aside, saying he's over a thousand years old. He's extremely bored. Why waste the effort after all this time if results can't be guaranteed? Meanwhile, Sookie is still entranced by what makes Bill different — from other men,

Nelsan Ellis, Carrie Preston, and Alexander Skarsgård contemplate whether Rutina Wesley's dress would fit Lafayette. (B. Henderson www.alexander-skarsgardfans.com)

and other vampires. But will goodness (his and hers) sustain her once they know all there is about one another? Bill has already lived many lifetimes over. He doesn't seek answers or knowledge so much as repentance for the acts he's committed. Sookie has only just begun to live, and will, in comparatively short time, die. Heady stuff.

In the meantime, this episode offers more than enough distraction from existential questions. Sookie infiltrates the Fellowship of the Sun with Isabel's human lover, Hugo, a partnership that does nothing to further the appeal of vampire-human relationships. If anything, it's the 1:1 ratio of human to vampire that provides the most hope for stimulation in this episode, when, in a flashback to 1926 Chicago, Lorena and Bill pick up a human couple, something that quickly dissolves into the biggest gross-out scene since Eric tore Royce apart. Lorena is one seriously disturbed woman who clearly doesn't need the aid of a man to get what she wants unless it's to provide musical accompaniment. ("Hard-Hearted Hannah" is also the song Bill was playing on the piano when Jessica was returned to him by Eric in "Nothing But the Blood.") Regardless, she still wears a necklace Bill gave her well over 70 years ago. While they may not have been equals, and even if Lorena's human impulses recede much further than Bill's, she chose him as her progeny, something she did assuming she'd spend eternity attracted to him. And while her assumptions may have been a stretch, this relationship depicts yet another example of someone much older sexualizing someone much younger to meet their own deprived needs.

Meanwhile, if there was ever any question that Eggs was manipulating Tara, that shell's been cracked wide open in shattered fragments of terrifying memories he struggles to piece together. Eggs's flashbacks are an interesting device in duality because they're what we might imagine being glamoured by a vampire to be like — parts of your life suppressed by another's will. The difference between his flash and glamouring is that vampires typically glamour to feed or erase details from a woman's mind to preserve the vampire's safety, whereas it would appear that Eggs may have actively participated in heinous acts himself.

How much of a relief is it to hear Sam say that Daphne is the most amazing person he's ever met? No longer pining for Sookie, he lies naked on a pool table in Merlotte's completely exposed, physically and emotionally, proud of who he is but still struggling with whether or not to advertise it. Daphne counters that we shouldn't keep secrets from the people we love, and we can hear Alan Ball's voice of reason shining through, that there's no point in knowing people if we can't share who we are with one another. So it's especially heartbreaking when Daphne not only betrays Sam, but leads him to the one person he's most afraid of: Maryann.

As we head into the next episode, Eric's observations stay with us. He's been around long enough to know the inevitable outcome of most any relationship. Is it a wonder why humans bother? Or is that what makes us so wondrous, that we keeping trying? Hoyt and his mother are a good example of two people who have withheld from one another for so long that it seems almost fruitless to try to connect. When Hoyt reveals to Maxine that Jessica is a vampire, the news is delivered more out of spite rather than the joyous occasion it should have been between a son and his mother.

Then there are those who make choices even though the aftermath will clearly be negative. Sarah Newlin abandons her devotion to God's gift to her, her husband Steve, by sleeping with Jason. And Tara opens Sookie's home to Maryann in the name of family (with Maryann's identity meanwhile revealed as the creature that attacked Sookie, Miss Jeanette, and Daphne), only to have it taken over by another depraved orgy, desecrating the memory of the woman who actually raised her.

Not only is everyone tied to an uncertain future, they're haunted by their pasts, unable to get away from visions or people. In a twist, Eric wants Lafayette to start selling V-juice again after they tortured him for doing so, showing up in an embodiment of Andy, a nice tie-in to shifting. It offers one of the best scenes in the episode, Lafayette consoled by Terry, a soldier whose demons and post traumatic stress disorder are very real.

Tribute: Mehcad Brooks (Benedict "Eggs" Talley)

> "One moment you're having an orgy in the middle of the woods and it's 45 degrees outside and you can see your breath. You're actually discussing Kafka and Puccini between pelvic thrusts. And you're pondering how it is you're being paid for this and trying to make it seem real!"
>
> — Mehcad Brooks

When Mehcad Brooks first appeared on *True Blood*, millions recognized him immediately. It wasn't from *Desperate Housewives* or any number of modeling campaigns: it was from the bedrooms of our childhoods, mirrored in the image of many unclothed action figures. Six-pack abs are for mere mortals; Mehcad Brooks has a superhero's physique. Yet his perfectly sculpted physique offers much more than eye candy, as pleasant as it is — it's key to his appeal as the perfect sidekick for Maryann. He's strong, charming, straightforward, and sensitive . . . so much so that his fall is even greater when we realize that he isn't capable of taking care of himself, that even those who appear to have everything going for them are still susceptible to influence.

Though images of Brooks' impressive derrière have shown up all over the internet, it's his smile (for real) that we've come to love most, along with Eggs' innocent love for Tara. Even when Sookie's house was packed to the rafters, it was like Eggs and Tara were the only two dancing, eyes only for each other. Their possessed lovemaking sessions are more than a ratings romp, even though there's more than enough to tune in for. But through Eggs' lens, we glimpse a vulnerable Tara, their trust in, and attraction for, one another reminiscent of Bill and Sookie's. Unlike Bill and Sookie, Eggs and Tara are not supernatural; they're just two everyday people who have suffered extraordinary circumstances in order to arrive at a place where they're ready to love, even if love sits waiting on the other side of insurmountable odds, least of which is possession by a mysterious hand.

Where you've seen Mehcad Brooks: *Boston Public, Cold Case, Desperate Housewives, Glory Road, The Game, Dollhouse, The Deep, Just Wright, Fencewalker*

As the episode ends, all hope seems lost. Faith, in particular, has seen better days, all but abandoned or its influence enforced against people's will. Maryann once told Tara that Carl's life of service was a selfish act because he wants to please people. But the orgy participants are empty and depraved, void of any emotion, joy, or fulfilment. Who are they in service to? Maryann? Or something higher?

Highlight: Andy [to Lafayette]: "You weren't on any damn gay cruise. 'Cause if you were you would've come back with *more* pizzazz, not less!"

Nightcap: This episode has also gone by the title "Friend Is a Four-Letter Word." "Friend Is a Four-Letter Word" is a song by Cake, but it does not appear on the episode playlist. The character of Lorena does not appear until *Club Dead*, the third book in the series. Jim Parrack (Hoyt Fortenberry) and Mariana Klaveno (Lorena) appeared together in the short-lived FOX show *Standoff* (2006).

Paging Dr. Creepy: The flashback in which Lorena and Bill devour the couple, then each other, is particularly disturbing, their female victim left to bleed out while they have sex beside her. Rolling over each other like swines in a mud pen, they're completely soulless, merely killing because they can, and heartless, forcing their victims to take the most horrific visions to an early grave.

Location, Location, Location: The Fellowship of the Sun church is actually the Sky Rose Chapel at Rose Hills Memorial Park, in Whittier, California, about 15 miles east of downtown Los Angeles. The largest cemetery in the United States, it has over 600 employees. In 1956, they opened the Rose Hills Mortuary and Flower Shop, making it among the first to offer all services required for memorialization.

Encore: "Hard-Hearted Hannah" is performed by Dolly Kay during the end credits, and by Stephen Moyer at the piano in Chicago in 1926. "Hard-Hearted Hannah (The Vamp of Savannah)" tells the story of a "vamp" or femme fatale from Savannah, Georgia. It's been recorded by many artists including Lucille Hegamin, Peggy Lee, the Ray Charles Singers, Patti Austin, Jim Croce, Bobby Darin, Ella Fitzgerald, Nancy Sinatra, Kay Starr, The Nitty Gritty Dirt Band, and Toni Tennille, to name a few. Both Dolly Kay and Belle Barker recorded versions of the song in 1924, each landing on that year's Billboard Top Singles. Its inclusion in the show is both timely and humorous. The song would have still been popular and recognizable in the 1920s, perfect musical fare for a vampire existing in plain sight.

2.07　Release Me

Original air date: August 2, 2009
Written by: Raelle Tucker
Directed by: Michael Ruscio

Eric: Tell me, what is that you find so fulfilling about human companionship?
Isabel: They feel much more strongly than we do. Everything is urgent, exciting. Maybe because their lives are so temporary.
Eric: Yes, they certainly don't keep well. Do you find the prospect of him growing old, sickly, crippled somewhat repulsive?
Isabel: No, I find it curious, like a science project.

Jason breaks ties with the Fellowship of the Sun. Bill struggles against Lorena's hold on him. And Daphne makes the ultimate sacrifice to Maryann.

Now we know for certain: Maryann is a maenad. In Greek mythology, maenads ("raving ones") were female followers of Dionysus, also known as Bacchus, the god of wine — notice that Maryann is most often seen drinking wine — who incites madness and ecstasy. Maenads worshipped Dionysus to the point of frenzy, often with dancing and intoxication. But this ain't no kegger. It's a Bacchanalia. And alcohol is a key ingredient to partying with Maryann. Tara first sees her while drunk. Andy falls off the wagon, drinking at one of her parties. Tara and Eggs are rarely seen without weed or alcohol. And Jane Bodehouse is almost always pickled, so perhaps that's why she's often among the first to "turn." She's the most susceptible.

Thank goodness for Jessica and Hoyt. Sookie's relationship with Bill, Sam's with Daphne, Tara's with Eggs, and Jason's with Sarah Newlin are so complicated that it isn't until Jessica tells Hoyt to take off his pants that we're reminded that things can sometimes be that simple.

It feels like everyone's chasing after something, or being chased, time always of the essence. Sam's been outrunning Maryann since he was a young man, pursued because she can't have him. As Daphne explains, Maryann challenged her to bring Sam to her. It would be a deflating end to a story that's been building since the end of last season if it weren't for Eggs stepping in to cut out Daphne's heart. It becomes clear that Maryann's fun has only just begun, not unlike Lorena's, which Bill once described as cruelty for sport. Sam is stuck in Bon Temps running from a goddess with nothing but time on her hands. He lost Sookie, Tara, and Daphne. The bar is no longer the establishment it once was and he runs the constant risk that someone else will find out he's a shifter. Will he give up? Or will Sam rise to the challenge like when his faith was tested and he shifted into a bird? Could his determination in that scene reveal a hidden conviction in Sam?

Lorena, like Maryann, has all eternity, holding Bill hostage in his Dallas hotel room. Meanwhile, Sookie gets to know Hugo, Isabel's human lover, while they're captured in the basement of the Fellowship of the Sun. A cowardly, unlikeable fellow, he nonetheless says to Sookie what only another human dating a vampire could, that vampires will always have the upper hand, that her willingness to change her whole

The mantel in Gran's home. (Jodi Ross, courtesy of The Vault www.trueblood-online.com)

life to accommodate his lifestyle is akin to addiction, and that unless she is turned, she'll become undesirable. For now, sex is an intoxicant, a temporary transcendence offered in exchange for a limit on her personal freedom. But what happens when time catches up to Sookie, she gets older, and Bill no longer finds her attractive?

Organized religion also limits the personal freedom of its followers. Jason is expected to be abstinent while Sarah and Steve maintain a public relationship, watching his every move, even in the bathroom where Sarah first seduces him. She challenged herself to sleep with Jason so she could replace one earthly man with another. They sleep together in the church balcony, after which she feels closer to God than ever before. (So does her hair.) Jason attempts to leave the church, literally chased first by Gabe who thinks Jason is working with vampires, then by Sarah who shoots Jason. It's like he's trying to turn back the hands of time, like a little boy who closes his eyes against a nightmare.

In a flashback to 1935 Los Angeles, we also learn how Bill came to be free of Lorena, and that he was prepared to kill himself to make it happen. This is where Maryann's logic, as absurd as it is, makes its point. Sooner or later, we all stop running, and we give in. She, and the Fellowship of the Sun, ask their followers to give themselves and their energies in the name of a greater purpose. Soldiers are expendable.

All season long, we've heard the same thing — that if we don't let ourselves be seen, what's the point of *being*? Regardless of the end, stand and be counted. We evolve through sharing. So it's no wonder that everyone's so messed up. Sookie defines herself based on her relationship with Bill, yet when they're separated they're all but useless to one another. Tara defines herself based on family, yet she's abandoned hers and allowed another to "squat" in her home. And Jason's identity is wrapped up in a hypocritical church that doesn't even fully subscribe to its own faith. Of course, the flip side of this is poor Andy Bellefleur, the one person who *has* seen everyone as they are, in all their depravity (read birthday suits minus the ribbons and bows), but is ultimately an unreliable narrator because he's a drunk and stripped of any authority. He can't even get a witness to his cousin, Terry, snapping his arm like a twig, giving Bill and Sookie a run for their money for the character least likely to catch a break.

While Maryann is a creature who has been around longer than everyone else, her argument is pretty basic: "Feeling sorry for things is just an excuse not to celebrate your own happiness." We're driven by shame. As civilization evolved, so too did our ties to humanity. Bill turned against his true nature as a vampire when he stopped hunting. Tara turned against her faith in family when she abandoned her mother. Sam only accepted his true identity when he thought he'd found someone to keep his secret. And Jason has been looking to others his whole life to make his decisions for him.

Which brings us back to Jessica and Hoyt. They turned away from their shame and presented themselves to one another truthfully. No shimmering influence, and no silver ring of honesty. Their belief in themselves is the antithesis of Maryann's nihilism. Bill and Maxine should be proud; after all, isn't it every parent's hope that the next generation will get it right?

Highlight: Sarah: "Just 'cause I broke my vows to my husband doesn't mean I'm ready to throw all my beliefs out the window."

Nightcap: Ashley Jones' expression when Eggs stabbed her was brilliant. Not just the shock and betrayal, but that she looked more doe-like than ever. It was like they'd killed Bambi! There are a few parallels in this episode worth noting. Jason almost got stabbed, but then got shot; Daphne almost got shot, but then got stabbed. Arlene thinks she may have raped Terry; Gabe almost rapes Sookie. The black-and-white movie that Tara and Eggs watch at Sookie's house is *The Screaming Skull* (1958), a horror film that claimed it was so shocking it could kill audience members! It tells the story of newlyweds whose home is haunted by skulls and the ghost of the groom's first wife, Marion. (Marion. Maryann. Coincidence?) It's revealed that the husband may have ulterior motives against his new bride, something the suspicious-natured Tara might relate to. The film was also spoofed on *Mystery Science Theater 3000*. In the flashback to 1935 Los Angeles, Bill is reading *Gods & Monsters of Ancient Greece*, which doesn't appear to be a real book, so we can only assume that it's a nod to the many parallels between the characters on the show and their Greek mythological counterparts. For this viewer, I just love that Bill is a big book nerd, and that for all he has to learn about the modern world, he still returns to the classics.

Relationship Crypt Falls: Is Tara so desperate for a man that she can't see Eggs, her King of Sheba, is messed up in Maryann's enabling ways? He plays the guitar a lot. But unless he's dropping an album sometime soon, why isn't she worried that he isn't looking for a job?

Paging Dr. Creepy: Maryann wanders in with a rabbit for stew. It's not that she's filthy. Or that she communed with nature all night. Or even that she caught a rabbit for stew. It's that in the absence of a snare I'm left with the disturbing image of her shimmering that rabbit into submission. And you know what they say about rabbits.

Encore: When Lafayette is on the phone selling V-juice, you can hear "Release Me," performed by Conway Twitty and Loretta Lynn. In 1971, Loretta Lynn and Conway Twitty began a professional partnership, scoring five consecutive #1 hits between 1971 and 1975, making them one of the most successful country duos in history. Between 1976 and 1981, they had seven more top 10 hits. Loretta Lynn has probably had more songs banned than any other artists in country music's history, penning lyrics about divorced women, sex before marriage, birth control, and the anguish of losing a loved one to war. Until 2006, Harold Lloyd Jenkins, a.k.a. Conway Twitty, had had more #1 Billboard country hits than any other act in history. He died in 1993 at the age of 59. There are multiple meanings behind the use of "Release Me" in this episode, along with the fact that it's a duet as it applies mostly to pairings: Sookie and Hugo are trapped in the basement of the Fellowship of the Sun; Bill asks to be released from Lorena; Sarah Newlin hopes to leave her husband for Jason; Sam remains in Maryann's grip; Jason escapes from the Newlins; Hoyt and Jessica escort one another out of Virginville; and in the scene in which the song is heard, Lafayette returns to his role as seductive pusher, dealing to people who want release so badly, they'll pay large to take a short cut.

2.08 Timebomb

Original air date: August 9, 2009
Written by: Alexander Woo
Directed by: John Dahl

> **Sookie:** Godric's your maker, isn't he?
> **Eric:** Don't use words that you don't understand.

Sookie: You have a lot of love for him.
Eric: Don't use words I don't understand.

Sookie is saved by an unexpected hero. Sam makes a horrifying discovery at Merlotte's. Maryann cooks an unforgettable meal for Tara and Eggs. And Jason makes good with the vampires.

One of the most enjoyable aspects of *True Blood* is how it explores civil justice when laws fail our personal agendas. Vampires have been able to take advantage of their secrecy to exercise their own laws. While vampire sentences are barbaric, their emphasis on loyalty is unparalleled even if some of their ideals are outdated. A human having an affair with another human's spouse would be a humiliation, the pending court battle an exercise in property division: house, car, children. However, if a vampire took what belonged to another vampire, we can imagine what might follow. And sometimes outrageous measures are exacted against innocents, such as when Jessica was turned as part of Bill's punishment. Or vampires act of their own accord. See Royce's untimely demise for throwing a silver cross in Eric's face. In this episode, Godric kills Gabe with an efficient snap. Unlike humans, vampires don't tie up their legal system with cases to hinder other vampires. We've yet to hear of a vampire who was taken to tribunal under false pretences.

Whether it's Sarah taking matters into her own hands by shooting Jason in the crotch with a paint ball pellet — "There are wolves in our henhouse. We must defend our flock" — or Steve calling for Armageddon with a plan to ritually sacrifice a vampire to the morning sunlight, most senseless death and persecution has been committed in the name of a god. The heretical Fellowship of the Sun justifies genocide, seeking to annihilate the entire vampire race and willing to martyr themselves in the process. When Eric steps in to replace Godric on the cross, he acts on behalf of another. But by killing Steve Newlin he would incite a larger riot. Meanwhile, Stan and his Dallas clan are nothing more than bloodthirsty gang members who would smite others sooner than make themselves vulnerable to harm, revealing that they were the ones to kill Steve Newlin's family.

Godric, older than Jesus, ends the scuffle noting that no one in the church's camp is willing to trade their life for Steve's. It's not a hopeful message of Kumbaya, but he later reveals to Eric that vampires are monsters who have only grown more brutal over time. While it's the most evolved logic we've heard, that's not to say that it didn't still feel good when Jason clocked Steve. Similarly, Godric shows mercy on Hugo even as a traitor. This gentlemen's law also extends to Jason and Bill who mend ways in the name of Sookie.

If Murphy's Law holds true, anything that can go wrong will go wrong. While Sam tries to defend himself to "The Law" for Daphne's murder, under just as much suspicion for not having a past, Andy, the unreliable narrator, steps in for Sam. He's as honorable as Eric, weaving a tale that sounds impossible, if true. With his badge on the line, he gets no respect, not even from the man he's protecting. And in a surprising turn, Jessica's hymen grows back, meaning every time she sleeps with Hoyt she'll have to relive the pain associated with losing her virginity.

So far though, nothing compares to the laws of nature as manipulated by the maniacal Maryann, feeding Tara and Eggs a psychedelic meal of Hunter Soufflé (containing Daphne's heart) that incites rage and passion, this being the second time in this episode we've seen an act of domestic violence, the other being when Bill hit Lorena over the head with a television. The more we nurture an act the easier it is to repeat. Maryann would no doubt say that we've unlearned how to respond to our most base instincts, whereas Godric believes that to choose to evolve beyond such vulgarities is to ensure the preservation of all kinds.

A nitpicking note: why does Sookie's telepathy always go on the fritz just as something big is about to happen? Did she not hear Luke approach? She also didn't hear Hugo's thoughts the whole time she was caged up with him. Both men would have been in a heightened state. If being with Bill has taught her anything, after all this time, it's that she is not safe. She needs to remain guarded at all times.

More scenes with Alexander Skarsgård and Anna Paquin! They are so much fun together. If only there'd been a full-on fight scene in the chapel. A church full of sheep trained to kill a vamp and his sympathizer and no one raises a stake? Eric may have that kind of self control, but after all this time of people hating on Sookie for dating Bill, it's surprising she didn't at least throw a rousing hissy fit. We did get some satisfaction from the brief fight with Lorena, but it's hard to hate Bill's maker when her penance is to forever love someone who doesn't feel the same.

Highlight: Lorena [to Sookie]: "Did you know your boyfriend hit me over the head with a 52-inch plasma television earlier tonight? Everyone says they're so thin and light, but let me tell you, when wielded properly, they're quite a weapon."

Nightcap: Oops. When Jessica and Isabel cry, tears of blood do not appear. Sarah calls Jason "Judas." Judas Iscariot was one of Jesus's 12 Apostles, best known for his betrayal of Jesus to Roman soldiers. Allan Hyde (Godric) is a talented voice performer. In his native Denmark, he's revoiced some of the most popular teen sensations in contemporary culture: Zac Efron's Troy Bolton in *High School Musical*, the character of Ron Weasley in all the *Harry Potter* films, and Joe Jonas's Shane Gray in *Camp Rock*. Maryann's Hunter Soufflé is actually a concoction of vegetables, tomatoes, and beef.

Relationship Crypt Falls: To never introduce your girlfriend to the "mother" you're estranged from is one thing. But to never talk about her is another. It seems that

Sookie hasn't exactly pressed the point about who Bill's maker really is. In the first episode of this season, Sookie got angry at Bill for not having disclosed he'd turned Jessica, yet when they were reunited they'd apparently talked about everything under the sun. How did they manage to skip over Lorena? That would be on par with forgetting to tell your new spouse you'd been married once. For over a hundred years.

Paging Dr. Creepy: A clear winner. That Hunter Soufflé was disgusting, from the first cut into Daphne's heart to the surge of blood when Tara served up a piece to the resulting mania between Tara and Eggs, not to mention the voyeuristic pleasure Maryann gets from watching these two knock each other's socks — and blocks — off.

Encore: "Timebomb," performed by Beck, is heard during the end credits. "Timebomb" is American alternative singer Beck's 2007 Grammy-nominated single, made available first on iTunes before being released on vinyl. Beck hoped it would be a "song for bonfires, blackouts, and the last hurrah of summer." The cover artwork for the single included Beck in an Aztec bird costume, which he'd become known for wearing on stage. So, it's no wonder the song appears at the height of Bon Temps madness, with Maryann's influence threatening to build to a horrific crescendo.

2.09   I Will Rise Up

Original air date: August 16, 2009
Written by: Nancy Oliver
Directed by: Scott Winant

Maryann: Few bumps and bruises. It's a small price to pay for bliss.

Eric finds a way to connect with Sookie. Lafayette and Lettie Mae plot to steal Tara away from Maryann. Hoyt introduces Jessica to his mother.

Incredible! The episode that will be remembered for inciting screams of "Team Eric!" Alexander Skarsgård is given everything he could hope for to throw Eric's hat in the ring as a worthy competitor for Sookie's attentions. And, oh, does he have her attention, entering her dreams and playfully arguing why she'd be a good vampire. He's radiant, godly, and relates to Sookie as if they've known each other for centuries. Fiercely loyal to Godric, Eric recognizes the same quality in Sookie, noting she'd do anything for the people she loves. In the dream, she's more worldly and self-aware then we've seen her in the past, comfortable in her skin, and against his. Eric says he has love for "only Sookie." Is this the truth, or just the words of a thousand-year-old vampire who knows what every girl wants to hear?

The episode begins with Luke detonating a suicide bomb, delivering His message — Steve Newlin's. The nest crumbles in on itself, taking Stan, who we never really got

Tribute: Allan Hyde (Godric)

"Can you imagine a guy like Godric — [he and Eric] spent a thousand years together, and they were kind of a tag team . . . Just imagine what kind of bond you achieve in not twenty-five years but eight hundred, nine hundred years. They have so much in common that they're almost the same person."

— Alexander Skarsgård

Becca's Initial Top Five Gut Responses to Godric:

1. He's awfully young to be a vampire.
2. I wonder if his mother knows he has those tattoos.
3. Eric likes him, therefore, I shall like him, too.
4. Oh, he's saving us from ourselves! He's a good vampire!
5. Get off the damn roof! Well, now, there you've gone and done it. I hate you. (But, look, Eric is crying. Therefore. I. Shall. Love. Him. Forever!)

Allan Hyde must get his cheeks pinched everywhere he goes. He jumps to the top of my list of cutie patootie teen vamps. I'm not talking about the *Twilight* crew or the studs from *The Vampire Diaries*. My widdle Godric falls more in line with the Midget Count on *The Hilarious House of Frightenstein*. Or, perhaps, Eddie Munster if he'd ever truly let his freak fang fly.

For extra kicks and giggles, check out www.hadleyk.com where you can find Allan's frequent collaborations with creative bon vivant Hadley Klein.

to know very well for such a strong personality. Godric wanders the house taking in the carnage. Only moments before Godric had denounced the savage behavior of vampires, yet Luke, a human, devalued his own life and the lives of his kind.

Godric seeks to establish order in chaos, but it looks hopeless. What use is it to deliver edicts from his chair? And what does it mean to be "alive" for a vampire who won't feed? He inhabits the same world as Maryann, who conversely believes we cannot evolve without chaos. The jail cells of Bon Temps are packed. How long would it take to process each case, let alone understand the alleged crimes? How much effort do we expend to maintain order? When do we change the order? And how much longer before another Luke straps a bomb to his chest to maximize the damage? Eggs

Fan Sarah Napier catches up with Allan Hyde (Godric) during the Masquerade Fangbangers Ball at the EyeCon Convention in Orlando, Florida. (Sarah Napier)

acted as Maryann's suicide bomber, taking Daphne's heart as Maryann thanked her for her service. Even as Eric put himself on the cross for Godric, the lines between true purpose and blind devotion are blurred.

Bill remains ineffectual, arriving late to the explosion as he did the church. For one of the most humane vampires, it's odd that he shows so little concern for other humans, barrelling past wounded bodies to find Sookie under Eric. Bill has some of the worst luck on the show. Even if Sookie takes the brunt of it, she emerges stronger after each battle, while Bill tries to sleep off the hangover of a miserable existence with Lorena and now the reality that his lover contains a booster shot of his nemesis. It's a shame to see Lorena leave so soon. She's dangerously seductive and petty. While there's more than enough to suggest she'll be back, we could have sacrificed one or two orgies, if it meant more scenes with her.

In the war for humanity, Sookie pulls out her best weapon, honoring the memories of those you love. Godric is perhaps too old to remember who or why he would keep fighting, but Jason and Sookie are surrounded by recent loss. Ryan Kwanten delivers his strongest performance to date, a boy finally struggling to become a man. He's always shown leadership skills, but by his sister's side he realizes that it's when he shares himself that he finds the connection he's been looking for. Like when he helped Luke up over the fence at the Light of Day camp, he's learning that when we link up, our bonds become stronger. Whether it's grief, or all out war, we order the chaos by navigating it together. (A conclusion that Sam also arrives at, reaching out to Andy to have his back.) The inclusion of the Newlins bickering on a television interview is hilarious.

Anna Paquin is spectacular in this episode, proving yet again that she has more range when she's not stuck in bed with Bill, talking about what a great guy he is. Her scenes with Eric continue to be among my favorites. Maybe it's because Eric towers over her, but she's a pint-sized fireball around him, going into the mouth of the lion whether she's berating him, offering heartfelt compassion, or a heartpounding kiss. Stephen Moyer, unfortunately, has been shackled to a character that has changed drastically in tone from the books, with the show writers emasculating Bill in exchange for a feistier Sookie and to set Eric up as more layered than a glorified goon. (Bill doesn't even get to go up on the roof. And when he hauls off on Eric, there's no satisfaction, whatsoever. Eric was so numb, he didn't feel it. A bit of a low blow.)

As Maryann would like people to give in to their ecstasy, uniting with their god, Godric arrives at a similar destination, giving up on self-knowledge in favor of the unknown. Put simply, he's done. Godric has many answers, but in the end he chooses one question. What awaits? He greets the morning, escorted from this world by what Steve Newlin called the greatest weapon of God, the sun, a 25-year old waitress as his only witness. Eric's farewell to his maker is heartbreaking. Eric bargains at the feet of a once-child, each so weary that it wouldn't have been a surprise to see Eric join Godric in his suicide. We never saw Godric turned, or much about his life before or after, so we're left to assume that his fatigue with this life, and his resolution to give himself over to a new one, is evidence enough that he's witnessed the worst that humanity has had to offer. He's left as much an enigma as when we first met him. Had the performances been left in lesser hands, we wouldn't have felt the weight or implications of Godric's decision to effectively euthanize himself. It's a touching moment, one that makes us hope for future flashbacks so we can glimpse the world alongside these fathers, brothers, sons. They're, by far, the most interesting maker/progeny team. Even as we mourn Godric, Eric begins to evolve in front of Sookie, shedding the past with his tears as Jason did earlier. Vampire and human connected through grief. There may be hope yet. Eric's devotion plays in stark opposition to Bill's farewell with Lorena, which was tinged with darkness and threat.

Although we've lost Godric, we've gained Nan Flanagan and Maxine Fortenberry, matriarchs who don't hesitate to hand down sentences, judgment, and one-liners. It's nice to see Nan "Just Try to Mess with Me" Flanagan step out of her good citizen television persona to remind us she's a bad-ass undead. And Maxine, one of the scarier humans around, is spot-on as a controlling mother, unwittingly giving Hoyt the best gift a momma could, the final straw it takes for him to man up and leave. (Go, Hoyt! Go, Hoyt!)

Speaking of manning up, Lafayette and Lettie Mae barge in on Tara's card game with Eggs and Maryann, stealing her off into the night. It doesn't feel in character for Lafayette, but it could be in response to his time in the dungeon. Terry has to live with haunting war memories, whereas Lafayette is able to make right what he can, right now. Leave no man behind.

This episode succeeds on many levels, at once a study in existential despair and cautious hope for the future. It also carries us into the final episodes of the season, one graceful man down, and one evil woman running the show. What kind of faith, retrieved from how many beliefs, is going to keep Bon Temps from erupting into one big hell hole?

Tribute: Ashley Jones (Daphne Landry)

> "[The writers] did a great job of making the environment a major character. You can feel the humidity and the heat, which is a great way to set the scene for passion and horror."
>
> — Ashley Jones

My initial reaction to Ashley Jones when she first appeared on screen as "The Worst Waitress in ~~Bon Temps~~ the World" Daphne Landry was how much she embodied the Sookie Stackhouse I had imagined from Charlaine Harris's novels. It was surprisingly easy to imagine Daphne Landry, so real as the Girl Next Door she was almost cartoonish, stepping in as Sookie's understudy. Coincidence? Perhaps. But for those of us who didn't mind the idea of a parallel universe in which Sam and Sookie hook up, just to see what it would be like, that pool table romp between Sam and Daphne was a safe way for all of us to get what Sam's always wanted.

Of course, as we got to know the other Daphne, her doe-eyed alliances revealed themselves, Jones gracefully pivoting Daphne from sweet to sour on the head of a pin without a misstep. And let's pay props to the freezer shot, a cinematic study in how to create a creepy tableau you won't wipe clean from your dreams for days.

Where you've seen Ashley Jones: *Without a Trace, Crossing Jordan, CSI: NY, FlashForward, The Bold and the Beautiful, The Mentalist, CSI*

Highlight: Godric: "A human with me at the end. And human tears. Two thousand years, and I can still be surprised. In this, I see God."

Relationship Crypt Falls: Even though Sookie has drunk a bucket of Bill's blood, she's surprised to learn that only a drop or two of Eric's blood will affect her. Again, I wonder what these two talk about in bed that he's never brought up his maker or told her exactly how vamp life works. It's exposition for the audience, we can't learn it all at once, but it weakens their connection, not to mention that it's difficult to believe he has only her best interests at heart when he hasn't given her a cheat sheet on the Dos and Don'ts of vampire relations.

Paging Dr. Creepy: While Sookie fellating Eric's chest was clearly good for him, I'll never get used to the gushing blood wounds on this show. It is, however, a big step up from the probing tongues of feeding vamps who have to look both menacing and sexy while they negotiate tricky dental work.

Location, Location, Location: Godric's death scene was not shot atop the Sofitel Hotel, which stands in as Hotel Carmilla, but further east at 1000 Wilshire Boulevard in downtown Los Angeles, California, next to the Harbor/Pasadena Freeway. For shooting, they added a "Hotel Carmilla" logo to the center of the helicopter landing pad. The scenes looking east toward the sun show the Dallas skyline, indicated by a large clock tower.

Suzuki Sets the Scene: Ingerslev wanted Godric's lair to have a modern feel populated with relics from a variety of cultures accumulated over the course of his life, reflecting the places he'd been and the wisdom he'd gathered. Most of the paintings were commissioned specifically for the location. Rather than create a new set for the bomb scene, the existing set was actually destroyed, a tough goodbye for the crew who worked so hard to build it from scratch.

Encore: "I Will Rise Up," performed by Lyle Lovett, plays during the end credits. Lyle Pearce Lovett is an American singer-songwriter and actor. He's recorded 13 albums since 1980, and won four Grammy Awards. "I Will Rise Up" is taken from his 2007 album, *It's Not Big, It's Large*, recorded live in studio by Lyle Lovett and his Large Band. Lovett explains the band's name, saying, "We've always done arrangements that border on blues music, that border on jazz arrangements, that border on what folks might think of as 'big band,' but we don't really play big band music. But we've always had a lot of people in the band so that's why I call the band the 'Large Band' and not the 'Big Band.'" The song itself is about death and only God knowing what comes next for a man who is resigned to meet his end.

2.10   New World in My View

Original air date: August 23, 2009
Written by: Kate Barnow and Elisabeth R. Finch
Directed by: Adam Davidson

> **Bill:** No offence, Sookie, but humans are shockingly susceptible to just about every form of thought manipulation.

Sookie, Bill, and Jason return home to Bon Temps. Hoyt and Jessica try to keep Maxine safe from Maryann. And Jason tries to save Sam.

While the Maryann Forrester storyline is to this season what Jason's V addiction was to last, Michelle Forbes is absolutely infuriating, which is a good indicator that she's succeeded in her portrayal. It's hard to care for Tara and Eggs after 10 gullible episodes of them getting high and blindly following "Reese's Pieces" clothing to orgy sites. And the tie to Tara's mother's addiction weakened the real world despair of Lettie Mae. But the storyline is rescued by Forbes's nihilistic, narcissistic, emotionally vampiric Maryann. I would sooner follow Eric to the other side than let this woman near me. She takes to the meat statue like she's arranging a floral bouquet. And now that Godric is gone, she's the smoothest kid on campus, the vamps looking like pre-schoolers in comparison.

Sookie and Jason come home from Dallas to find Bon Temps in complete chaos. While you can always go home, there's no guarantee that it will be the same. Even Gran's house is unrecognizable. The siblings suffer more loss, virtually everything from their pasts replaced by crude effigies. (Even Tara's not the same.)

But this is the war Jason's been waiting for, and after two seasons, we finally get to see him own it! Even Bill gives him the thumbs-up. As Merlotte's descends into a scene out of *Lord of the Flies*, Sam sacrifices himself to a fate sure to be less pleasant than Godric's sunshine farewell. Jason becomes a mythical warrior, likely a combination of the demigod Heracles — masculine, courageous, and sexual — and Jason of the Argonauts, a friend of Heracles trained in combat (see pp. 187–188). He's still hilarious, pulling from Steve Newlin's arsenal of one-liners to smite the ravenous crowd. It's an inspired turn of writing, and Ryan Kwanten looks to be having the time of his life as the king of the castle overlooking his dirty rascals.

Sam, after waiting for a distraction before changing, at last outs himself as a shifter. Most of the town won't remember. And it won't matter if he ends up dead, anyhow. But Jason and Andy now know. One's not the sharpest tool in the shed, and the other is drunk. Sam couldn't have imagined two more unlikely wingmen.

Poor Bill is unable to protect Sookie — again — poisoned by Maryann's blood. He pukes out the window as Sookie drives, feeding on her arm in order to heal. In Eric's only scene, another dream, he doesn't say a word but still gets the girl. The only action Bill gets is a young frat girl he scares like it's Hallowe'en after overhearing her try to buy V from Lafayette. Armed now with the knowledge that he's dealing for Eric, Bill may have been given the upper hand.

Even though I miss the flamboyant Lafayette, new Lafayette is not without his charms. He's evolved (there's that word again) beyond his self-serving entrepreneur into a family man. All he needs to complete the picture is "a lil' cocoa! A lil' cocoa!" (Still one of my favorite lines from way back in the pilot) By staying put, Lafayette's prepared to try to heal what ails Tara, and it won't come from a plastic bag or vial. He's always possessed understanding and wisdom, but now he has compassion. When Tara comes to, she is not alone; she's surrounded by her entire family, blood and extended. And it's been a long time coming to see Tara and Lettie Mae reunited. It was as if

Tribute: Valerie Cruz (Isabel Beaumont)

"[Isabel] has a penchant for humans and a vulnerability. She wants to try to find a way to coexist with them."

– Valerie Cruz

Bill, Jessica, and Isabel Beaumont have all taken mortal lovers. Bill's hurdle is to adjust to a strong-minded young woman, while Jessica is forced to reason with her state of perma-virginity, making gender a pervasive player in both of their relationships.

However, Isabel's relationship with her centuries-younger companion, Hugo, gives the viewer a subtler glimpse into the ageless trials of universal love. Unlike articles that open with a physical description of a woman as aging well or otherwise, we're liberated from that old sexist measurement of a woman's worth, because, as a vampire, it's Isabel who will remain, always, in her prime. (Let's face it, there aren't a lot of elderly vampires walking around.) This clears the path for us to ask the curious questions – for Sookie and even Eric to ask theirs, as well – because by all accounts Isabel and Hugo appear to be in a healthy, happy partnership, which, while not natural by some standards, is nonetheless normal. So much so, that when Hugo is revealed to be a coward and a traitor, you can't help but feel that even after 600 years on this planet, the only cure for Isabel's heartbreak remains a night on the town with the girls – nothing but Bellinis and preferred blood type.

Where you've seen Valerie Cruz: *Nip/Tuck*, *Las Vegas*, *Grey's Anatomy*, *Cellular*, *Invasion*, *Hidden Palms*, *The Dresden Files*, *La linea*, *Dexter*, *Dollhouse*

Rutina Wesley had emerged from a thankless storyline, although a brave performance, into the arms of Adina Porter and the hope that in the coming episodes we'll get to see more of the old sarcastic Tara.

The vamps took a back seat in this episode. Jessica shows us her dark side, attacking Hoyt's mother, something that's bound to go over poorly. While Eric, with no dialogue, exudes more charisma than Bill's entire appearance, he's all but absent after having featured heavily in the last episode. And is it just me or does Bill sound more and more antiquated every time he speaks? Eric's been around a lot longer, and it could be argued that he's far more social than Bill who has chosen a reclusive lifestyle. But even Godric had adapted. Perhaps it's because Bill's so literary that we're supposed to equate his speech patterns with class, moreso than the time period that he comes from. It really works when he's talking about his desire to undress Sookie from a petticoat; it's swoonworthy. But when faced with Maryann, in the time it takes Bill to express his deeply felt belief that Maryann should immediately vacate herself from these premises built on a balmy day one June afternoon, *I believe Mahalia Jackson was playing on the radio* — BAM! Not to be too hard on Bill, his affectations are some of the only remaining Southern gent touches left in Bon Temps. And there are bigger issues at hand, because between a vampire, a maenad, and a waitress, none of them has any idea what Sookie just did to Maryann, or where that energy came from.

As we gear up for the last two episodes, it's hard to believe that Bon Temps will ever move past any of this chaos. But with the introduction of a powerful and unexpected character on the horizon, the certain return of newly sensitive Eric, and Sookie's ongoing dreams about him, something supernatural is en route to Bon Temps to restore order to chaos.

Highlight: Terry: "Bullshit. God has horns!"

Nightcap: Maniacal Maryann showing up is definitely one of the best parts of this episode, with that over-the-top crazy-as-a-loon laughter like she's just having the time of her life. At Bill's home, Maxine Fortenberry plays the Wii game *Dead Space Extraction,* a first-person rail shooter game about a group of space colonists working to fight against the infection of a group of re-animated, human corpses. The connection between the game and *True Blood* runs even deeper, with many of the characters suffering from hallucinations. The game is used to hilarious effect with Maxine because, while we know she has a fighter inside her, she'd never go out of her way to find herself in a scuffle. Dionysus is known by many names. The alternate names and their meanings shown in Bill's book are: Bromios — noisy or boisterous; Dendrities — he of the trees; Eleutherios — the liberator; Enorches — denotes Dionysus as a fertility god; Bacchus — name used by the Romans for Dionysus. When Terry says that the EPW is secured, he's using a military acronym for "Enemy Prisoner of War."

Relationship Crypt Falls: Jessica, we are right there with you about Hoyt's mother. And I can't believe I'm going to paraphrase Maryann, but where on earth did you get the idea this was about you? It takes at least half a year of dating until you can tell off someone else's mother, and, at that rate, at least a few years before you go biting her and expect forgiveness. Maxine's a trip alright, but Hoyt's the one who will have to deal with the aftermath. You weren't working in his best interests; you were finishing what you started with your father. As a result, you've proven to Hoyt what his mother always expected, that, at heart, you're a monster.

Paging Dr. Creepy: We've seen just about everything. Organ soufflés. Gaping chest wounds. Naked bodies of every shape, size, and cleanliness. And exploding vampires. But we've yet to see a vampire throw up. Out a car window, no less. That's like hearing your dad throw up for the first time. He's supposed to be invincible; what are those wretched noises? And with nothing but synthetic blood to line his stomach, it was probably pretty foul-smelling to boot.

Encore: During the end credits we hear "New World in My View," performed by Sister Gertrude Morgan and King Britt. Sister Gertrude Morgan (1900–1980) was 38 and living in Columbus, Georgia, when she heard a voice from God telling her to preach the word on the streets. She left her family to move to New Orleans, which she believed to be "the headquarters of sin," and created an orphanage with two other missionaries. She received another message from God to begin painting, and yet another to call herself a Bride of Christ. She wore a nurse's uniform and established "The Everlasting Gospel Mission." Sister Morgan also enjoyed a degree of fame as a prolific folk artist, often working in crayon and using whatever surface she could find. In the early '70s, Sister Morgan recorded *Let's Make a Record* comprised of nothing more than her singing — often repeatedly chanting words like "power," "hallelujah," and "amen" — and a tambourine. Twenty-five years after her death in 1980, the Ropeadope record label brought Philadelphia DJ King Britt on board to revisit her music. The result was 2005's *King Britt Presents Sister Gertrude Morgan*, which added contemporary beat programming and instrumentation to Sister Morgan's sparse vocals and tambourine. In this episode, the prayer that Lettie Mae recites is from Psalms 103:1–4: "Bless the LORD, O my soul, And all that is within me, bless His holy name. Bless the LORD, O my soul, and forget none of His benefits; Who pardons all your iniquities, Who heals all your diseases; Who redeems your life from the pit, Who crowns you with loving kindness and compassion." Bon Temps, Louisiana, is the new headquarters of sin, utterly lost and without hope, flailing in a battle not divided between mortals and demons, but true good and pure evil. Maryann, in a strange turn, takes her vision for a new world to the streets, guided by forces outside her, chanting and drumming her preferred mode of musicality.

2.11 Frenzy

Original air date: August 30, 2009
Written by: Alan Ball
Directed by: Daniel Minahan

Eric [to Sam]: Why should I trust you?
Sam: Because until somebody starts trusting somebody, we're all single targets, just ripe for the picking.

Bill seeks the advice of Sophie-Anne, the vampire Queen of Louisiana. Tara goes after Eggs. Sam turns to an unlikely ally. And Maxine stretches Hoyt to his limit.

There are varying definitions of "hero." Greek mythology describes a hero as a demigod, the offspring of a mortal and a deity. The etymology of the word is "protector" or "defender." There are also "seekers," heroes who have had something stolen from them by a villain, and "victim-heroes," kidnapped or driven out to initiate a conflict. The modern hero is often simply someone ordinary placed in extraordinary circumstances, who typically prevails, no matter the odds. Then there's "hero-identification," the notion that we as viewers are compelled to experience the story as ourselves.

Alan Ball and his writers have stuck close to classic Greek mythology, an admirable effort to sustain solidly for two seasons. In the last episode, Bill glamoured Tara long enough for Sookie to get all caught up on what they'd missed in Dallas. But it's Bill's bookishness that proves most useful when he recognizes the chant Sookie heard in Tara's head — Bromios. Dendrites. Eleutherios. Enorches. Bacchus. He goes to New Orleans where he consults with the Queen of Louisiana, Sophie-Anne (played by Evan Rachel Wood).

Sophie-Anne is a seductive, self-involved strategist. She's 500 years old, supposedly turned when she was in her teens, but here looks a fair bit older. Thinking back to Kirsten Dunst as Claudia in *Interview with the Vampire* or Lina Leandersson as Eli in *Let the Right One In*, what works in those performances is that because the actors themselves are so young, their gaze is eerily mature. They're at once intense and child-like. Older actors can bring a lot of posturing to their roles, because they think they've seen a lot when, in reality, they're still growing up. Evan Rachel Wood, while a fine actor, doesn't imbue Sophie-Anne with the wisdom we'd expect from a vampire of her age and influence.

She's a poser, porcelain skin lavishly displayed like she's a cross between a '30s film siren and a present-day Hollywood starlet, unlike Bill, a warrior who once burned to a crisp in the name of bravery. And for all her alleged power, she's unconvincing. Bill, for the first time this season, looks more competent than his peers. Her logic that mae-nads are just deluded humans is muddled. By now, we've all come to accept that there's more in this world than we could ever imagine, but the point is that it's not fake. Rene Lenier would be an example of a deluded human, but his murder streak was very real. And Maryann, while getting desperate, is extremely powerful. If there's something else in Sophie-Anne's message, it's nearly impossible to retrieve. So is the reasoning behind forcing Bill to sunbathe. If he was going to be held against his will (see above definition of "victim-hero") it seems unlikely he'd kick back, no matter how awkward.

Conversely, Jessica, and Deborah Ann Woll, is getting stronger with each episode. The evolution of her character from whiny brat to purposeful young woman is among my favorite transitions. And after finally seeing her come into her own with Hoyt, what a brilliant twist to turn her against Hoyt's mother. As Jessica lets out a blood-curdling scream, we know her "change" isn't complete. To be accepted for the first time as a vampire is euphoric. To

Gran's kitchen sink in happier days, sans creepy naked guy. (Jodi Ross, courtesy of The Vault www.trueblood-online.com)

be rejected, soul-crushing. What will her next incarnation look like? Beauty or beast? And as much as we want Hoyt to choose Jessica, he wouldn't be the man we know if he abandoned his mother. As one of the only people in Bon Temps who hasn't been consumed by Maryann — why? — he's able to watch over Maxine. His choice brings consequences, when his mother tells him the truth about his father's suicide.

Lafayette has become a whole other entity. He takes a solid run at every demon, even if he's quivering in his boots the whole time. It has yet to get old to see him cower in the presence of Eric, or swoon just the slightest at the dreams he's been having. Through him, we're reminded that even in Lettie Mae's porch dress, Eric is the man. It's a great comment, that fear, power, and strength are not engendered. Lafayette and Eric are each in their own rights men not to be reckoned with, but both have taken their turn in ladies' garb. That's fierce confidence. (Maybe the trick then is to put Sophie-Anne in a suit.) So, it's a tremendous disappointment when Lafayette falls under Maryann's spell. Not only is it difficult to accept that after all he's been through he's too weak to resist her, but he would have made a formidable soldier alongside Andy and Jason.

We can't fault Tara for running after Eggs; after all, she's spent so much time running from men. And it's touching that her mother helps her escape, even if she means to keep Tara from running away from her. If you love something, set it free, and she does, the first truly motherly thing Lettie Mae has done. We don't own our children, we support them. But Tara's decision is a difficult one: did she turn her mother's faith against her in a move reminiscent of Maryann's mind games, or is this in fact Tara learning a thing or two from Lettie Mae, keeping her close when she needs something, then tossing her aside when she doesn't? It's clear that Eggs has a good, if conflicted, soul. But there are times when it's hard to believe that Tara actually loves Eggs, a stereotypical slacker. By blaming her mother, how is Tara any different from what Maryann accused Lettie Mae of being? Someone who looks to credit anything outside of herself rather than accept personal responsibility for her own life? Tara's measures are heroic in that she refuses to leave Eggs behind, but Eggs isn't like Sookie locked in a church basement, or Eric burning on a cross, or Jason facing a mob. He's barely capable of taking care of himself. If it's the strong who survive — and it sure feels like that's what it's going to take — as ironic as it may seem, Eggs' muscular exterior is no match for true strength of character.

Where Tara put down her edge, Sookie picked it up and hasn't looked back. Girl is fierce sans Bill. In just the past few episodes she's gone from a self-conscious pretty girl to one hot mama who knows how to keep her cool in the face of uncertainty, hatred, and whacked-out coroners. While Jason prepares to lead the troops into battle, Sookie's our sniper — one moment at a safe distance, the next right under your nose. Which clearly doesn't leave enough time for her to listen in on anyone's thoughts, or she would have known Lettie Mae planned to help Tara escape. Sookie's telepathy is too distinct a trait to only employ it occasionally as a narrative device. We know she tries not to listen in on family and friends, but, just once, I'd like someone to confront her about it. Seems lately more people are getting hurt than not. It kind of makes her a strange accessory to the fact, don't you think?

Religion in all its forms has been scathingly critiqued since last season. The Newlins are portrayed as self-righteous extremists, whereas Maryann's paganism is met with equal disdain and distrust. While it's difficult to accept Sophie-Anne's assertion that Maryann is just a pathetic human, we do see a large crack in her veneer when the mob arrives to say that her God came, but she'd missed it. And by crack, we could say hissy fit. If last season was about trying to find moderation, in particular drugs and alcohol, this season's addictions are fear and self-loathing and what practices and communities we can cling to to carry us out of the darkness.

Thank God or whomever else you pray to for Alan Ball and his team of writers, because nothing is ever served up without a side of something truly ecstatic, namely humor. Jason and Andy's confrontation in the truck was hilarious. Chris Bauer and Ryan Kwanten are remarkable actors, and it's an inspiring turn to have both of them play the straight man in their scenes. As always, Pam is delightful, as is Eric in full lounge position, a hulking man trying to come down to the level of Arlene's "teacup humans." It was also quite touching to see Sam take such good care of the children, something he didn't get growing up and can't easily offer anymore at Merlotte's because, let's face it, no one needs a roof over their heads to party when the great out-doors is your dancefloor. It's a bittersweet sentiment that leaves us wondering if there's anything left for Sam, or if it's time for him to pack up and move on.

Highlight: Sookie: "I am gonna kick that bitch's evil ass out of my Gran's house, and then you are going to shoot her."

Nightcap: Eric can fly! When Sam is at Fangtasia with Arlene's children, Pam says, "*Jag avskyr dom. Dom är korkade,*" which in English means "I hate them. They're so stupid." To which Eric responds, "*Men delikata.*" "But delicious." When Jason mentions he read a book about the oral history of the zombie war, he's most likely referring to the 2006 novel *World War Z* by Max Brooks, the post-apocalyptic follow-up to Brooks's 2003 book *The Zombie Survival Guide*. *World War Z* is a series of character interviews about a 10-year war on zombies, noting specifically the aftermath of the war and its impact on religion, politics, and the environment. *World War Z* was directly inspired by *The Good War*, an oral history of World War II by Studs Terkel. Referenced here, it's funny because Jason's so gullible, it's hard to know if he does or doesn't actually believe in zombies, but he's willing to strategize nonetheless. *Frenzy*, this episode's title, is also the name of a 1972 movie by Alfred Hitchcock. It was the penultimate film of his career. Coincidence that this is the penultimate episode of the season? Probably, but it's fun to make the connections! One of Hitchcock's signature moves was to reveal a mystery's answer (such as a killer's identity) early in a film so that the remainder focused on building dramatic tension around the audience knowing something the characters didn't. It was around this time in season 1 that the audience learned Rene was the killer before his intended victim, Sookie, did. It is a stretch to consider this Alan Ball's way of tipping his hat to closing in on the end of another fine season? At the very least, Bon Temps is barely a shadow of itself, certainly lost in a frenzy.

Relationship Crypt Falls: Hoyt's mother cooking him preservative-laden, confec-tionary casseroles is a far cry from what Gran used to make: fresh biscuits and sausage, a warm plate always waiting for you in the oven. Maxine's failure is as much to herself as it is to her son. She's spiteful and angry, and her truth is ugly and selfish. But her profound loneliness does draw a small amount of sympathy from viewers.

Paging Dr. Creepy: The entire scene in which Sookie re-enters Gran's house is pretty creepy. First she encounters Jane Bodehouse who has just sacrificed her finger to offer to the god; then she's greeted by a man bathing in her sink fondling what appears to be part of an intestine; then the town coroner, Mike "Makes You Feel More Alive Bein' in the Presence of Death" Spencer spoons her on the floor where her grandmother lay bludgeoned to death while he chastises her for letting Bill put his "dead dick" inside her, far too reminiscent of the dearly departed Uncle Bartlett.

"Maxine Fortenberry's Broiled Cheese and Chips Sandwich"

Country Crock margarine spread
4 slices white Wonder Bread (in Dallas it would be Mrs. Baird's)
2 slices of Kraft American Cheese
Lay's Potato Chips

Preheat broiler on lowest setting. Spread margarine on one side of each bread slice. Place four bread slices buttered side up on an ungreased baking sheet. Place under broiler until golden, about three minutes.
Remove and turn bread slice over and spread margarine on that side, then top each with a cheese slice. Place under broiler until light golden, about three minutes.
Remove from oven, place Lay's potato chips on top of melted cheese on one bread slice, then top with other slice, cheese side down. Repeat for other sandwich.
Then MASH down with the palm of your hands (breaking all the chips).
Serve.
Visit www.lovingtruebloodindallas.com for more great recipes!

Location, Location, Location: The hotel Andy stays in (which was used in season 1 as Tara's temporary home) is Crescenta Motel, located in, you guessed it, La Crescenta, California, in the foothills northwest of Pasadena. Originally called the May Lane Motel, it is on Route 66.

Suzuki Sets the Scene: Queen Sophie-Anne's home is an existing location in Malibu, California. Ingerslev loved the nostalgic feel of the outdoor pool. The crew spent a few weeks setting the scene. Inside, the crew created custom-made dioramas for each window to create the illusion of an ocean view for Sophie-Anne — what she might want to gaze out on, if she could survive in daylight — a brilliant detail. To ensure that the audience didn't misunderstand the dressings as poor attempts at reality, they made each diorama slightly surreal, almost like the set-ups one would find in a museum of taxidermy. The gorgeous interior already had an art deco feel. Ingerslev notes this as one of her all-time favorite locations for the degree of existing detailing. They even used the furniture, subbing in only new cushions, a few additional planters, and authentic period *Vogue* magazines, purchased from eBay.

Encore: When Jason and Andy arrive at sheriff's office, you can hear "Frenzy," performed by Screamin' Jay Hawkins. Jalacy Hawkins (1929–2000), a.k.a. Screamin' Jay Hawkins, was one of the original shock rockers, known for his operatic vocal stylings, theatrical stage performances, and flashy wardrobe of leopard skin, leather, and hats. When his plans to be an opera singer fell through, he served in the U.S. Army during World War II, mostly as an entertainer. He claimed to have been tortured by the enemy; it's rumored that upon release he exacted revenge by taping a hand-grenade inside his captor's mouth and pulling the pin. As an entertainer, "I Put a Spell on You" was his most famous song, selected for the Rock and Roll Hall of Fame's 500 Songs that Shaped Rock and Roll. During that song's recording session, the band was so intoxicated that Hawkins blacked out, unable to recall how what was originally intended to be a ballad became a "raw guttural track," one that sold over a million copies. Soon after, he was offered money by a disc jockey to come out of a coffin on stage. What emerged was Hawkins' next persona, the coffin becoming a fixture along with a variety of outlandish costumes and voodoo props. Later in his career, Hawkins performed with The Fuzztones, Dread Zeppelin, Nick Cave, and The Clash. By the time of his death in 2000, he was responsible for 19 albums and (allegedly) up to 75 offspring. Is there any better song than "Frenzy" (1957), or any better artist than Screamin' Jay Hawkins, to represent this episode? Bon Temps is operating under a mob mentality, ravaging themselves and one another. As sensual pleasure steps in for intimacy, and bodies are reduced to crude vessels, even Jason looks chaste compared to his fellow citizens.

2.12   Beyond Here Lies Nothin'

Original air date: September 13, 2009
Written by: Alexander Woo
Directed by: Michael Cuesta

> **Maryann:** Come on, Sookie, it'll be our little secret. What are you?
> **Sookie:** I'm a waitress. What the *fuck* are you?!

Maryann prepares a sacrifice for her God. Eric meets with Sophie-Anne. Hoyt has had enough of Maxine. And Sam and Bill momentarily put aside their differences.

Did you spot the author? The woman at the bar who said, "Well, I certainly never expected anything like that to happen here!" is none other than Charlaine Harris, author of the Sookie Stackhouse novels. The comment could have been in response to

Maryann's storyline, which is much more minor in the series, surely a surprise to the originator of this character. Expanding the maenad story offered more material, more interpretations on a theme, and certainly made for better use of a large and outstanding cast. After investing an entire season in Maryann's antics, and genuinely believing that there was no known power that could destroy her, it turns out her death wasn't *that* hard to come by, which is a bit of a let-down. We do, however, draw a lot of satisfaction from knowing it's Sam who looks her in the eye in the moment she realizes there's no god, her eternity sealed in one crush of her heart. In fact, it's really quite heartbreaking. It's not so much about what it took to kill Maryann, but how much it took for Sam to be the one to do it. Like for most true heroes, there's a risk. Sam's victory is not so much that the town has been saved, or that he used his gift to secure that safety, but that flesh-and-bone Sam, the guy who doesn't want any trouble from anyone, is the person to put it all on the line. There isn't an ounce of ego in his decision. It's a good, good moment for Everyman Sam.

Michelle Forbes was consistently fantastic throughout the entire season. Not one misstep, and hers was a supremely good death scene. Unlike Godric, who gave himself over to the possibility of a god and punishment if there was one, Maryann's last words are pitiable. To see herself as merely human would have been humbling, so it wouldn't have been out of character to expect some degree of bargaining. Then again, she had just been harpooned by a bull's horn, so it may not have been a top priority. Even if Sophie-Anne's conviction that Maryann is just a mortal guided by a delusional sense of purpose is still unconvincing, the idea alone of a kind of self-curated supernatural experience is incredible. To think that Maryann would be capable with only sheer force of will, of controlling the deepest urges of an entire town.

To wrap up the season by having half the town wander in a stupor, with no memory, is a leap, if only because we've been spoiled by writing that takes a hard look at humanity. There's so much material to work with. Then again, Rene's arc at the end of season 1 drew to a swift close too, so having the second half of this series finale left open to set the scene for the mysteries of season 3 is perfectly in keeping with the pace Alan Ball set in motion from the very beginning. Every episode ends with a cliffhanger that forces the audience to ask even more questions of what's to come.

Risk accompanied by consequence is one of the most prevalent themes of the series, so it's unclear for now how, or if, the people of Bon Temps will ever reconcile what they did to themselves and one another. But it's, again, in perfect keeping with Hitchcock's philosophy that "There is no terror in the bang, only in the anticipation of it." Whereas Maryann's death didn't come with a huge bang, everything leading up to the moment kept us on our toes. It's also what makes Eggs such a passionate and unlikely dissenter. After all this time, he wants to accept responsibility? It makes his

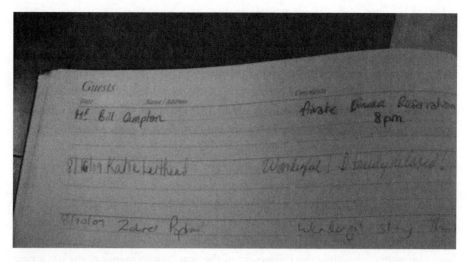

Bill Compton's reservation at the French restaurant where he proposes to Sookie. Note the superscripted "r" in Mr., just like they did in the olden days. It's all in the details! (Eleanor Tivnan)

death even harder to accept, because it took something so horrible to make him the man Tara could be proud of.

One obvious consequence of all the baby-making will be a baby. Money's on Arlene and Terry, the one truly hopeful relationship that came out of Maryann's destruction. Carrie Preston and Todd Lowe were consistent highlights this season, even though it was hard to accept their devotion to Maryann. It did give Terry a chance to play toy soldiers though, which was quite heartwarming, and amnesia is the only safe place to leave those memories.

One final disappointment is that we didn't get to see Jason and Andy save the day. It was a good ending for Sam, however tortured. But like Lafayette being taken over by Maryann, it seemed like a writers' device to reduce the number of characters to write for. It made sense for Tara and Eggs, less for Lafayette, but not for Andy and Jason, who had spent a good chunk of the show prepping for their big invasion.

The greatest evolution of the season, funnily enough, was our shifter, Sam. Has he finally learned how to accept his own body? (Can shifters suffer from body dysmorphic disorder?) Sam puts all his faith in Bill, essentially risking his life with no certainty that he'll survive on the other side. Is this another allusion to Godric, who chose a peaceful death over a violent world? In this case, Sam chose a violent death in hope of a more peaceful world. The moment where he contemplates a doe, his pain and exhaustion forming in tears, is a breaking point. There's simply no other direction for Sam to go but home. When he visits his foster parents, he truly is risen, left for dead, and back from the war. Whereas Godric died hoping for answers, Sam came back to insist on some. In season 3, we hope to get those answers too.

After Maryann's death, Sookie sees Bill limping down the road like a wounded dog. He falls into her arms and she supports the man who has, yet again, foiled her. Must she always be the last to know? Thank goodness, Stephen Moyer embeds such intense honor and loyalty into his performance of Bill, who spent most of this season in a no-win situation, save for his scenes with Deborah Ann Woll as Jessica — Daddy Bill is far more appealing than Vampire Bill and he owns that field. The proposal scene is quicker than we'd expect, but Anna Paquin's portrayal of Sookie as utterly conflicted is perfect. Everything has been quicker than she'd expected. From the night she met Bill she's never been without him. Now she's never without two vampires, Eric much stronger and potent than Bill. She's a surrogate mother to a newly turned vampire. She has yet to properly mourn her grandmother's death. And they all have targets on their backs for going up against the Fellowship of the Sun. Not to mention, she has a new power. Before she met Bill, she was just a telepathic waitress who lived with her grand-mother, had never had a boyfriend, never had sex, and never swore.

Sookie's telepathy was a major plot point in season 1. In season 2, her gift seems to come and go, more out of convenience to the writers, who otherwise wouldn't be able to put her in the same room with anyone. It's also what drew Bill to her. Without it, she's no less extraordinary, but she's not the girl we fell in love with either. There's also the question of genetics. Maryann can't possess Sookie but she can possess Jason. We know that Sookie probably received her gift from her grandfather, but the show hasn't discussed whether Jason has any powers. Is it possible he just hasn't tapped into his gift?

We know that to drink a vampire's blood is to get a different part of the vampire each time. Sookie has drunk from Bill several times, and in large volumes, yet she hasn't had any erotic dreams about him since they started having sex. Now that she's dreaming about Eric, will the dreams continue so long as they don't have a sexual rela-tionship? Are these things connected or just the writers ditching one wet dream for another? Sam drank a lot of Bill's blood. If Bill senses Sam in danger, will he come to his rescue too? And will Bill appear to Sam in his dreams as well?

Queen Sophie-Anne's scenes with Eric were marginally better than those with Bill. But she still doesn't possess enough presence to convince us she's a threat to anyone, let alone Eric. It feels like the writers are still trying him on for size. The monster in him seems to have subsided in favor of Yahtzee. It wasn't that long ago he was chewing on a man in his basement. Tara has matured, but is now more frightened than ever by the world. Just a taste of her original sarcasm would be a welcome return.

When will *True Blood* tackle race? Tara hooks up with what appears to be the only other black man in town, someone Lafayette even thought he had a shot at. Now he's

Tribute: Dale Raoul (Maxine Fortenberry)

> "Dale is so brilliant. If there were an award for most transformative performance it would go to her. For such a mean close-minded character, she is the most open and caring person."
>
> – Deborah Ann Woll

There's plenty in *True Blood* to make you cringe. Blood, gouged-out hearts . . . feeding those hearts to unsuspecting innocents. Personally though, nothing gets the hair on my neck standing straight as Maxine Fortenberry and her endless string of insults against her son, Hoyt Fortenberry. It was with strange relief that I watched her dancing crassly around her once-pristine kitchen, under Maryann's influence as most of Bon Temps. I was so happy to see her freed from her strict regimen of domestic perfection, that I thought, naively, it would unleash a litany of love, acceptance, and adoration for her son. Well, there's always next Christmas, right, Santa? Holy Hannah, if she didn't become even *more* venomous and *more* spiteful.

Some characters you love to hate, whether it's because they're so good at being so bad, or because you hope that, deep down, they're wounded little self-loathing birds with shockingly high levels of bad cholesterol. Dale Raoul, you scare the bejeezus out of me. That can only be the mark of a great performance. But, you, Maxine Fortenberry, you get 10 glass houses out of 10.

Where you've seen Dale Raoul: *Seinfeld, NYPD Blue, Party of Five, Six Feet Under, Friends, The Office, Seven Pounds*

dead. The bulk of the hard drama this year focused around addiction, cannibalism, faith, and enslavement, stories featuring one or all of the African American characters. And the only gay character also happens to be a drug-dealing, gender-bending black man who services closeted men on the down low. For a show that has captured just about every flag, race would be the most relevant and topical taboo Alan Ball could tackle next.

So who kidnapped Bill? Lorena seems like a good suspect. She did say that their paths would cross again, and she's already taken him hostage at the request of Eric.

Now that we know that Eric is working with Sophie-Anne, it wouldn't be a stretch to suggest that if it is Lorena, she isn't working alone. We'll find out in season 3!

Highlight: Bill: "I'm grateful that you would reveal your gift for the sake of the town." Sam: "It took me this long to realize that you suffer a lot more hiding something than you do if you face up to it."

Nightcap: The T-shirt Terry Bellefleur wears at Merlotte's reads: "WARNING: Beaucoup Dien Cai Dau. I suffer from occasional loss of mental stability and become very violent with only slight provocation. The Veterans Administration has determined that both mental and physical harassment of my person may be hazardous to your health and well being. So stay the hell out of my face. Thank you." "Beaucoup" is French for "very much," and "Dien Cai Dau" is a Vietnamese saying that is the equivalent of "crazy as a kicking rooster." The saying was adopted by U.S. soldiers during the Vietnam War. When Jason says that he loves the smell of nail polish in the morning, it's a bastardized allusion to Francis Ford Coppola's epic war film *Apocalypse Now* (1979) in which Lieutenant Colonel Bill Kilgore (played by Robert Duvall) says, "I love the smell of napalm in the morning," one of most memorable lines of American cinema dialogue. In the scene, Kilgore almost bears resemblance to an older Jason Stackhouse, unblinking as bombs fall all around him, distracted by the surf, his sense of play just as important as his duty to his country. Jason would be at home in that chaos. The original title of this episode was "Before the Night Is Over," a Jerry Lee Lewis and B. B. King song that plays while Sookie and Bill dance.

Location, Location, Location: The French restaurant in which Bill proposes is a bed and breakfast called The Stockade Bed and Breakfast, located on the south side of Baton Rouge, Louisiana. The property is listed as an archaeological site on the National Register of Historic Places. The Highland Stockade was a Civil War–era Union fortification and camp site, built in 1862 by Union troops as a check-point to protect the southern entrance into the city.

Suzuki Sets the Scene: For the destruction of Sookie and Gran's home, Maryann's paganism, not to mention invasion, was explored by bringing the outdoors inside. Shooting the scene proved to be a challenge, however, as the set dressers had to remove all the dirt, clean the set, then bring it back in. Can you imagine the challenge of continuity on mud and branches? As for Maryann's "meat tree," yes, real meat was used, replaced every day as it began to decompose. The crew even coined a nickname for the tree: Demetri. (De Meat Tree.)

Encore: The song that plays during the end credits is "Beyond Here Lies Nothin'," performed by Bob Dylan. Born Robert Allen Zimmerman on May 24, 1941, Bob Dylan is one of the most influential singer-songwriters in American history. Songs such a

"Blowin' in the Wind" and "The Times They Are a-Changin'" became anthems for the civil rights and anti-war movements. In 2008, the Pulitzer Prize jury awarded Dylan a special citation for his impact on popular music and American culture, "marked by lyrical compositions of extraordinary poetic power." Dylan's musical tastes span a wide breadth of genres: folk, blues, country, gospel, rock 'n' roll, and even traditional Christmas songs. He's been inducted into the Rock and Roll Hall of Fame, the Nashville Songwriters Hall of Fame, and the Songwriters Hall of Fame. "Beyond Here Lies Nothin'" is the lead single from the 33rd studio album from Bob Dylan, *Together Through Life,* released in April 2009. The song was produced by Jack Frost, Bob Dylan's pseudonym of late. The song also appeared in the HBO second season teaser, making it the perfect way to bookend the beginning and end of a season that showed us that while love may not conquer all, it's a powerful tool when wielded — be it for good or evil.

An Exclusive Interview with *True Blood*'s Patricia Bethune (Jane Bodehouse)

There are a number of character actors on *True Blood* who are all but unrecognizable out of costume: Adina Porter, Carrie Preston, and, another one of my personal faves, Patricia Bethune as Jane Bodehouse, Bon Temps' resident drunk. Initially a mix of sadness and desperation, Jane became the very picture of uncensored abandon when she was under the influence of Maryann. Yet Jane relishes in this state, and is one of the first people in Bon Temps to fall under Maryann's mystical embrace. What makes Jane most appealing, aside from Patricia Bethune's fierce commitment to playing her, are her vulnerable under-pinnings, her childish glee that Sookie gives her extra pickles offset by an overcompensating need to please as evidenced in the finger she cut off in offer of sacrifice to Maryann.

When I heard Patricia Bethune (*CSI*, *Grey's Anatomy*, *Desperate Housewives*) in a radio interview, I was surprised to hear how level-headed she was in her approach to her performance and what it requires of her physically and emotionally. What follows is my chat with Patricia about playing crazy Jane:

When Jane Bodehouse initially appears, she's quiet and understated. When we see you again, you're a firecracker. Can you explain the evolution?

I was cast as Jane Bodehouse in a potentially recurring role. The first season was rich with the development of Sookie and Bill's story, Sam, Jason, and their immediate worlds, and there wasn't a place for me in the story early on. Luckily for me, the second season began the further development of another main character, Maryann, and the whole town of Bon Temps and its residents, including Jane. The viewers were first introduced to Jane at the bar after many an hour of drinking, but in the second season Jane is already shown the effects of Maryann's presence right from the top. That enabled the writers to have Maryann bring out a side of Jane that had been stashed away for a long time.

What do you like most about Jane?

I love Jane's courage. She's still out there working it when a lot of women would be at home watching a Lifetime movie.

Do you pull from any influences, or even your own past performances?

Everything begins with the writing. Alan Ball and *True Blood*'s writing staff are the best of storytellers. They provide plenty of seeds to grow these characters. Then the directors make sure we all stay in the same episode, at the same point in time. Their guidance is essential. But once I perform a role, I let it go and allow whatever new character that comes my way to be her own. Jane's laugh is mine on a good day. As far as other influences, let's just say I have enjoyed time with the locals in a variety of establishments around the world . . .

Do you have a favorite scene of Jane's?

Of course, the scene where Jane cuts off her finger is a favorite. I also loved us all being duped by Jason and Andy when they were rescuing Sam.

Going into the show, did you have any idea that your character would become so deeply involved in the orgy scenes?

No, I didn't. I received a call from the director to ask what I would be comfortable doing. On the set, we were all given as much privacy as could be given. I was also fortunate to work with John Billingsley, a respected professional, whom I trusted completely. And Michelle Forbes is a doll. She is a powerful actress. She respects the craft and it shows in all her roles.

How is it working with Alan Ball? His reputation for giving actors a lot of room to play is well known.

There are many worries that actors have when creating a character. When you have the opportunity to work with Alan Ball, most of them are erased. You know it will be a good story; you know the writers have a vision far past where the individual actor can see; you know you will be surprised, at times, gleeful with each turn of the story. His presence creates both calm and energy on a set.

What do you think Jane wants in this world?

A good laugh and a good lay – not necessarily in that order. Jane wants company, even if it is just for a little while.

Could you picture Jane as a vampire?

If Jane was drunk enough, I think she would consider hanging out with a vampire for an evening. But she's not 25; becoming a vampire at her age is a long-term commitment to menopause. God help the planet if that happened!

Visit Patricia Bethune at www.patriciabethune.com.

True Blood on Twitter

The Roleplayers

By extending such reach to fans before season 1 of *True Blood* had even begun through a massive viral marketing campaign (see page 77), HBO had succeeded in fabricating an entire narrative around the brand of their show based on storytelling, humor, and something just a little out there. In doing so, they effectively embedded the world of *True Blood* into ours, normalizing the presence of vampires while piquing our curiosities.

They also jumped aboard the Twitter train by creating the profile @BonTempsGossip to dole out teasers and plot points. And the fans followed suit, borrowing the voice of the show and its characters to astonishing effect. "*True Blood* on Twitter" (www.truebloodtwitter.com) organized a troupe of almost 200 *True Blood* roleplaying identities, all characters from the books and/or series. These didn't include the countless more profiles created under similar usernames, or, in some cases, to subvert the characters, such as @GayVampireBill or @ButchAssSookie. Even locations and wardrobe have a voice — @FangtasiaBar, @GrabbitKwik, @LafayettesThong, and @Erics_Racerback. The list gets even more "just for fun" with tools, cell phones, food items, and iconic hairstyles all represented. Bill's bangs alone are the source of much-heated debate (@BillsBangs), so to see them reenacted on Twitter — bangs! — is a nod to those of us who love the series and worry at times for Bill's hair.

"We may be declaring our love or ripping someone's head off or serving a customer at Merlotte's or going to the GrabbitKwik for a gallon of milk," says the description on the website. "Some call it role-play, but we like to call it Twitterfic. Unlike typical RPGs, our characters don't just interact with each other. We respond to anyone who talks to us, and often they join our stories."

For their efforts, the players have been featured by *TV Squad*, *Geek Speak*, *American Way Magazine*, *Screamtress*, and *Entertainment Weekly* — where TV writer Ken Tucker notes that the roleplayers prove "once again that *True Blood* and Twitter are taking over the culture."

Unlike the AMC network, who suspended all *Mad Men* roleplaying Twitter accounts only to reinstate them after realizing how much free publicity they were losing, HBO openly endorses the *True Blood* players, stopping just short of full affiliation. The real testament to this troupe, however, is their dedication to their craft, extending the show further into our realities in the shape of real-time conversations with the likes of @EricNorthman, just when we want and need him. (Which, based on the level of activity on any given evening, is quite often!)

When I interviewed a number of the roleplayers for my site, there were moments when I could fully imagine the characters sitting on the other end, typing (or pounding) out their replies. I asked them about their reactions to recent events in Bon Temps. Here's a taste:

@SookieBonTemps: All the folks in town were actin' like black-eyed zombies what with their lo-lo-chanting. I swear it was like some unholy zombie Kumbaya they were singing to Bacchus.

@MerlottesBar [Sam]: I like it here. Life's pretty quiet usually. I got good customers, and I can own a little piece of land. Everybody gets in everybody else's business and I hear most of it at some point because it all comes through the bar, but that's a small town for ya. If folks stopped gossiping, they'd be dead, and we've had enough of that around here lately.

@JasonBT: To be a man is to fix what ya broke. Make what ya done wrong right. Maudette would scream, "Man your so damn good" so ya have to be good too.

@LafayetteTB: I woulda blow da witches head off but when ya don't know what your fightin' might as well be shootin' blanks. Maryann did her vibratin' thang and that was all she wrote.

@JaneBodehouse: Ifn' i rememberin' correctly when Mr. Compton came inta tha bar i was pritty good inta mah cups, but i vaguely rememba thinkin' he was a hot piece a new ass. *fans self*

@EricNorthman: I see only the difference between Godric and myself. He turned me to give me what I love most: life. He obviously did not feel the same. When I reach his age in another thousand years, perhaps I will understand his decision more than I do now.

@GodricofBlood: Immortality was not my choice. I too was turned and had to accept the new path I was given by my maker. My existence was not right. I did not live long enough as a human to fully understand what it meant. I should have died the day I was turned.

@LorenatheMaker: William is Mine and will always be Mine! He loves me, even if he doesn't realize it, right now. He is enthralled by that blonde blood bag, but she will grow old and he will lose interest.

@SteveNewlinJr: Vampires have no Soul. The Soul has long since departed when the human was killed to make way for the vampiric parasite. The empty husk that remains is simply a vessel for the Hell Beasts to inhabit. We simply execute the Lord's will and return the demons to Hell. It is neither murder nor mercy, it is pest control!

@SarahNewlin: It's important to me to help young women grow within our church, learn who they are, and how Jesus fits into their lives. Loving and supporting Steve in his endeavors is a huge part of my purpose on this Earth as well. *thinks* But I don't think I'd ever change hairdressers, even if Jesus asked me to.

Tweeting with @VampireBill

@BeccaWilcott: Accounts from the night you and Sookie first met at Merlotte's suggest that you had an almost immediate bond.

@BeccaWilcott: What's your attraction to Sookie?

@VampireBill: *eyes glaze over and tongue darts out to taste my lip* *turns and looks at you with eyes aglow* *a hiss escapes my throat*

@VampireBill: Sookie has re-awakened feelings in me, I never thought to experience again. She brought me my past, present, and future.

@VampireBill: I do believe that is all a gentleman should say on this particular subject. I am sure you understand.

@BeccaWilcott: What's your relationship to your maker, Lorena?

@BeccaWilcott: What place does she have in the world as you've come to know it?

@VampireBill: *spits the word* Lorena. She is my maker and I will not deny the allure and pull of such a force, or what I did while in her thrall.

@VampireBill: I am vampire. The blood lust is strong when one is newly made and I wished to please her.

@VampireBill: In the end, I could not endure the misery and had to be free or put to my final death. A place in my world? No. Never.

@BeccaWilcott: You, in turn, never planned to become a maker. Now, you have Jessica in your charge, a young woman with needs.

@BeccaWilcott: Do you trust Hoyt's intentions toward her?

@VampireBill: My hesitation was never with the Fortenberry boy, but rather with Jessica being newly made vampire.

@VampireBill: She is not in control of her hunger and urges and will not be, for quite some time.

@BeccaWilcott: As a Sheriff, Eric has more authority than you, yet there's clear tension between the two of you.

@BeccaWilcott: Now that he can boast that he's in Sookie's blood, are there "bad things" you'd like to do to Eric?

@VampireBill: I am honor-bound to him as a vampire in his Area. He is my Sheriff and I am in his debt for helping to save Sookie.

@VampireBill: Are there bad things I would like to do to him? *smirks* *lengthy pause*

@BeccaWilcott: Do you think Sookie's brother, Jason, is a help or a hindrance in the fight against the Fellowship of the Sun?

@BeccaWilcott: For instance, if you were to think back to the Civil War, would you have wanted Jason by your side in battle?

@VampireBill: I believe Jason did, indeed, prove helpful in the church. I find him mentally deficient.

@VampireBill: I have not commented as Sookie loves him and he is all she has left.

@VampireBill: In a battle of brawn, I would accept his help eagerly. In a battle of wits, I do believe I would have to pass.

@BeccaWilcott: Finally, if you could describe your relationship with Sookie in one word, it would be . . .

@VampireBill: Unexpected.

@PamVampTB: Eric is my maker. I owe him my loyalty. I have to obey him, but I do it willingly. I would retaliate against anyone that harmed him, which includes Sookie. I am a vampire first, and survival is my ultimate motivator. Well, that, and a great pair of pumps.

@JessicaHamby: NOT bein' a virgin was one of the only things I wanted when I was still alive. And then my new "life" starts and I find out that's the only thing I won't EVER lose. Hoyt doesn't understand that pain. It ain't just physical . . . it's just remindin' me over and over and over that I can never have what I want.

The sheer volume of followers the players have amassed is testament to the chord they've struck in fans. The accounts for Sookie Stackhouse (@SookieBonTemps), Bill Compton (@VampireBill), Eric Northman (@EricNorthman), Jason Stackhouse (@JasonBT), Jessica Hamby (@JessicaHamby), Lafayette Reynolds (@LafayetteTB), Sam Merlotte (@MerlottesBar), Pam Ravenscroft (@PamVampTB), Arlene Fowler (@ArleneFowler), Ginger (@FangtasiaGinger), Andy Bellefleur (@AndyBellefleur), and Terry Bellefleur (@TerryB_Fleur) bring in a combined 75,000 followers. And that's just the *tip* of the iceberg; it doesn't begin to do justice to all the other players who make up this dynamic community.

@MerlottesBar and @MaryannForreste are the *"True Blood* on Twitter" roleplaying accounts for Sam Merlotte and Maryann Forrester respectively (for the sake of the users' privacy, they will be referred to as "Sam" and "Maryann" throughout this chapter). Sam has been involved in roleplay since high school, and has played everything from a scientist to a revolutionary to a doctor, a spy, and an assasin. He had already devoured Charlaine Harris's books when he stumbled across the *True Blood* players on Twitter. "I liked the portrayals and the nascent story-lines and noticed that there was no Sam, so I thought I might give it a shot." As part of his obligations, he's also responsible for the upkeep of Merlotte's Bar and Grill, so included in his tweets are work schedules for other characters, serving up virtual drinks for visitors, and sounding out the all-important last call.

Maryann came to her roleplaying as a newbie, but was attracted to the character for her no-nonsense attitude. "She enjoys life and when she wants something she goes for it," she says. "It's an admirable trait; she's my idol."

Maryann spends around five hours a week roleplaying, more if other users continue to engage her in interesting ways — keep in mind, this is Maryann. You'd have to be about good times to keep her interest. Sam treats his roleplay as another job, online approximately 20 to 30 hours a week, in keeping with how much time regular patrons of Merlotte's would expect to spend with Sam. "But I don't mind at all," he says. "I just like Sam . . . He reminds me a lot of the men I knew when I was growing up in the South. They were simple, good, honest, country folk that would give anyone the shirt off their backs but would also not hesitate to point a gun at an intruder to protect their own."

Both roleplayers enjoy using Twitter as a challenging and creative outlet and understand its value to the *True Blood* audience. "I've been involved in creative writing and other performing arts since I was young," Sam explains, "and this is another angle on them both. I think the audience enjoys having their favorite (or not so favorite) characters around to get a beer from, ask questions of, or just chew the fat with." Maryann agrees, expanding on that to say, "[The audience] also gets a place where it can voice frustrations. It's like watching the football game on TV and yelling and screaming when something you don't like happens. But the TV never talks back. Here they can actually get a response back from us."

The popularity of Twitter is undisputed, but its 140-character constraints make it difficult to elaborate. The roleplayers have to find their way around it, but so far it hasn't proven to be problematic. "Obviously it's hard to get everything into the little box, but it does help you be concise," says Maryann, "which is perfect for my character because she doesn't beat around the bush too much." Sam, too, has learned to craft his tweets to their best advantage, something he believes has improved his overall writing. The immediacy of the medium can sometimes be a challenge, however. "[R]eaders sometimes expect us to be there all the time and real life does not always work very well with that."

So, how do they engage with other users? And do they often encounter people who believe them to be their characters? Sam says, "It was more common in the beginning. Most people seem to realize by now that we're just fans like they are." Fans, not employees of HBO? No, says Sam. "Payment would taint the fun of it for the players and the audience, in my opinion. My only 'payment' has been an advance bottle of Tru Blood soda."

As for the other people in their lives knowing about their roleplay, Sam says that his family and close friends know. Maryann says that not many people in her life know about her "alternative lifestyle" because "it's hard explaining what makes you want to play a maenad on Twitter."

There's also a lot of racy material on *True Blood*. But how do these players monitor their storylines in a public venue where they can't know the true identities, or ages, of the people they're engaging? "I prefer to avoid storylines that are gratuitously violent or sexual because I'm not personally comfortable with that," Sam says. Users who constantly play out "adult situations" typically lock their accounts, but Maryann prefers to remain as true to her character as possible with the caveat that if something is out there, anyone can see it. "You can suggest minors not follow but they can put on a face and follow anyway," she says. Sam generally tries to keep his tweets family-friendly, "but there will always be one or two things that aren't suitable for juvenile eyes. That's the nature of the internet, though," he continues, "it's not really my job to police anyone."

Besides, for Sam, who works for an equipment manufacturer, he dislikes drama as much as his character. "We're both interested in living our lives and being happy . . . However, I am not a bartender and have never been a bartender, much less a shapeshifting bartender."

Perhaps the most admirable quality of these players is how they use their presence to inform and motivate, as well as entertain. When they set up "Bites for Blood," a virtual blood drive, HBO took notice. Behind the scenes, the players constructed a simply sophisticated page on their site, their goal being to fill a vial of 500,000 virtual drops of blood. To donate, users were asked to click on the image of a number of participating characters. Doing so generated an automatic tweet including the Twitter handle for both HBO and the American Red Cross, and the message that you'd received a kiss (from a human) or a bite (from a vampire).

One-shot campaigns such as this rarely do anything to build lasting awareness for a cause or organization, but in this case numbers talked. @SookieBonTemps, the roleplayer account for Sookie Stackhouse, confirmed over 86,000 individual tweets were created in the first four hours, something that caught the attention of HBO, who stepped up to pledge $10,000 to the Red Cross if the players and their followers reached their goal, a seemingly insurmountable feat. "Sookie" said that to do so they had to generate approximately 45,000 "donations" *per day*. She confirms that not only did they reach their goal, but tripled it as word of mouth for the campaign spread from Twitter to Facebook, resulting in over 1.5 million digital imprints for both HBO and the Red Cross. Further to that, the participating roleplayers took the extra step of crafting individual responses to as many tweeters as possible, in keeping with their appreciation for fan loyalty.

Months after I'd interviewed a number of the roleplayers for my site, I received an excited tweet from a young man who had engaged his first roleplayer and couldn't believe when he responded. The following day, he wrote again, this time to say that he'd created his own character and had spent the evening tweeting back and forth with the other players. He was beyond jubilation; he said he felt included. During our exchange, another dozen tweeters had already posted in the hope of grabbing the attention of @EricNorthman or @JasonBT. @SookieBon Temps and @ArleneFowler had shown up for their shifts @Merlottes Bar, where @LafayetteTB was firing up the grill. It was fast, fun, and sexy. Just another day in the *True Blood* Twitterverse.

Tweeting with @AndyBellefleur

@BeccaWilcott: Now that things are starting to get back to normal around Bon Temps, do you feel vindicated?

@AndyBellefleur: No, 'cause still nobody's seen the peaag but me and Tara Thornton.

@AndyBellefleur: And I always know what I seen, even after throwin' back a few Abita Lights.

@AndyBellefleur: That damn peaag had me fallin' on my face in mud wallows.

@AndyBellefleur: If it ain't turned into Paul Bunyan bacon by now, it oughta be.

@BeccaWilcott: How has your view of Jason Stackhouse changed now that you know he isn't a killer?

@AndyBellefleur: Stackhouse is a half-decent guy when he ain't incriminatin' himself with vamper sex tapes.

@AndyBellefleur: He ain't the brightest bulb in the drawer, but it don't take a very bright bulb to trick a buncha demon zombies. Just some flares.

@AndyBellefleur: Hell, he saved my ass from freezin' to death. Plus, he wields a weapon better than some of our BTPD officers . . .

@AndyBellefleur: . . . even if it is just a frickin' nail gun. Never thought I'd be relyin' on Stackhouse for help — more like helpin' him into a cell.

@AndyBellefleur: Maybe that Marlboro bible camp really changed him.

@BeccaWilcott: Have your feelings on vampires changed at all now that Sookie's involved with one?

@AndyBellefleur: It still don't seem right that Miss Stackhouse wants a date where she's the damn appetizer, entrée, and dessert, . . .

@AndyBellefleur: . . . specially when there's lotsa normal, decent, hard-working, uh . . . living guys around here.

@AndyBellefleur: We ain't never had any vamps in town 'til vampire Bill moved into the Compton place.

@AndyBellefleur: Gives me the creeps, even when he is handin' out free frescas. *shudder*

@AndyBellefleur: I'm alright with him bein' here, just keep abidin' the law and stay away from my sister.

@BeccaWilcott: How do you think Sam is holding up after all this excitement?

@BeccaWilcott: He's been through a lot, but he's not talking about it with anyone.

@AndyBellefleur: Sam might be mysterious, and a sometimes-nudist, but he's still a helluva humble guy.

@AndyBellefleur: Not too many people that mighta made the same choice he did.

@AndyBellefleur: Sure wasn't anything in the Bon Temps Police manual trainin' 'bout how to handle a mob full of saucer-eyed zombies.

@AndyBellefleur: If Sam's the one-eyed man in the kingdom of the blind, guess that makes him Cyclops.

@AndyBellefleur: I'm just glad a damn Cyclops has my back.

In Conversation with Screenwriter Karen Walton

In season 3 of *True Blood*, werewolves emerge in Bon Temps. Karen Walton is the screenwriter of the cult indie film *Ginger Snaps* (2000), a huge fan of *True Blood*, and knows only too well what it's like to incorporate folklore into mainstream entertainment with convincing, relatable results. What follows is my interview with Karen, in which she explains her writing process, monsters as metaphor, and those we create.

What was it about supernatural creatures, in your case werewolves, that appealed to you when you began to write the script for *Ginger Snaps*?

It was the chance to examine all the crooked little lines between humans, our own beastliness, and beasts. Portraying creatures doomed by their own transformations is a kind of theme in all my stuff. And to be perfectly honest, my take on werewolves was really about who it happened to, a girl like Ginger, a self-declared outsider becoming something she did not choose to be.

How closely did you stick to werewolf folklore? Charlaine Harris played with vamp lore to great effect when creating her vampires, and Alan Ball also likes to play beyond the traditional definitions. Are there uses in stepping away from folkloric constraints?

Of course, there isn't one version of the lore. All the rules about what a werewolf should look like, behave like, where it comes from, what it wants from us – these are the inventions and enhancements of ages of storytellers from many cultures. Every culture has a story about something "half man–half beast," and almost every culture has a story about something that appears out of the wilds of nature, deadly to humans who "stray from the accepted or safe way" through the wilds. Or, living among us, there's the "wolf in sheep's clothing." So if I diverged, I suppose it was from letting the classic Hollywood version be my defining model.

Which is precisely how vampires have been treated in *True Blood*. Many of those "rules" have been put aside in favor of a more modern interpretation. The lore evolves alongside our metaphors, it seems.

In *Ginger Snaps*, we weren't so interested in towing a story over a set of preconceptions. Rather we connected our version of the phenom of becoming a werewolf to unhappy adolescent benchmarks, for young women specifically. For example, the decision to build the narrative around that first, single transformation linked up neatly with my take on the horrors of coming-of-age: wake up and find hair that wasn't there before, find you're driven by nasty impulses you can't explain, or in some cases even like about yourself, yet cannot seem to control, the outbursts, the lash-outs, the budding potential for real violence and harm – to yourself, to people you care about, to people you don't care about – the desire, and then the scary ability to take your society apart and being unable to resist that. And then what both these phenoms can do to your childhood relationships.

It's not dissimilar to the transformation Jessica makes from human to vampire in *True Blood*. It was great to see that first turn through the lens of a young woman.

At the time, *Ginger Snaps* was unusual because my main werewolf was female. In the Hollywood versions, that was pretty much unheard of: teen boys, yes, had been werewolves. But the whole brute force and snapping jaws and behaving like a horny dog-wolf on 'roids – the more visceral aspects of becoming a werewolf (and becoming a young woman) – were designed largely by and for men, with a distinctly male perspective. Hollywood was/is ever adverse to admitting young ladies too grow hair, anywhere but on their pretty little heads, etc.

Vampires have always been with us, but it seems as if werewolves are finding their way back into the supernatural consciousness. What do you think is the lasting appeal of any of these creatures?

I suppose the lasting appeal of all our monsters is, speaking only for myself, that they are a reflection of the cultures who create them, the funhouse mirror for the side of our psyches reality tends to socialize away. To me, we are what we fear, we define ourselves by our relationship with what threatens or terrifies us. The case-by-case, and decade-by-decade, versions of what we fear are all as old as the human race, in essence. Where honesty or prudery or morality tempers us, the monsters step in. And exorcise. Vigorously.

Different species – vampires or werewolves – fulfill by design different roles in the world of terror, and both are as flexible as icons to be made to serve any human relationship you want to challenge. Once fully manifested as creatures, they are both in theory tormented with some partial recognition, some fluency in the human condition, which they use to their own advantage, motivated by their own survival. Both often find that affinity with humanity bites them in the ass, if they get too involved with the treacherous empathy pure human beings ooze – they're both stuck with the unreliable limitations humanity likes to impose on them. I guess we do that to inspire the hope that the irrational, the Other, the Unknowable is somehow manageable, perhaps even defeatable. Though what we *really* all love is their possibility, that there are yet beings and worlds we cannot ever truly know, but that know us – too well.

What do you think about *True Blood*'s representations of the supernatural?

I am a great and long-standing fan of all the creative talents involved, am chomping to read the books, and I follow the fan fiction on Twitter. It's really quite brilliant and I can't wait for more. I favor horror that openly relates to the status quo, and sets about challenging it, with teeth.

Written in Blood

Talking to Author Kevin Jackson
(*Bite: A Vampire's Handbook*)

When I approached Kevin Jackson for an interview, my reasons were three-fold. I adore his book *Bite*, and was worried I'd copy it note-for-note (out of jealousy or spite, I don't know) if I didn't create some familiarity between us; his Canadian publicist happens to be a good friend of mine, and the contact seemed too good to waste; and, finally, I was born in England and have never returned save for a quick stopover en route to Nairobi many years ago. I think I've always wanted a British pen pal.

What happened after that is simple, as these things go. The correspondence came easy, and while I keep Google nearby at all times, I've learned a lot from Kevin. His enthusiasm for his subject is fused directly with his knowledge of it. It only confirms my belief that vamp lovers are some of the coolest kids around.

It's been suggested that as modern society became more individualistic our view of vampires softened. Once used as scapegoats, we now sympathize with them as lonely rock stars, less like monsters and more like our own alienated selves. Do you agree? And, if so, can you point to a moment in time or popular culture that reflects this?

"Softening." Broadly speaking, this is, of course, true – a majority of the vampires in the most commercial and/or artistically successful films and books of recent years have had sympathetic and even admirable qualities, and in some cases are shown to be ethically superior to humankind. Examples: Eli, the androgynous 200-year-old boy in *Let the Right One In*, who saves poor lonely Oskar from murderous bullies; or the existentially agonized priest-hero of Park Chan-Wook's utterly brilliant take on Therese Raquin, *Thirst*. I'd also like to point out how many contemporary vampire tales take place not merely in modern-day surroundings, but in positively dull, ugly, quotidian locations – a working-class housing estate in Stockholm, a business district in Seoul, a scruffy Bristol suburb (*Being Human*) . . . even *True Blood*, though it reads as exotic to those of us not from Louisiana, is deliberately set in an unglamorous backwater. This anti-exotic aspect of the mythos is fairly new; whereas the idea that vampires might be attractive and sympathetic has been with us at least since Polidori's tale of 1819. The vampire as Romantic lead is much more a re-discovery than a discovery.

I'd say that the Barnabas Collins character has a fairly good claim to being the progenitor of this kind of vampire. (He is, incidentally, all but unknown in the UK; I had heard about *Dark Shadows* in my childhood via comics and pastiches – maybe in *Mad* magazine? – but only saw episodes a couple of years ago, thanks to my novelist friend Matt Thorne, who loves the show and has it all on DVD.) I'd say, though, at the risk of repeating a small chapter in my book, that the softening up was being done for years before, thanks to (a) reruns of the Universal films on television, so that they became familiar and charming instead of frightening, and (b) comedy shows of the mid-'60s such as *The Munsters* and *The Addams Family*. (Was Morticia a vampire? In my mind she was. Lily Munster was obviously a true vamp, as were Eddie and Grandpa, but that show was much less interesting.)

The softening tendency obviously isn't universal – think, say, of the vampire horde in *30 Days of Night* (nice touch: the vampires have their own language), or the mutated, post-viral vamps in *I Am Legend*. These incarnations look back to the pre-Romantic, folkloric vampires, who were largely disgusting, incapable of human speech, none too clever and certainly not dashing. Some of the potency of Stoker's myth-making is that he combined the terror and loathing of the folkloric vampire with the melancholy elegance of the Byronic vampire; so that his Count may be by turns charming and terrifying. Recent versions of the myth have split up that inspired union, so that Edward Cullen is charming, aloof, melancholic, pretty – in a word, Byronic – but not even remotely frightening to most grown-ups; while the *30 Days of Night* mob can be rather chilling if you're in the right mood, but you definitely wouldn't want to go on a date with them. It would be interesting to see if writers and artists in the near future can combine the two, as they were combined in, say, the Christopher Lee Dracula series – well, the first couple of them.

The fact that so many people dream about these beings suggests any number of things. One appeal – a very potent one, I'd guess – is that the most fervent audiences dream of a life less ordinary. And an undead life, presented in sufficiently glamorous lights, is an attractive version of such an existence.

What do you make of Stephenie Meyer's defanged vampires? Do you see an agenda at work?

Ah, the Meyer phenomenon and its "agenda." The latter, I take it, refers to the whole biz about Stephenie Meyer being a Mormon and the books being propaganda for sexual abstinence or postponement? Well, it doesn't sound wholly implausible, though I have a hunch that there must be something at least a touch theologically wobbly for the Church of JC and the LDS about vampiric heroes. What, for instance, would Edward do if you waved a crucifix at him? (I haven't read past the middle of the second book; perhaps Meyer has written this scene? Though I doubt it.) One of the reasons why he is not frightening is that, whether or not you have religious faith, a vampire has to be *unclean* as well as *undead*. (Again, the Park Chan-Wook film plays an ingenious set of variations on this theme, not least because its hero becomes a vampire as an indirect result of seeking Christian martyrdom.)

My almost complete lack of ability to answer this question appropriately may be due to the fact that I JUST DON'T GET IT. Had I been the publisher's reader who had first received the manuscript, I would have binned it within 20 minutes. On the rare occasions when I have spoken to young girls who love the series, they have unanimously used the word "romance"; my hunch is that the vampiric component of the tales, though not negligible, is more like the wrapping paper than the present itself. Emma P., the 16-year-old daughter of my friends, explained to me with remarkable self-insight that she loves Edward, the character, not Robert Pattinson, the cute actor. And she emphasized that one of the things that makes her dream of Edward as a beau is that he has Nice Manners. Question: is one of the motors of the Meyer phenomenon a mass craving on the part of teenage girls that teenage boys would stop being oafish, childish idiots?

Now, Bella as a feminist? Well, I suppose if I were pretending to be a media studies lecturer, I might say something to the effect that the ideological positioning of the character is as much, or more, a question of how she is consumed as how she is produced. (Stripped of bibble, I mean that if her fans think she is a feminist heroine, then she is. End of argument.) I'd like to add that the young actress who plays Bella is terrific, I think; so inward-turned and troubled and subdued that she almost risks monotony, but sheers away from it at the last minute. A lesser talent would have done more scenery tearing. I haven't heard much about boy Bella fans flocking to the films to swoon over her – but I suspect that, at 17, I would have done just that.

If you've had a chance to see any of season 1 of *True Blood*, what do you make of vampires mainstreaming? Do we need our vampires to remain subversive, or is this precisely what the series is pointing to, that visibility exposes everyone's subversions?

I speak cautiously here, as I have only seen a few episodes; it struck me as at least pretty damned good, at times verging on terrific, from the dazzling opening sequence (I simply can't think of a better one in the whole history of TV series, not even the one for *The Sopranos*) onwards. It seems to have dragged in a fairly healthy audience who otherwise wouldn't go near vampire fodder, some of them drawn by the raunchiness, some just by the general air of knowing cool that suffuses the whole enterprise. I'd read a few of the Charlaine Harris novels out of a sense of duty, and found them passable but forgettable (this is praise of a kind – a lot of the vampire fiction I dipped into turned out to be unmitigated drivel); this series is decidedly a case of the visual medium improving on its written source.

One of the things that most people who are not blind drunk when they watch it soon twig to is that it uses vampirism as a successor to the Civil Rights, Gay Rights, and other emancipatory movements (this includes lovely touches in the credits, like "God Hates Fangs," and the child dressed in KKK robes) to make drama and comedy – it's a very witty show – of the Otherness question. A delicious moment in an early episode: Sookie, who is a *nice* Christian (thus off-setting the vamp-hating Christian fundamentalists and bigots we see both in the cast of characters and on news-show style clips from TV), says that Jesus would have embraced vampires in divine love. Theologically dodgy, perhaps, but spot-on in terms of Sookie's warm-hearted character. As even my cat has figured out, the series dances elegantly around the question of Otherness, and how much of it we will welcome/tolerate/stand. In the early episodes, at least, questions of ethnicity and sexual orientation are treated as trifling if not invisible in the context of a homo sapiens/homo Nosferatu divide; thus, the series doesn't feel liberal-preachy in the mode, say, of early dramas about race relations, but sucker-punches you with a juicy, sexy yarn and lets the play of values go its own way . . . I look forward to becoming addicted.

During research for your book, did you encounter any real vampires (i.e. sanguine, psi, psychic)?

Yes, in the sense that I hung out with, and then joined, a crowd of fanged and dark-dressing types who call themselves vampires or more exactly vampyres, and am now a fully paid-up member of the London Vampyre Group. They can look rather alarming, especially in full regalia – one of them recently showed up at a talk I gave in dark body armor, a giant helmet, a face painted like a human skull and a genuine ram's skull as a codpiece – but, you will hardly be surprised to learn, are entirely sweet and gentle people, almost to the point of bathos. (At one of the meetings I attended, there was an '80s pop trivia quiz. I do not know whether I am boasting or confessing when I say my team won.)

However, at the launch for my book at a fine emporium called Wynd's Little Shop of Horrors, I did become aware of a rather more sinister sub-group in attendance who were bragging about more dubious practices than trivia quizzes, including the ritual consumption of actual human blood. The main braggart was someone I had already identified as a bore and a jerk, and I wasn't altogether surprised. It didn't fill me with horror, just mild contempt.

What is your earliest memory of vampires? Was it literary? Animated? Cinematic? Do you recall how it impacted you? And how else has your interest in vampires manifested itself in your life?

Well, I ask again, was Morticia a vampire or not? I was about 10 when I first saw her, played by Caroline Jones I believe, and it was something very much like love at first sight. But it was only a matter of months after that, if I recall correctly, when I discovered a wonderful publication called *Famous Monsters of Filmland* – wholly unaware that countless thousands of other baby boomers were also feasting greedily on it – and encountered both the Bela Lugosi and Christopher Lee incarnations of Dracula. The identification with the latter was instant, though I knew Lee's Dracula only through black-and-white stills and posters; *this* was who I wanted to be when I grew up. (Further sordid confessions can be found in the introduction of my book. Though slightly tweaked for would-be comic effect, they are otherwise shamefully true.) Not every aspect of my life has been shadowed by that encounter, but I would be lying if I were to deny how potent the fascination has been from time to time. About four years ago, I founded an informal vampire seminar in Cambridge; it is still going strong, and we are all going off to see *Daybreakers* next week.

If I had to pick a favorite vampire, though, I'd say undoubtedly the one I made up myself for a little promotional film, *Bite: Diary of a Vampire Housewife*, Laura. (Her name, and some of the pretentious symbolism of this squib, comes from Christina Rossetti's poem "Goblin Market," which I choose to read as a displaced vampire fable.) Like me, like thousands or millions of others, Laura finds that vampires are not a threat but a promise – a promise, again, of a life less ordinary. But in the long term: Christopher Lee's Dracula. Never bettered.

Our formal interview ended there, but our personal correspondence continued, and a few weeks later Jackson emailed me the following anecdote:

So, there I was, yesterday afternoon, talking to a bunch of 17-year-old lads about vampires . . . and I include a clip from the very opening of *True Blood*'s series premiere. Only about a quarter of them had even heard of the show, let alone seen it, even though they have all kinds of communications gizmos. This is odd, as it has been playing on satellite channels here for well over a year and more recently has been screened on Channel 4. As far as I could judge, most of them seemed to be captivated by this initiation, though there was one kid who scornfully dismissed it as stupid and "smut" – what's wrong with this kid? At the age of 17 I would have been grateful for the mildest glimpse of a well turned ankle (well, you know what I mean) – and thus a terrible collapse from the high literary standards of the 19th century. I think the kid was essentially trying to wind me up, and didn't give a hoot about the smut factor. So I replied to him that a characteristic product of alleged 19th-century Nosferatu stuff was *Varney the Vampire*, an astoundingly ill-written, bloated, inchoate, and simply idiotic potboiler, compared to which *True Blood* is Ibsen, Chekhov, and the Marx Brothers all rolled into one. Don't think he bought it; let's call it a draw.

Interview with a Sympathizer

sym·pa·thize: *intr.v. sym·pa·thized, sym·pa·thiz·ing, sym·pa·thiz·es.*
1. To feel or express compassion, as for another's suffering; commiserate.
2. To share or understand the feelings or ideas of another.

I asked. Over 300 of you answered. Here's a selection from some of your responses to my "Interview with a Sympathizer" questionnaire at www.rebeccawilcott.com. Do you recognize yourself?

Q: How do you feel about the casting on *True Blood*?

So far, the casting has been exceptional. I'm especially impressed with the casting of Nelsan Ellis as Lafayette and Rutina Wesley as Tara. They are such unique characters who defy traditional African-American stereotypes. Casting Anna Paquin was also a great choice; my God, she's hot! And she really captures Sookie's naivete.

I'm extremely glad that the decision's been made not to do any stunt casting or get any A-list names for guest shots. That is an extreme distraction from the plot and feel of the story, and I think the show comes off a lot better without it.

Alexander Skarsgård is absolutely perfect as Eric. PERFECT. He gets this character completely and many, many book Eric fans feel the same. Any complaints we have about Eric on the show have nothing to do with Skarsgård's portrayal. The way the character is being written is the bugbear, not the actor. Every now and then Skars gives us an Eric we recognize (the bullet sucking scene, the dream sequences) and we lap it up.

Stephen Moyer – love the guy, he comes across so well in interviews and he has the acting chops. But he is too old for this role. Watching him and Sookie have sex feels incestuous. His whole presence feels so much older than her and I just don't like it. Book Bill was about 30 when he was turned, and so was Eric. They've stuck to that with Eric but then added 10 years onto Bill. It's odd.

Although Pam's character on the show is much older than her character in the books, Kristin Bauer plays the part perfectly. Pam is funny in the books and I hope to see more of that on the show. I love Anna Paquin, don't get me wrong, but sometimes she doesn't quite get it.

Like many others, I was not a fan of Evan Rachel Wood as Queen Sophie-Anne. In the novels, she was described as the world's most dangerous teenager. The Queen in the TV series came off more spoiled and entitled than dangerous.

Q: Do you have a favorite character on the show?

It's real toss-up for me between Lafayette and Eric. Both are such complex characters. Lafayette is a gay character who at times acts more "straight" than the heterosexual characters. He's tough, brash, and self-made. Oddly enough, despite his drug use and risky behaviors, he is still a voice of reason. Eric, on the other hand, is pure id. His pursuit of Sookie in the face of Bill's warnings is exciting.

Eric is definitely my favorite heartthrob. He is so dark and brooding and mysterious. Not to mention his undeniable sex appeal. Lafayette is also amazing. I love his flair and how he is so comfortable with himself. He cracks me up. Oddly enough, I also like Andy Bellefleur. He is strange, but lovable in his own way. He really came through in the end of season 2.

Gran. I know she was only around for the first five episodes of season 1, but she was so sweet and endearing. I was *shocked* to see her go so early . . . and how she did.

Eric. I could give a long and winding analytical reason (of which all would be totally true), but for time's sake, I'll just say he's *smokin'* hot.

I love Hoyt for his wholesomeness and boyish courtship tactics. But my heart − scratch that, my *neck* − belongs to Eric. He is the very essence of a vampire, right down to the instantly seductive good looks. He is lust, personified.

Lafayette. I would peg him as the narrator. From his post at Merlotte's, he can see the town without having to jump up in it all the time, though that wouldn't really stop him if he wanted to. He's fun, confident in his skin, adventurous, and *gorgeous.* I love the way he talks, from his drawl to how he simply cuts down the shit in a situation and tells it like it is.

I'll say Sookie . . . because she can read my thoughts.

Q: Are you squeamish about any of the more graphic elements of the series: blood, sex, or violence?

I was so disturbed as Tara and Eggs ate Maryann's Hunter Soufflé that I curled up on the couch in horror. I think that was one of the more horrific things I've ever seen, especially with the way it was shot. Watching Tara, a character I really like, gorging herself on a human heart, was frightening.

Not at all. What would be left if you took away the blood, sex, and violence? *Little House on the Prairie*? *shudders*

Mostly the blood. Everything else I can tolerate — as long as my parents are fast asleep and the volume isn't too loud.

The only time I ever got even remotely squeamish was when Tara and Eggs stared digging into that Daphne Pie. I shudder even to think about that. And I swore off raspberry dessert syrup for a long time after it.

The sex and nudity is so overdone it's humorous . . . It's probably good for reducing costume expenses. I will stick to my belief that sex is not a spectator sport, and looking at bare bodies is not all that interesting. And on other shows vampires turn to ash when they become definitely dead. I don't understand why the show wants it to be as messy as possible. Nobody's going to do a post-mortem on a vampire.

I've had a few "I can't believe they went there!" moments, but it's not the blood or sex that get to me, it's the visceral stuff like the sound of the vamp's teeth as they puncture skin. There's the scene when Lafayette is being held in Eric's dungeon, shortly after Eric has ripped off the other prisoner's leg. Lafayette is looking for anything to help him escape. He spots the ripped-off leg and remembers that there's an artificial joint in it. He picks up the leg and thrusts his hand inside the bloody flesh, trying to pull out the joint, so he can use it as a tool. It was the concept of being that desperate and the "squelchy" sound that bothered me.

No. I got bored, though, because so much of it was pointless and poorly portrayed. On the other hand, when it was good, it was excellent. An example of the latter is the scene in the basement of Fangtasia with Royce, Eric, and Lafayette. Damn. It always reminds me of that exchange from *Pulp Fiction*: "Who's Zed?" "Zed's dead, baby. Zed's dead." (I wish Quentin would take over this show. That would be epic.)

Q: Do you believe vampires exist?

I'd like to believe that they exist . . . There are UFO sightings . . . the Elvis stories haven't died down. And maybe it's just that my interpretation of a vampire isn't what they actually are and they already do exist. What if they're these ugly troll people? What if someone like Amelia Earheart was a vampire and her disappearance was just her changing from one name to another. I mean, if I was a vampire, I doubt I could keep my name without tweaking it for centuries.

No, I don't think they're real — even if my parents always said I was a creature of the night.

I know for a fact that vampires exist; they just aren't like the ones we read about. And no I am not one.

Unlikely, although you just don't know. I think it's more likely that the vampire is an archetype built on something, maybe drawn from people who were misinterpreted, then turned into monsters, people who invaded the stability and livelihood of tiny villages by attacking their cattle, etc. The contemporary vampire has struck a chord from a place of loss, the forbidden, and a sexualized sadness.

I believe emotional vampires exist, but they're just humans who like to thrive on other's pain.

"There are more things in heaven and on earth than are dreamed of in your mind, Horatio," to paraphrase the Bard. The universe is too vast and life too short to discount anything. My guiding light is "Imagine everything; believe nothing, and then all things are possible."

It's all fantasy, a way to escape the doldrums of an everyday existence. While it would make the world a far more interesting place if in fact they did exist, I'm going to have to go with no, they don't.

I believe that there are people out there who believe they are vampires and drink blood from others. I do not believe that those people are immortal, supernatural beings.

Q: Have you ever fantasized about being turned?

No. Living forever can't be all that it's cracked up to be.

I wouldn't say fantasized about it; more like imagined what it would be like to see all those centuries of life experiences.

I actually have given being turned some thought and I'd definitely go for it. I'd be a kick-ass vampire too.

Yes. The idea of immortality has appealed to everyone at one time or another, right? And the idea of sharing blood with someone and really having a deep bond with them is appealing in its own right.

Yes, I have fantasized at great lengths about being a vampire, and being turned. I have a deep desire to be Nosferatu. Maybe not the really ugly ones, but a vampire, for sure.

Not at all. Sorry, I'm not down with all the blood. And I love food too much.

Hell, yes. All of that power, no more papers for graduate school, not having to cook anymore. I think about it all of the time.

I've probably wanted to be one for Hallowe'en one too many times! To live an eternity would be lonely. And endless life means always having to be self-motivated. That kind of liberty can keep you up at night, or you can say, "Fuck it." Take Godric, for example. His anguish was to witness all this passage of time, yet to see very little accomplished. As mortals, we live with the same eternal questions, but at least we know we'll die before we get to answer any of them. I also feel for vampires, because the things humans fuel themselves with — in particular, food — are part of a larger connection to community. Something as simple as breaking bread is lost.

No, but I have fantasized about being ravished by a certain Viking.

Q: Do you feel the series diverges from traditional vampire lore?

The series doesn't seem to diverge much, except in its general premise. Vampires, by nature, are solitary creatures, lurking in the shadows. *True Blood* provides them with an infrastructure, a secret society in which they answer to higher powers. I actually like this. It makes sense that they would need to stick together at some point. It also creates more conflict as boundaries are broken.

I think it sticks pretty closely to the lore. It doesn't make a mockery of the standards, like other teen-girl-aimed atrocities that currently dominate the market (Cough!*TWILIGHT*!Cough!). A lot of the lore is in place: aversion to sunlight, stakes to the heart, fire. Fortunately, they did away with the holy water, mirrors, and garlic. I always thought those were silly. Every vampire universe comes up with its own rules and I like *True Blood*'s a lot.

I'm not terribly familiar with vampire lore. But I'm pretty sure fangs don't make a little popping noise as they appear and disappear.

It doesn't bother me that they don't seem to react strongly to crosses or stuff like that. At least they don't sparkle. What I do like are details — like, for instance, when a vampire cries, he or she cries blood. And what I've always liked is that the vampires in Harris's stories are out in the open. That's a welcome deviation for sure.

I've done some research and what caught my attention was that vampires are not supposed to do any kind of penetration except for the bite. No sex! But I like them better having sex.

I am so glad that they kept the "I have to be invited in" part of the lore, together with the sunlight and silver. The ineffectiveness of religious icons worked fine as well; it made a lot of sense when it came to the scenes with the Fellowship of the Sun.

I think the development of the Tru Blood beverage solved the problem of having to be in constant seclusion and hiding. If it were me, the sunlight rule could stay as it is. I really don't like being out in the sun to begin with. The world doesn't stop at sundown, so why fight it?

Vampires in this series are different from Dracula and I have no problem with that. Just as I don't mind that Merlin and Harry Potter are two completely different types of wizards or that elves and dwarves in the Forgotten Realms are just like elves and dwarves in Middle-earth.

The most obvious divergence is the ability to survive on synthetic blood. I'm okay with this, because it obviously facilitates the whole coming-out-of-the-closet scenario. It also gives vampires a choice in how they sustain themselves. Their view of themselves as predators is based on their need for human blood to survive. Remove that need, and you have vampires who still have a vampire nature to struggle with, yet they don't have to be predators anymore. That opens up some interesting possibilities for the way they interact with humans.

I think the blood bond theme that runs through the books is a very intriguing new addition to vamp lore, even if it's still a little unclear as to what it means for Sookie. That's been altered a little in the show, with the drinking of vampire blood in large quantities leading to sexual fantasies. In the books, there has to be a pre-existing attraction for those fantasies to occur, in the show, there doesn't. I'm a little annoyed by that.

Q: Do you see any ties to minority rights in *True Blood*'s depiction of vampires?

Oh, absolutely I see the connections. I think it adds a very interesting subplot/undertone to the story. Hopefully, if there are any homophobes watching the show they see the connections too and realize how stupid it is for them to discriminate based on something that individuals can do nothing to change (not that they should even try).

The media has put a lot of emphasis on the gay and lesbian interpretation of the VRA, probably because Alan Ball is gay. While lines like "out of the coffin" support this, I don't think the show is that obvious. Civil rights are to be shared by all, yet do not come without consequences. One of the show's greatest assets is its willingness to show both sides of the issue, creating a greater context to the events that take place. We see this especially in season 2 as the vampires of Dallas have to take on the Fellowship of the Sun.

I think it is a great way to send a message without being overbearing or controversial about the topic. I also think it gives a show that is clearly very make-believe a very real-world connection.

I'm not sure it adds value to the show. It's like dodging anvils really. It's like every other scene sometimes. We get it already!

The connections are there, but do not overwhelm the show. I think it is a nice undercurrent, but not overly allegorical. They add their own little bit of value to the show because gay rights are something that we as Americans are, unfortunately, still struggling with. I think people are afraid of what they don't know or what makes them feel uncomfortable and they would rather hate than accept those things. I'm glad Alan Ball and the writers have chosen to address this important issue that we all need to continue to work on.

The world treats LGBT people as if they are something unreal or unnatural, much like the way people (in this series) treat vampires.

Being gay myself, it was pretty hard not to see that connection. If anything, I think it endeared me to the show even further, as the fight for equality and acceptance has always been important to me, and it's nice to see that fight in another context.

Q: Do you have any rituals when you watch *True Blood*?

I record the show and watch it several times after each showing. Always alone so I can concentrate.

My ritual is to watch it as it airs. I don't care what my boyfriend says, we're watching it. He could take it or leave it. Sometimes if I have to DVR IT, I actually enjoy it more alone since I can exclaim and also drool over Eric as I please.

I watch it alone, *never eating*, because I was eating when I watched Eric dismember that poor guy in the basement. Won't make that mistake again!

I watch it alone on my laptop. My parents saw a few bits and the characters were having sex at those moments! So my parents think that it's some nasty, gory show. That's great, I really don't want my parents next to me when I'm watching it!

My husband and I always used to watch the show together before he left for basic training. We both used to work nights, so if one of us was off before the other we would read the title of the episode and text it to one another to prep us for the episode, but we would never watch it alone.

Dark room, no exceptions. I think the darkness adds to the ambience and feel of the show, plus I feel a little bit more "in the story" that way. I will wait 'til the episodes are available to download, then my boyfriend and I watch at the same time, and connect via Skype so we can talk and share in every last surprise.

I watch with my best friend who has also read all the books. We imbibe a lot of alcohol. Then we spend an hour laughing, screaming, swearing, swooning, and sometimes throwing things at the television. Afterwards we spend about two more hours conducting an autopsy of the episode, and then the next week we get together and do it all over again. After the season finishes we have a marathon — all 12 episodes. When that is over we cry for a bit, and then we go back to our books.

Q: Who have you been surprised to learn watches *True Blood*?

One of my teaching colleagues is also a big fan, which is a bit more interesting, since she appears to be a goody-goody teacher. I guess there's a little more bite in her than I expected.

My very conservative, Catholic niece who is raising small children, and even objects to the diversity on *Sesame Street*, never misses *True Blood.*

A priest.

Funny story. When my mother came to visit, I hooked her on *True Blood.* On her flight back home, she was bumped to first class, where she was seated next to porn star Ron Jeremy and they watched an episode of *True Blood* together on the flight.

I found out my über-conservative boss watches the show! It's a little creepy thinking about him watching some of the scenes.

Sometimes I can get my husband to sit in the room with me, and I think he enjoys it even if he says he is just watching it for the boobs.

Sources

Alexander-Skarsgardfans.com

AllStephenMoyer.com

Alston, Joshua, "Give HBO Some Credit." *Newsweek*. September 22, 2008.

AmericanVampireLeague.com

AndySwist.com

Armstrong, Stephen, "*True Blood* Is Latest in the Vampire Trend." *The Sunday Times*.
Online. June 21, 2009.

AskMen.com

AusielloFiles.EW.com

Barber, Paul, *Vampires, Burial and Death: Folklore and Reality*. New York: Yale
University Press, 1988.

Barnes & Noble Studio. BarnesandNoble.com

Bernstein, Abbie, "Alan Ball Interview." *Buzzy Multimedia*. Online.

———. "*True Blood*'s Rutina Wesley Gets Freaked Out by Orgies." *iFMagazine*.
Online. August 21, 2009.

Bierly, Mandi. "*True Blood*'s Pam, Kristin Bauer, Talks Meeting Her Maker (and
Alexander Skarsgård)." *PopWatch*. Online. September 11, 2009.

BillsBelles.wordpress.com

BiteClubShow.com

BlogTalkRadio.com/True-Blood-in-Dallas

Bloodbondsblog.com

BloodCopy.com

Bloody-disgusting.com

Boursaw, Jane, "Interview with a Vampire: Stephen Moyer of *True Blood*." *TV Squad*.
Online. June 12, 2009.

Braxton, Greg, "Rutina Wesley Hopes Her *True Blood* Role Is a Stepping Stone for
Other Black Actresses." *Los Angeles Times*. Online. September 11, 2009.

Buchanan, Kyle, "The Verge: Rutina Wesley." *Movieline*. Online. June 1, 2009.

Bunson, Matthew, *The Vampire Encyclopedia*. London: Thames & Hudson, 1993.

CampBlood.org

Carbone, Gina, "*True Blood* Star Ryan Kwanten Socks it to Jimmy Kimmel."
SeaCoastOnline. Online. September 10, 2009.

CharlaineHarris.com

Claremont, Chris and Michael Golden, *Avengers Annual 1*. Marvel Comics, August 1981.

Cling, Carol, "Las Vegas Academy Grad a Shooting Star." *Las Vegas Review-Journal*. January 29, 2008.

Cohen, Daniel, *Encyclopedia of Monsters: Bigfoot, Chinese Wildman, Nessie, Sea Ape, Werewolf, and Many More*. London: Michael O'Mara Books Ltd, 1989.

Créméné, Adrien, *La mythologie du Vampire en Roumanie*. Monaco: Rocher, 1981.

D'Arbonne, Jess, "Jace Everett Wants to Do Bad Things With You, in a Nice Way." *Blast*. Online. July 11, 2009.

D'Avalon, Vivienne, "The Truth about Modern Day Vampires." *Instant Magick*. Online.

D-Kitchen.com

DeClemente, Donna, "HBO Promotes Season 2 of *True Blood* with Sweepstakes & Social Media Created by Vampires." *Donna's Promo Talk*. Online. June 27, 2009.

Dethloff, Henry, C., "Our Louisiana Legacy." *Steck-Vaughn Company*: 1980.

Doyle, Chelsea, "Anna Camp Chats about Her Role on *True Blood*, Getting Nude with Daniel Radcliffe & More." *Starpulse Entertainment News*. Online. September 3, 2009.

EricNorthman.net

EW.com

Facebook.com/TrueBlood

Faivre, Antoine, *Les Vampires. Essai historique, critique et littéraire*. Paris: Eric Losfeld, 1962.

Fangoria.com

FellowshipoftheSun.org

Ferber, Lawrence, "Out for Blood." *Windy City Times*. Online. October 9, 2009.

Féval, Paul, *Les tribunaux secrets: ouvrage historique*. Paris: E. et V. Penaud Frères, 1851–52.

Frayling, Christophe, *Vampyres: Lord Byron to Count Dracula*. London: Faber, 1991.

Freezedriedmovies.com

"Fresh Vein of *True Blood*." *Fangoria*. August 2009.

Goldberg, Lesley, "Exclusive Interview with *True Blood*'s Kristin Bauer." SheWired.com. Online. November 11, 2009.

———. "Fresh Blood." *Advocate*. Online. October 26, 2009.

Goldberg, Michelle, "Vampire Conservatives." *The Daily Beast*. Online. July 18, 2009.

Goodhart, Benjie, "Interview with Alexander Skarsgård." *Channel4*. Online. August 2009.

Harris, Charlaine. *All Together Dead*. New York: Ace Books, 2007.

———. *Club Dead*. New York: Ace Books, 2003.

———. *Dead and Gone*. New York: Ace Books, 2009.

———. *Dead as a Doornail*. New York: Ace Books, 2005.

———. *Dead to the World*. New York: Ace Books, 2004.

———. *Dead Until Dark*. New York: Ace Books, 2001.

———. *Definitely Dead*. New York: Ace Books, 2006.

———. *From Dead to Worse*. New York: Ace Books, 2008.

———. *Living Dead in Dallas*. New York: Ace Books, 2002.

———. *Touch of Dead, A*. New York: Ace Books, 2009.

Hawbaker, Laura, "Actor Nelsan Ellis Vamps it Up on *True Blood*." *Time Out Chicago*. May 2009.

Haynes, Lorien, "Rising Vamp: Anna Paquin Back in the Limelight." *Daily Mail*. Online. July 19, 2009.

HBO.com/TrueBlood

Hernandez, Lee, "Valerie Cruz on Her *True Blood* Character: 'I Modeled Her Accent after Penelope Cruz.'" *Latina*. Online. July 21, 2009.

Hudson, Stacey, "Vampire Mastermind." *Metro Spirit*. Online. January 2009.

Humphreys, Justin, "Rosy Outlook: From Satires to Vampires with Alan Ball." *The Hook*. Online. November 5, 2009.

Hurwitz, Siegmund, Gela Jacobson (trans.). ed., *Lilith, the First Eve: Historical and Psychological Aspects of the Dark Feminine*. Einsiedeln, Switzerland: Daimon Verlag, 1992.

IamNotaStalker.com

IMDb.com

Jackson, Kevin, *Bite: A Vampire Handbook*. London: Portobello Books, 2009.

Jones, Ernest, "The Vampire." *On the Nightmare*. London: Hogarth Press and Institute of Psycho-Analysis, 1931.

Juergens, Brian, "Interview with Nelsan Ellis from *True Blood*." *After Elton*. Online. October 26, 2008.

KristinBauer.com

Lacob, Jace, "Blood Bath: Televisionary Talks to *True Blood* Writer/Executive Producer Alan Ball." *Televisionary*. Online. September 14, 2009.

Laker, Freddie, "HBO's *True Blood* 'Viral'/ARG Campaign." *Social Media Today*. Online. September 8, 2008.

Laycock, Josephe, "*True Blood*: When Marketing Goes for the Jugular." *Religion Dispatches*. Online. June 10, 2009.

Littlezas.net

"Louisiana History." *Destination 360*. Online.

LoveBitten.net

LovingTrueBloodinDallas.com

Marcg.fr

Marigny, Jean, *Vampires: The World of the Undead*. London: Thames & Hudson, 1993.

Martin, Andrew, "*True Blood*." *Interview*. Online. June 11, 2009.

Matthews, K. J., "Interview with Alan Ball." CNN. Online. October 5, 2009.

McNally, Raymond T., *Dracula Was a Woman*. New York: McGraw Hill, 1983.

McWhiter, Erin, "*Home and Away*'s Ryan Kwanten Finds Success in *True Blood*." *The Courier Mail*. February 17, 2009.

Montoya, Maria C., "HBO's *True Blood* Star Sam Trammell Finds His Way Home to Louisiana." *The Times-Picayune*. June 27, 2009.

Murray, Rebecca, "Alexander Skarsgård Interview." About.com. February 2009.

Nemecek, Larry, *Star Trek: The Next Generation Companion*. New York: Pocket Books, 2003.

NewWorldEncylopedia.org

Nicholson, Rebecca, "*True Blood* Creator Alan Ball on Season Two: Sink Your Teeth into This." *The Guardian*. Online. February 26, 2010.

Obrecht, Mitch, Omahastar.livejournal.com

Paskin, Willa, "Please, Amy Heckerling, No More Vampires." *Black Book*. Online. November 9, 2009.

PatriciaBethune.com

Phillippi Ryan, Hank, "On Vampires." *Jungle Red Writers*. Online. September 30, 2008.

PopWatch.com

Pretty-scary.net

"Project Paranormal," PenguinGroup.com.

RandomHistory.com

Raymond, Joan, "Alexander Skarsgård Is a Neck Man." *Newsweek*. Online. September 11, 2009.

"Reconstruction: A State Divided." *Louisiana State Museum*. Online.

RedHotJazz.com

ReligiousTolerance.org

Riley, Duncan, "Nine *Home and Away* Actors Who Went on to Stardom." *The Inquisitor*. September 6, 2009.

Riley, Jenelle, "Scene-stealer Nelsan Ellis Returns to the South as a *True Blood* Breakout." *Backstage*. June 11, 2009.

Rochlin, Margy, "Flesh and Blood in a Town of Vampires." *New York Times*. Online. October 30. 2008.

Schwartz, Howard, *Lilith's Cave: Jewish Tales of the Supernatural*. San Francisco: Harper & Row, 1988.

Seeing-Stars.com

Sharp, Dave, "*True Blood*'s Lafayette a Glamorously Shady Character." *Alabama Live*, August 9, 2009.

Skal, David J., *The Monster Show: A Cultural History of Horror*. New York: Penguin, 1993.

———. *V Is for Vampire*. New York: Plume, 1996.

Skarsgardnews.com

SookieBonTemps.com

SookieStackhouse.com

SpookyFiles.com

"Spotlight: Training to Act." *Backstage*. January 17, 2007.

Stewart, Andrew, "Main Title Designs Set Mood for Show." *Variety*. Online. August 3, 2009.

Summers, Montague, *The Vampire in Europe*. Gramercy Books: New York, 1996. (Originally published as *The Vampire in Lore and Legend*, 1929.)

———. *Vampires and Vampirism*. New York: Dover, 1928, 2005. (Originally published as *The Vampire: His Kith and Kin*.)

"Take 10: Girl Power." *Marvel News*. Online. February 2009.

Tarnoff, Brooke, "*True Blood* Vampire Valerie Cruz: 'The Coolest Shows Are on Cable.'" *Pop Eater Canada*. Online. June 30, 2009.

TheLatestEpisodes.com

"The Wrong Eyed Concept." *Liftingfaces*. Online. September 2008.

"To Die For." *Nylon*. September 2009.

Topel, Fred, "12 Big-Ass Spoilers for *True Blood* Season 3." *SCI FI Wire*. Online. November 3, 2009.

TruBeverage.com

"True Blood." *The Art of the Title Sequence*. Online. November 21, 2008.

"*True Blood* Title Sequence." *Communication Arts*. Online. October 21, 2008.

"*True Blood*'s Michelle Forbes Talks Maryann, the Statue, and What's Next." *The TV Addict*. Online. July 12, 2009.

True-Blood.net

TrueBlood-News.com.

TrueBlood-Online.com.

TrueBloodNet.com

TrueBloodTwitter.com

TrueBloodWiki.HBO.com

TVGuide.com

TVWatch.People.com

Wikipedia.org

Wieselman, Jarett, "Rutina Wesley: 'Maryann's Chaos Is Only Beginning!'" *New York Post*. Online. September 4, 2009.

———. "*True Blood* Star: 'Things are About to Get Real Krunk!'" *New York Post*. Online. July 13, 2009.

Williams, Kam, "Rutina Wesley *How She Move* Interview." *News Blaze*. Online. January 20, 2008.

Wilson, Katharina M., "The History of the Word 'Vampire'." *Journal of the History of Ideas*. 1985.

Woerner, Meredith, "*True Blood*'s Rutina Wesley Tells io9 She's Not The Huxtables." io9. Online. November 20, 2008.

Wright, Dudley, *The Book of Vampires*. New York: Causeway Books, 1973. (Originally published as *Vampires and Vampirism*, 1914.)

Acknowledgments

Virtually anyone I could thank is probably contained somewhere within the pages of this book, either a sign that I know some of the coolest people around, or that people who like vamps are generally the coolest people around.

That said, to my friends and family, wow, you put up with a lot. Thanks for loving me. But you have some catching up to do because I love you even more.

To the peeps at ECW, especially Jack David and my editor Jen Hale, thanks for taking a chance and continuing to publish upstarts like me, people who love this stuff as much as you. (Which is saying something, 'cause you mad crazy for it!) Also a big holla to Crissy and Jen K who love vamps, personally and professionally. And to the publicity team, notably Simon, who is going learn more about vampires than he ever deemed possible.

To Lola, here's to our next scary movie, and the hope that I won't swear through the whole damn thing.

D, I will concede that that quip you made about switching to plastic cutlery so it wouldn't scrape the plates was pretty damn funny. I'm sorry I surgically removed your pores as you slept — the thunderous sound of perspiration a constant distraction. All that to say that, shucks, I like you just fine.

A special note to the fan bloggers and podcasters. You know what you do is special, but that you do it with such earnest passion, regularity, and professionalism deserves a rousing round of applause, high fives (up high), back slaps, and butt pats. Because, believe me, you saved this writer's life on more than a few occasions. If I ever wasn't sure about something, I knew where to turn for confirmation, putting you at the top of my search engine list. That's right; you trumped Google. I owe you a debt of gratitude. Whenever you want me, I'll be here.

A very, very special thank you to the Twitter *True Blood* players and @Sookie BonTemps. When I first approached you, you didn't know me from a hole in the wall. Thanks for letting all us strangers in.

Finally, a big head butt to Rudy and the longest game of Tortilla Tie Tag your little kitty heart could hope for. You were by my side for at least 85,000 of these words, written three times over. For all you know, I was just sitting there, but, I thought you should know, you kept me sane, occasionally providing lumbar support. You're the best damn cat even if you aren't the fastest cheetah.

Shamon.

B.

(Carl William Heindl)

Becca Wilcott

Becca Wilcott can be found at www.rebeccawilcott.com and www.twitter.com/beccawilcott. She lives and works in Toronto, ON, as a publishing professional.